Hidden Gold

HIDDEN GOLD

A True Story of the Holocaust

ELLA BURAKOWSKI

Second Story Press

Library and Archives Canada Cataloguing in Publication

Burakowski, Ella, 1957-, author
Hidden gold / by Ella Burakowski.

Issued in print and electronic formats.
ISBN 978-1-927583-74-6 (paperback).—
ISBN 978-1-927583-75-3 (epub)

I. Title.

PS8603.U72H54 2015 jC813'.6 C2015-903297-0

C2015-903298-9

Edited by Kathryn Cole
Designed by Melissa Kaita

Printed and bound in Canada

Although this is a true story, some of the characters' names have been changed to protect their privacy.

Second Story Press gratefully acknowledges the support of the Ontario Arts Council and the Canada Council for the Arts for our publishing program. We acknowledge the financial support of the Government of Canada through the Canada Book Fund.

Canada Council for the Arts
Conseil des Arts du Canada

Funded by the Government of Canada
Financé par le gouvernement du Canada

Canada

Published by
Second Story Press
20 Maud Street, Suite 401
Toronto, ON M5V 2M5
www.secondstorypress.ca

In memory of my mother, Shoshana, her sister, Esther,
my grandparents, Leib and Hanna Gold,
and the six million Jews who perished in the Holocaust
as part of Hitler's final solution.

This book is dedicated to David Gold,
the youngest and only remaining survivor of the Gold family.
It is through David's memories that writing this story was possible.

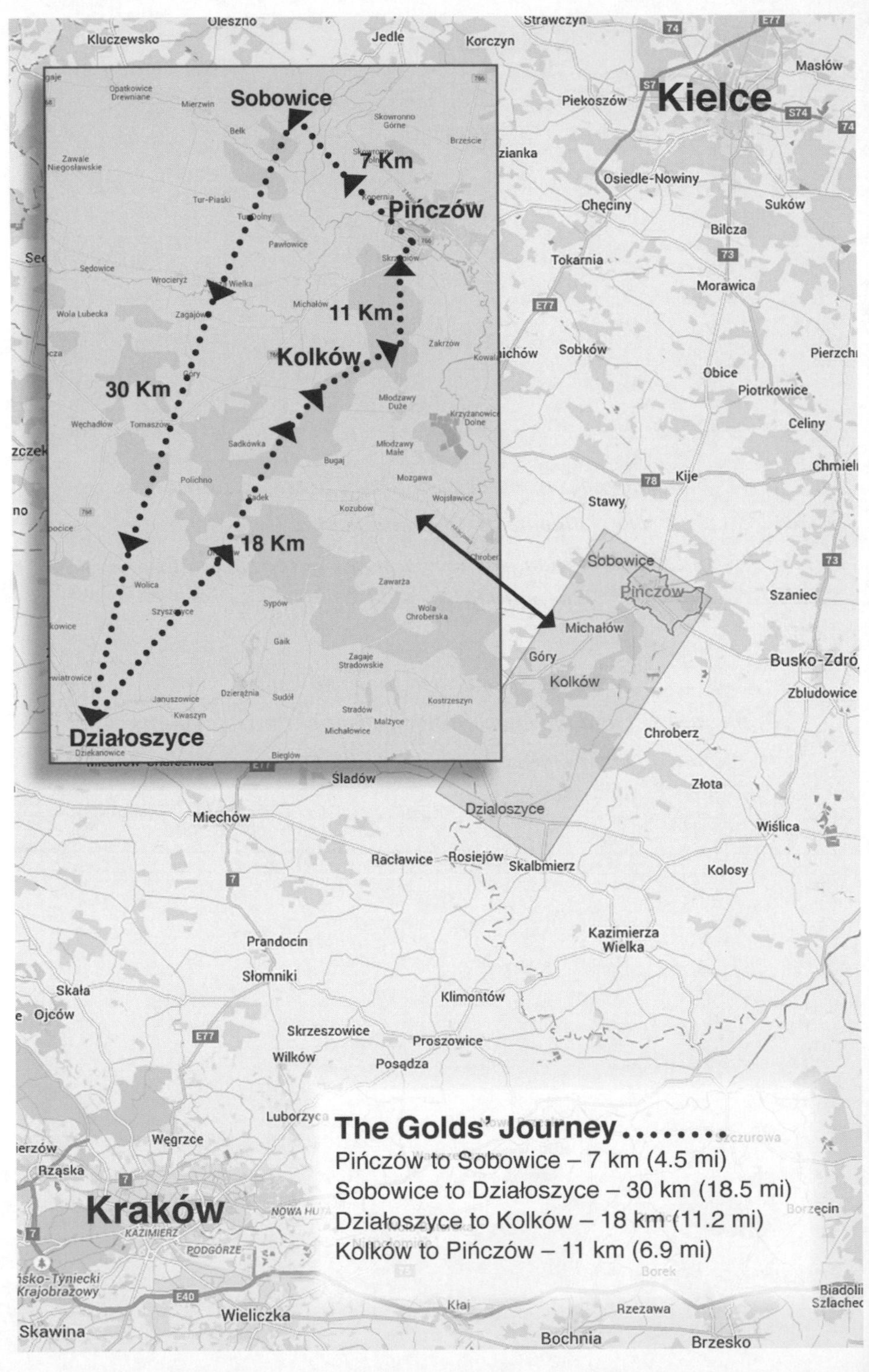

Sobowice
7 Km
Pińczów
11 Km
Kolków
30 Km
18 Km
Działoszyce
Kielce
Kraków
Sobowice
Pińczów
Michałów
Góry
Kolków
Dzialoszyce
Miechów
Chęciny
Busko-Zdrój
Wieliczka
Bochnia
The Golds' Journey........
Pińczów to Sobowice – 7 km (4.5 mi)
Sobowice to Działoszyce – 30 km (18.5 mi)
Działoszyce to Kolków – 18 km (11.2 mi)
Kolków to Pińczów – 11 km (6.9 mi)

PART ONE
Life in Pińczów

CHAPTER 1

A Son, 1930

Leib heard Hanna's screams from the street. He bounded up the stairs two at a time and paced back and forth.

Why is it taking so long?

Finally Hanna's shouts stopped and so did Leib's breathing. The melody he'd waited so long to hear ended the momentary silence; *weh, weh, weh*. He closed his eyes and mumbled a quick prayer of thanks. The baby had strong lungs.

The bedroom door creaked open slowly, and the midwife emerged, wiping her hands on her apron. "You have a son," she announced.

"A son?" he asked. "I have a son?" Leib wasn't sure he could trust his ears. "How is my Hanna?"

"Your wife is fine. Give me a little time to clean things up, and then you can come in and see them both."

Unable to control his excitement, Leib lifted the midwife off the ground and twirled her around. Realizing how inappropriate this was, he placed her back down and watched as she straightened her dress.

"I'm sorry Pani Glowinski, but I have a son!" He laughed. "Thank you. Thank you so much!" Leib ran down the stairs to the front door of the apartment building. "I have a son!" he yelled into the street. *Mazel tov* echoed back to him.

It was freezing out, but Leib paid no attention to the frigid temperature or the snow as he ran to his general store. Shoshana had been left alone in the store to keep it running. He was very excited to give his eldest daughter the wonderful news that she had a baby brother.

Shoshana knew her mother was in labor and anxiously waited for her father to return with some word. It seemed to be taking forever. Her mind was not on serving the customers, it was on the broken clock on the wall whose hands didn't seem to be moving. *What's taking so long,* she thought just as her *tateh* burst through the door. A wave of nervous excitement surged through her.

"Tateh, did *Mameh* have the baby?"

"Yes, yes Shoshanaleh, you have a little brother." He squeezed his daughter tightly and planted a kiss on her head. When he released her from the bear hug, he held her at arm's length, staring at his firstborn; the pride evident on his face. She was so grown up. Where had the time gone? She was already eleven and a responsible young lady.

"A little brother," Shoshana said, "How's Mameh? Can I see him, Tateh? Did you tell Esther?" There was so much she needed to know, Shoshana didn't know what to ask first.

Making sure to answer all her questions Leib said, "Your mother's fine Shoshanaleh. Of course you can see him, but not yet. I haven't even seen him yet. Pani Glowinski is fixing things up, so we can go in, but she said your mother and the baby are doing well. I'm going to tell Esther before I go back up. Stay here, sweetheart, and mind the store. You're doing a great job; Mameh and I are very proud of you," he reassured her. "I'll come get you very soon *mayn tyreh meydele*, my precious girl." And he was gone.

Absorbing what her father had just told her, Shoshana stood still for a moment, then took a deep breath. She giggled and began to sing loudly while she went back to work straightening the jars on the shelf.

Esther was at the family's second store, the tobacco wholesale next door. Leib stood at the door watching her before he walked in. She sat on her knees, a pencil tucked between her teeth, counting each item from the delivery that had arrived earlier. Her hair pulled back in a kerchief, she used the back of her hand to brush away one escaped lock of hair. She was a bright child with her mother's ability to understand the workings of a business. Leib watched his daughter concentrate on her task. She took her job seriously and loved working even more than playing. The first time he realized it was when he watched her make change for a customer. The man laughed as Esther, at age four, counted out the *zloty* into his palm. To Esther it was a game.

Today, at the age of nine, Esther had lost her status as the baby of the family and made no secret of her disapproval. She didn't notice her father walk in. Leib crouched down to his daughter's eye level. "Esther, you have a new baby brother," he said, watching for her reaction.

There was a moment of hesitation before she dropped the pencil from her mouth and threw her arms around her father's neck. They stood together and he held her, rocking back and forth like he used to when she was a baby.

"Tateh is Mameh okay?" Esther asked.

Leib laughed, gave her a big kiss on the cheek and put her down. "Everyone is wonderful," Leib said.

Ania, the family's housekeeper was in the store with Esther. Even though his youngest daughter could run the place herself, Hanna insisted the housekeeper be there. "Mazel tov," Ania said to Leib from behind the counter. Leib smiled and thanked her for watching the girls.

"Esthershe," Leib said endearingly, "I'm going to see Mameh and your new brother. I haven't seen them yet. I'll be back to get you soon."

Word traveled quickly in the town of Pińczów, Poland, and Leib could hear shouts of mazel tov coming from all directions. He waved at people as he made his way back to the apartment. He stomped the snow off his shoes as he ran up the stairs. Just as he approached the door to the bedroom, the midwife opened it and gestured for him to enter. He stood at the entrance for a moment surveying his wife and new son, who was swaddled in a soft cotton blanket. He went over, smiled at Hanna, and took his son in his arms. He looked down at the baby with so much joy in his heart he thought he would burst. Leib sat down on the edge of the bed next to his wife.

"Hanna, you gave me a son," he said gently, his eyes filled with tears. Hanna beamed. Although she was exhausted, she relished this moment. Leib kissed his her gently. He stroked her hair with one hand, and held the tiny bundle in the other. "I love you Hanna," he whispered, as she succumbed to exhaustion.

Darkness set in while Leib sat next to his sleeping wife, rocking his newborn son. Leib looked at his wife, her long hair draped around her shoulders, loose and flowing. It wasn't often he saw her with her hair down; she always wore it tied back in a tight bun. Without those tortoise shell glasses that rarely left her face, she looked calm and beautiful.

He couldn't believe how fortune had shone on him. His mind wandered back to the past and how he'd met this remarkable woman who had borne him three children and become his soul mate.

It was 1918, and Leib was twenty-four. Gittel, the matchmaker, approached him about arranging a *shidduch* for marriage. The young woman was twenty-one-year-old Hanna Finer of Wislica. Leib asked around about the Finer family, and the feedback was glowing.

After just one meeting, Leib realized they had much in common. There was a spark between the couple, and Hanna was drawn to Leib's charm and confidence.

The match was a success. The children of two prominent families joined forces to become a power couple to be admired.

Hanna complemented Leib's life perfectly. She knew what her husband needed even before he did. Even with her small stature, when Hanna spoke, people listened. This diminutive dynamo of a woman was well ahead of her time. She handled the family businesses, while Leib was away on buying trips or entertaining politicians. She oversaw their general store and tobacco wholesale, while keeping a tight grip on the home front. She hired a housekeeper to help with chores and she taught her two daughters, Shoshana and Esther, to help her after school. She ran her home and the businesses like a seasoned orchestra conductor.

Leib had charisma and intelligence. He surrounded himself with important notables and made sure they were not only business associates, but also friends. He greased palms when necessary and won the hearts of many with his charm and wit.

He played the political game well. He was shrewd enough to know he needed to befriend not only the higher ups, but the working class as well, and often threw parties for the Polish police of the town.

Yes, everyone knew Leib Gold. He was an elected alderman, a member of the Alegminer Zionist Movement, a successful businessman, a family man, and now he had a newborn son to carry on his name. Leib had it all.

CHAPTER 2

David

Leib sat next to his wife all night. He had held the baby in his arms, gazing at him for a long time and had finally placed him in the little wicker bassinet beside Hanna's bed. As she began to stir, he picked up the sleeping infant and placed him in his wife's arms.

"*Guten morgen,*" he said wishing his wife a good morning.

She smiled at her husband and said, "Leib, what should we call him?"

They bounced a few names back and forth but always came back to the name David. So David Gold it was, a good strong name. Pure and innocent, with his whole life ahead of him, he was the son of a wealthy, respected family in Pińczów, Poland. Hanna, who normally doted on no one, couldn't stop herself. She adored this little miracle in her arms. She felt something different toward this little boy that she hadn't felt after the birth of her two daughters.

The festivities surrounding David's birth lasted for a week. It wasn't until after his *bris,* the religious circumcision ceremony, that things returned to a more normal pace, and the realities of life set in.

ᔕ

The Great Depression caused growing anti-Semitism, and more restrictions were imposed on Jews, but life went on normally for the Golds. Leib conducted business as usual. He traveled a lot and, for now, was able to move around the country freely for politics, business, and vacations. But Leib's yearning to live in a Jewish homeland grew as anti-Semitism increased throughout Poland.

It wasn't till after the stock market crash of 1929, and the Great Depression spread over Europe, that Adolf Hitler's party gained power. In 1933, when David was a toddler, Hitler became Chancellor of Germany.

ᔕ

By the age of six, David had begun *Cheder.* One crisp fall afternoon, he finished his half-day of studies and started home. Kicking stones and picking up every pebble that twinkled in the sun, he took much longer than he should have. He broke into a run when he spotted Yoel scratching at his front door. He scooped up his cat and walked into the apartment. David stood still for a moment, stroking Yoel and listening to Shoshana practice her mandolin in the salon. Her instrument was not to be touched, which enticed him all the more. But the spanking he'd gotten the last time he was caught playing with it was still fresh in his memory. Shoshana heard his steps and called out, "David, is that you?"

"Yeah."

"Come here, please."

David entered the salon cuddling Yoel in his arms. His sister began nattering instructions at him. "When I'm finished practicing I'll play with you. Right now, go straight to the kitchen, and ask Ania to give you lunch. When you're finished, we'll go to the park, and I'll take you to see Mameh at the store."

David barely heard his sister's words. His thoughts were about his next adventure. He was a mischievous child, and his curiosity often got the better of him.

He was hungry and could smell the *kotletin* frying. Ania was a wonderful cook whose juicy meat patties were award-worthy. Since David was a picky eater, she tried to have his favorite foods ready for him. He would start with a *forshpeits*, an appetizer of his favorite schmaltz herring, often followed by some type of soup, like sweet beet borscht with potatoes, and finally the main course, those succulent kotletin with a side of *kluski* noodles and fried onions.

On his way to the kitchen he got sidetracked and found himself in front of the forbidden cabinet. He knew very well that cabinet was off-limits, but its magnetism was overwhelming.

David put Yoel down and surveyed his surroundings. The music was still coming from the salon, Ania was busy in the kitchen; the coast was clear. He very carefully opened the cabinet, which was where the family kept their medicines and other forbidden items. The first thing to catch David's eye was a bottle of deep red iodine. He was just about to open it when Ania screeched, "David, what are you doing!"

Startled, David dropped the bottle, and the cap popped off. Ania and David watched helplessly as the red iodine leaked onto the floor. David instinctively jumped to pick it up. His clothes, hands, and face became a canvas, as the red dye became an abstract design all over him. It was too late for excuses. Shoshana assessed the mess on the floor. Her little brother had literally been caught red handed.

"I can't leave you for five minutes without you getting into some kind of trouble!" she bellowed.

David lowered his head and accepted the scolding he knew he deserved, but Shoshana saw a smirk emerging at the corners of her little brother's mouth.

"Come with me," she said, grabbing him by the back of his shirt collar and holding him at arm's length. Shoshana tried to clean up David, as Ania got down on her hands and knees to scrub the stain on the floor.

Once he was cleaned and well fed, Shoshana took David out, hoping this boy would get into less trouble outside. On the way to the park they stopped at the tobacco store to see Esther. She was busy with inventory and customers and didn't have time to play. She took her job very seriously and, at the age of fifteen, ran the place with the efficiency of a professional manager.

There were many government rules that came with running a tobacco concession, and Leib was lucky to have the opportunity to own one. Jews were usually not allowed to hold certificates to run such establishments. He'd purchased the concession from the wife of a deceased Polish World War I colonel. One of the rules was that the concession had to be open on Saturdays. So, in spite of being an observant Jew, Leib was obliged to open the store on the Sabbath. He hired a gentile worker to handle Saturdays. Leib and Hanna did not let religion get in the way of prosperity.

"Hi Esther," Shoshana announced as they entered the store. The girls began discussing an incident that had happened the night before between two of their neighbors. They were so occupied with their gossip, that they forgot to keep an eye on their brother.

Shoshana turned in time to see a whole pile of boxes falling from the shelf. "DAVID!" she screamed.

"Get him out of here!" Esther hollered. Shoshana knew they'd overstayed their welcome. David couldn't be left unattended for a second before he was into something. Lucky for him he was cute. He had a smile that would melt a heart of stone. Instead of punishment, he often got off with a rueful smile and a "What are we going to do with you?"

With Hanna at the store most nights, it was Shoshana who tucked David into bed. David would get cleaned up, put on his pajamas, and crawl into his narrow bed, which was pushed against the wall of the room. On the other side of the bed, Shoshana would place the netted rail in place, and David was securely tucked in. Most nights Yoel jumped over the rail and stretched out along David's body. In a trance-like state David would fall asleep gently stroking Yoel's soft body. The cat would purr, and the two of them would drift off together every night.

Hanna, who was very conscious of appearances, controlled

the children's social lives. She did not approve of David's close friends Adeck and Lieleck, two brothers who lived in the neighborhood. David came home filthy every time he was out with those boys.

"Look at you, you're a mess," Hanna said to her son. "David, I want you stay away from those two boys. They're a bad influence."

"But I have fun with them, Mameh," David whined.

"Get upstairs right now, and Ania will clean you up."

David walked slowly to the entrance of the apartment, his head hung low as he pawed at the ground trying to waste time.

Then there was Mulik. He was David's friend too, but alas, the son of a tailor would not be good enough for David to play with either. Tailors and shoemakers were considered to be of a lower class, and Hanna felt that David should be associating with children whose families were of the same social status.

To offset everyone's busy schedule, Hanna attempted to add a little normalcy to their hectic lives. Every Friday night it was mandatory for the family to have dinner together. It was a time to rest, regroup, and to talk. It gave the children a chance to tell their stories about their week. Hanna would light the *Shabbos* candles, and Leib made *Kiddish*, the prayer over the wine. He passed his silver Kiddish cup around the table so everyone could partake of the blessing. Then Ania served dinner, as the family sat around the large dining table discussing their friends, school, and social activities. It was the only time in the week when business took a backseat, and the Golds all came together as a family. It was a custom each one of them loved and looked forward to.

Being a traditional Jewish family, the Golds did their best

to obey Jewish law. On Saturday morning, David and his father dressed in their best clothes and went to synagogue.

This was the only day the girls had the time to explore their social lives. Shoshana was very popular and had many friends. She was a typical teenager and enjoyed having fun.

Unlike Shoshana, Esther preferred to have a few close friends. She spent her Saturdays going for a walk and talking with one of her girlfriends. But her favorite pastime was to plant herself on the bench under the huge willow tree in the park and immerse herself in a book. Often her walks would take her right past the tobacco store, so she could peek in and make sure everything was running smoothly. The store was her real passion, and she didn't like handing control to a stranger, even if it was for only one day a week.

Hanna spent Saturday mornings relaxing. She sat in the salon on the rocker by the window, a bright sunbeam lighting her newspaper as she read. With Leib and the children out, this was her quiet time, and she cherished these few precious hours.

The Golds lived a comfortable, happy existence.

☙

After *shul* on Saturdays, Leib would stay and talk with the congregants while David ran off to Marian's farm. Marian Wicinski, a fellow council member and close friend of the family, often joined the Golds for their Shabbos dinners. Marian was a Polish bachelor with no children of his own. His sister Frania and her husband, the chief of the Polish police, lived on the farm with him.

David did whatever chores Marian assigned to him and did

them with a smile. He helped round up the chickens, collect the eggs, and clean up around the barn, but his favorite job was taking the horses down to the Nida River to be watered. There was no greater feeling than riding his favorite horse, Bolek, bareback down to the water's edge. Bolek was huge, and David was on top of the world when he rode the majestic animal. Their special bond was obvious to anyone who watched.

Marian loved to observe from a distance. David had an innocent, mischievous manner. He reminded Marian of himself as a young boy, always trying hard to be good, but never quite succeeding. The temptation of something off limits was just too great to resist, and David, like Marian before him, always managed to find trouble in every task. Instead of getting angry, Marian would often laugh out loud at some of David's antics. When they were together, they had an unspoken connection. Others noticed it too. They both seemed to come alive in each other's presence.

Before Shabbos ended, Marian would walk David home and stay for tea. It wasn't long before the conversation would turn to business, and Leib and Marian would discuss matters that were boring to the rest of the family. The two men spent hours playing chess and talking. While in the rest of the country the division between Jews and Poles widened, these two men grew closer.

CHAPTER 3

Anti-Semitism Grows, 1936

By the summer of 1936, anti-Semitism had increased the tension and fear felt by the Jews of Poland. The government ordered all Jewish shops to be visibly labeled. Attacks on Jewish businesses surged. Jewish children were beaten regularly by their Christian classmates. Their alleged crime? The killing of Jesus Christ.

Leib's dream of moving to the Jewish homeland and re-establishing his family in Palestine grew. Hanna's cousin Isaac already lived there and planned to help with the transition. Every business dealing, every new connection, every thought – all were steps to achieve Leib's goal.

The situation in Pińczów became ugly. One Easter night, a large mob surrounded the home of Moshe Fishel, the tailor. He had the unfortunate circumstance of living very close to the church. Rumors spread that Moshe held a Christian boy captive in his basement and was using the boy's blood to bake *matzos* for Passover. The mob, led by the police, broke into Moshe's home. On the premise of conducting a search for the tortured boy, they destroyed his house. When they found no sign of any Christian child, they moved on to two Jewish neighbors and did the same to their homes. Nothing was ever found to substantiate the ridiculous rumor, but the incident fueled fear among the Jews and provoked more hate among the Poles.

It was time for Leib to put his plan into action. This would involve his sister, Leah, and her family. On the day before Leah's oldest daughter, Blacha, was to marry, Leib took a bus to Jędrzejów to visit her. Leah lived modestly, and Leib had the power to make her far more comfortable. His sister would play an important role in his plan to move to Palestine, and she would benefit greatly in the process. He would sell his businesses and his house to her for a fair price. Leib knew he would never enjoy the same level of comfort in Palestine, but he didn't care. The luxury of feeling secure could not be bought in Poland.

Blacha's wedding was lively, and everyone rejoiced and danced into the early morning hours. The next morning Leib sat down with Leah to finalize the plan. Leah would send Blacha to Pińczów to learn how to run the businesses. It was important that she be trained properly and be introduced to all Leib's contacts. Blacha was anxious to get started, as this was her opportunity to better her family's future.

Within a month, Blacha arrived ready to work. Both Hanna and Shoshana taught her about inventory, dealing with customers, ordering, and restocking. They introduced her to every supplier and explained their quirks and how to get the most out of each of them. She learned to joke with the customers and make them feel welcome. Blacha stayed with the Gold family during the week, and Leib paid for her to travel back to Jędrzejów every Friday so she could spend *Shabbat* with her new husband and family.

The move was on schedule, and the plan was working. Leib spent most of his days tying up loose ends while keeping a close eye on the news, both at home and in Palestine.

The news was not good on either front. One Friday night after Shabbos dinner, Hanna handed her husband a letter she had received earlier in the day. Hanna had a premonition that this letter held horrible news and held off giving it to Leib as long as she could. It was from Isaac in Palestine. Leib opened the letter, assuming it would tell him about the final arrangements for their arrival. Instead, the letter read:

Mayn tyreh Leib, My dearest Leib,

Things here in Palestine have taken a turn for the worse. There has been severe fighting between the Arabs and the Jews, and there is much chaos and bloodshed. After discussing this with the rest of the family we have decided this is not the right time for you to bring Hanna and the children to Palestine. It is too dangerous. It would be best for you to postpone this move until the fighting quiets down.

Your cousin, Isaac

Leib felt like someone had punched him in the gut. The color drained from his face. He buried his head in his hands as the letter fell to the floor. His dream was disintegrating.

Hanna crouched down beside her husband. "It's not forever, Leib. We will get there one day. Don't lose hope." Her encouragement seemed to bring him around. He sat back in the chair and put his hand over his wife's.

"You're right, I just need to rethink the plan, that's all. It doesn't mean we can't go next year, right? The safety of the family must come first."

Hanna kissed her husband, and they held each other as the disappointment churned inside them.

∽

Things in Pińczów went from bad to worse. The Polish Endeks, who were the national democrats, became very vocal. They were a militant group whose main preoccupation was making life difficult for Jews. They would regularly demonstrate outside the Golds' grocery store, shouting for people not to buy anything from Jews. They caused fear and chaos in the streets and looked for Jews to beat up on a regular basis. Eventually the young Jewish men, mostly from the university and Zionist parties, formed an alliance and fought to take their streets back.

Leib had to resign himself to the reality that he was staying in Pińczów, for now. He would have to wait for the day his dream would be fulfilled, and he and his family would make a new life in the land of Israel. He was prepared to wait for that day, no matter how long it took.

Once Leib emerged from his dejected state, he knew he had to do something positive for his family. It was time to move forward; if not in the Holy Land, at least he could make things better right here.

As the children grew, the space in the apartment shrank. *This would be a great time to move the whole Gold clan into a house of our own,* he thought.

In the spring of 1937, a new house was built at 30 Plac Wolnosci, attached to the apartment building they were presently living in. It was a large, well-built house with a yard. Shoshana's room was up a winding staircase on the second floor. The rest of the family had rooms on the main floor. A kitchen at the front of the house led to a formal dining room where many holidays would be spent together as a family. There was even a maid's room in the house. The location was right in the town square, across from the same beautiful park where the kids always played. Life was looking up again. The children loved their new home and settled in easily. Hanna enjoyed the extra space and the distinction of owning her own dwelling. With each passing day, the thought of moving to Palestine slipped farther away. Fighting continued among the Arabs and Jews of the Holy Land, with no end in sight. Time and choices were running out for the Jews of Poland.

CHAPTER 4

The Churchyard, 1939

Violent incidents were on the rise, but even though the growing tensions were disquieting, day-to-day routines in the Golds' new home masked the dangers emerging around them. Then one day everything changed.

Leib and Hanna were listening to the radio in the salon, when the announcement came. The Germans had infiltrated Polish borders. Leib and Hanna looked at each other and sprang to their feet. Hanna moved quickly around the house collecting all the silver, gold, and other valuables, while Leib worked on a hiding place for the family. Hanna did not pack Leib's silver Kiddish cup or her mother's Shabbos candle holders. She would hide them somewhere in the house. Leib prepared a deep hole in one of the alcoves of the cellar beneath the adjoining apartment building. When he was sure no one was watching, he put most of their material valuables into a large burlap sack and buried them. Leib marked the spot with a white rock, which he trampled into the earth so it was level with the ground. At a glance it would be visible to him, but was obscure enough not to draw attention.

They returned to the salon to listen to more reports. The Golds were one of the few families in Pińczów to own a radio, and they spent every waking hour listening for news of German activity. They were tuned into a German station when a panicked announcer broke in and said that the town of Gleiwitz, which was a German town situated on the border of Poland and Germany, had been invaded by Polish rebels. The airwaves went silent.

It was later discovered that Hitler staged this invasion to make it look like the Poles had invaded Germany. It was the excuse Hitler needed in order to make his move.

The next day, Friday, September 1, 1939, Germany launched the Fall Weiss operation, the invasion of Poland. This was the first military operation of World War II in Europe. Thirty-five days later, on October 6, German and Soviet Union forces, working together at that time, gained full control of the country.

Life would never be the same for the Jews of Poland.

On Thursday, September 7, the Golds, along with a Polish soldier and others from the same block, hid in the large brick wine cellar under the apartment building. Pandemonium had taken over the streets. People ran for their lives, searching for anywhere to hide. While gunfire could be heard from the street above, the silence in the shelter was rocked by a deep commanding voice.

"*RAUS! RAUS!* OUT! OUT!"

Panic set in. Leib knew if they did not obey, they would all be shot instantly. The Polish soldier who was hiding with them was prepared to go out shooting, but Leib grabbed his arm as he attempted to dart up the stairs. He had to try to reason with this man. Their lives depended on it.

"What's your name?" asked Leib.

"Feliks."

"Feliks, listen to me." Leib was only inches from the man's face, and he spoke with authority. "We have no time to argue. You can't go out there in this uniform waving your gun around. You will get us all killed. If the Germans think we're hiding armed Polish soldiers down here, what do you think they'll do to us? Go hide behind the others, and get rid of that gun."

Leib turned to the man standing beside him and said, "Find him other clothes to wear, he has to look like one of us."

Leib then turned to face Shoshana, who stood against the wall watching and trembling. He hated what he was about to do to his daughter but knew she was their only chance. He put his hands on her shoulders and looked directly into her light blue eyes, "Listen to me, Shoshanaleh. Pull yourself together. You are going to get us out of here. I promise you, the soldier won't do anything to you." As the words came out of his mouth, he knew he was lying. How could he promise his daughter she would not be shot? But if this was going to work, his words would have to instill strength in her.

Esther could see the panic on her sister's face. "Tateh, I will go," she said. "I can do this. Leave Shoshana alone."

Leib looked at Esther and tried to dismiss her request. In that instant, he realized two things: first Esther was reinforcing Shoshana's fear; second, he knew Esther could not pull this off. She didn't have the language skills or Slavic look that was needed.

He thanked his daughter for trying to help and motioned for Hanna to take over. Hanna understood immediately and tried to change Esther's focus by asking her to watch over their little brother, who was absorbing everything happening around him. David, confused and frightened, was only nine years old.

Leib continued speaking to Shoshana. "You're a beautiful young woman, and you're the only one who speaks perfect German. They will never suspect you are Jewish, and with your blue eyes and fine features, you have nothing to be afraid of," he said, trying to convince her.

"Go out, and plead for them not to hurt us. Tell them we will cooperate with whatever they want, and make sure they understand there are children in here."

Shoshana had no choice. She glanced past her father and saw all eyes glued on her. She nodded her head slightly, straightened her dress, and started up the stairs. She had no idea how many German soldiers were out there, but she heard only one voice.

On her way up she shouted in German, "I'm coming out with my hands up, please don't shoot."

She made her way from the dark dungeon, toward light and the high leather boots of a German soldier. She was relieved to see only one pair of legs, but her relief was short-lived, as she stared down the barrel of a gun.

She did her best not to squint so the soldier could see her eyes were blue.

Shoshana spoke clearly and confidently in German. "There are people and young children down there prepared to come up and cooperate with whatever you want. There's no need to shoot anyone. We'll follow your orders and give you no trouble."

The Nazi soldier looked at her carefully and replied, "Tell them to come out now with their hands in the air. If I see anyone carrying anything, I will shoot immediately."

Shoshana's eyes, now fully adjusted to the light, looked beyond the German soldier to see dead bodies scattered in the street where she had walked just a few hours ago. Although she consciously made the effort not to show any panic, she was sure her acting was not that good.

"I'm going down to convey your orders, and we will all come up and give you no trouble."

"Schnell!" he commanded.

Leib stood partway up the stairs, listening to the conversation. Shoshana had done well – really well. He caught his daughter coming down the stairs as she fell into his arms and broke down.

"You were wonderful *mayn tyreh meydele*," he reassured her, but they had to move quickly or their opportunity would be lost.

He rounded up his family and instructed all the people in the cellar, "We need to go up, quietly and with our hands held high in the air. Do not take a single thing with you, and do not try to be heroes. One wrong move from anyone, and you will cost us all our lives." They lined up and slowly, apprehensively, made their way up the stairs.

Once at the top, Leib quickly assessed the situation. They were shooting people in the streets for no apparent reason. David was first to spot Mr. Zimmerman. He was the cheerful shoe salesman he saw in shul every Shabbos. Easily identifiable by his long white beard, he was teetering like a drunk as he moved past. The intense gravity of the situation enveloped them when they witnessed the blood pouring from between Mr. Zimmerman's fingers. He had been shot in the stomach. David listened to his mournful cries as he staggered away.

Leib did not scare easily, but he was scared now. He positioned himself to walk behind his family so he would be aware of their circumstances at all times. He made sure David was walking directly in front of him as they were led quickly down the street. Leib tried to shield David from seeing the dead bodies lined up in the middle of the road, some of whom he recognized. The acrid smell of gunfire filled the air. David spotted a horse lying with its guts exposed and a river of blood flowing from its wounds. He was clearly shaken at the gruesome sight of the mutilated animal, and he recoiled and stepped backward. For a split second, Leib lowered his hands and gently pushed David forward. He whispered to the back of his head, "Don't look, turn away, look straight ahead, and keep going." For a change David did not have to be told twice and obeyed his father's orders.

Leib's focus moved from his petrified son to the destination ahead. In the courtyard of the town church, he could see a crowd being assembled. He saw soldiers with machine guns surrounding the people grouped together and recognized many faces. As they were pushed into the churchyard, a soldier commanded Shoshana, Esther, and Hanna to go left and David and his father to move right. Hanna begged the soldier for the life of her son.

"Please let him go, he's only a child," she cried. Esther could sense the impatience of the soldier and quickly grabbed her mother away before the soldier had a chance to react.

David clung to his father so tightly his fingers were numb from the pressure.

"*Auf den knein!*" commanded the soldier with the machine gun. They obeyed and went down on their knees. They remained in that position for so long, people squirmed from the intense pain. David remained stoic. After what seemed like an eternity, they were permitted to sit on the concrete blocks of the churchyard.

Leib tried to absorb the scene and listen to what was being said by the soldiers. They didn't know he understood German and didn't censor their words in any way. Their speech was continuously interrupted by the thunder of German tanks and trucks driving by.

Half the town was in the church courtyard, but the silence among the terrified people was unnatural. Everyone focused on the flames. Their town was being destroyed, their homes, businesses, synagogues burned all around them. Hours passed like days. The heat was intense. David inched very close to his father. Leib could still see his girls sitting on the ground on the other side.

"Tateh, I'm so thirsty," David said, looking up at his father's soot-stained face. With all that was happening around him, this was the first complaint Leib had heard from his young son. Leib was parched too, but he was helpless.

Leib wrapped his arm around David, bringing him in closer. He bent forward, touched his lips to the top of his son's head, and whispered, "It's okay, Davidle, this will be over soon, and we'll all go home." Leib knew very well there would be no home to go back to, but he would deal with that later. "Put your head down on my lap, and close your eyes. Think about your favorite place, and try to imagine you're there. Sleep and dream, my sweet child." David tried hard to obey. He closed his eyes. He imagined the heat on his face was the sun on a warm summer day. He was hanging on to Bolek's mane bouncing on his back as the powerful horse galloped through the tall grass and flowers.

There was a large submachine gun propped in the middle of the courtyard pointed straight at them. The German soldier manning the gun teased the trigger to scare the already petrified victims. As time passed, the guards became more complacent. The courtyard gates were locked, so there could be no escape. They spent their time talking to each other and waiting for orders, their guns – no longer pointed directly at the prisoners – were held down at their sides.

As the tension in the courtyard eased, Leib motioned for Hanna to meet him inside the church. She rounded up their daughters, and, when the soldiers weren't looking, they entered the church. Relieved to be reunited with her husband and son, Hanna held on to David and didn't let go.

With David safely in his mother's care, Leib had an idea. He found a door at the back of the church, where he assumed there might be a storage area. He knew exactly what he was looking for. When he eyed a barrel in the corner of the room he knew he had hit gold. It was the holy water, collected from the main well and kept in the back for services. He immediately drank. The water doused the dagger-like sensations in the back of his throat. Hanna stared at the door her husband had disappeared through. Finally, Leib opened it slightly and motioned her in.

She and the children moved quickly. Leib directed them to the barrel. "Drink! Others will be here soon to drink as well."

He knew once the thirsty crowd made the same discovery, there would be a stampede to the barrel. He wanted his family out of the room before that happened. As Leib watched his family alleviate their discomfort, the panic that had such a strong hold on him subsided, and he knew they would survive this.

Leib found a spot against a wall where they could all prop themselves up and eventually fall asleep, but he remained awake. He needed to know what was going on, what the Germans were up to. One by one, he watched his children escape the reality of their ordeal as they slipped into the safety of their dreams. Hanna was still wide awake. Leib rose slowly and moved as unobtrusively as he could back through the crowd. He needed to get closer to the soldiers to hear what they were saying.

"*Wir gehen in den Morgen*, we will move in the morning," he overheard one saying. Leib saw one soldier bring a small glass bottle to his lips and, from the man's careless demeanor, realized he was intoxicated.

His more sober comrade became impatient with his drunken partner's laughing and joke-telling. He raised his voice, "Heinrich, you idiot, stop it. We need to stay sharp and be ready for our orders."

Heinrich fumbled with his ammunition belt. "Relax," he said. "Look around you. Our mission here is a success. Our orders will come in the morning, and we will be just as successful in the next town."

With that knowledge, Leib made his way back to his family. He lifted David onto his lap and allowed himself to drift off.

At daybreak the rumbling ground woke them, as the tanks rolled out. The ground beneath them shook like an earthquake.

Leib saw trucks driving to the east, filled to capacity with German soldiers. The locks on the courtyard gate had already been broken by some of the townspeople. They were free.

CHAPTER 5

Rebuilding

The crowd filed out of the churchyard, uncertain if the troops were all gone. The reality of their unexpected freedom began to sink in. Leib was afraid of what he would find.

He kept constant count of his family – one, two, three, four – while at the same time seeing rows of twisted bodies lying in the street. Piles of cinder smoldered where his family's favorite stores and restaurants stood just a day ago. An unusual noxious stench melded with the heavy smoke. Leib realized he was inhaling the smell of burnt flesh from the people who had been too afraid to leave their homes.

"David, come here to Tateh," he said and pulled his son closer, attempting to shield him from the gruesome sights. But David wriggled away. He wanted to see. His happy, sheltered life had come to an abrupt end. He did not cry. He just walked, like a ghost, eerily quiet and slow.

Completely numb and lost in their own thoughts, the family navigated the few blocks back to their home. Shoshana stared at a pile of charred debris. This was all that was left of the family's stores. For a second she remembered how she'd just finished straightening everything on the shelves. Esther walked straight ahead. Surveying the scene, it suddenly struck her how fortunate they were to still be together and unharmed. She thanked God for saving her family.

David spotted Yoel sitting in front of what used to be their home. He broke away from the pack and ran ahead. He scooped up his cat and held her so tightly a high-pitched meow squeezed from her little body, yet she did not try to escape. She, too, was safe.

Leib broke the silence. "I'm going in to see if there's anything left. Hanna, take the children across to the park, and wait for me there. I'll be back soon."

Hanna didn't often argue with Leib, but this time was different. "I'm coming with you," she announced.

Shoshana immediately interjected, "We'll wait for both of you near the large willow in the park." She hoped her favorite bench was still there. It would be a safe and comfortable place for them to await word from their parents.

Leib and Hanna began their trek through the rubble to the entrance of what had been their home. They held on to each other as they balanced on the burnt scrap that was once their walls, their furniture, their pride and joy. It was then that Hanna saw the corner of an ornate picture frame she recognized. She teetered through the rubble to get to it. When she picked it up, she stared at the family portrait, which was only slightly damaged. She let her thoughts carry her back to the day when they all dressed up and took the bus to Działoszyce to have that photo taken.

Her thoughts were broken by Leib's hand on her shoulder. He gently took the picture from her and wiped the tears from her cheek. She hadn't realized she was crying.

They stood as one among the ruins. Leib wrapped his wife in a tight embrace. "I'm going to fix this," he promised. Even as he said it, he wasn't sure how, but he would move heaven and earth to get his family back to their happy home. He just needed time to devise a plan.

"Come, let's go to the children. We'll get through this, and together we'll find the strength to move forward. No one will defeat us, Hanna, not if we don't let them."

Hanna did not speak. She simply took the photograph back from her husband and held on to him as they made their way out of the wreckage. Hanna and Leib walked past the devastation to the park and saw their children at the bench under the willow tree, surrounded by green grass, beautiful foliage, and colorful flowers. It was like an oasis in the middle of an apocalypse, a sign of hope where they thought none existed.

David ran up to meet his tateh and wrapped his arms around his father's waist. "Tateh, why did they do this to us? Why do they hate us so much? I didn't do anything wrong, did I, Tateh?"

Leib held tightly to his son's trembling body. How was he going to explain senseless hatred like this to a nine-year-old boy when he didn't understand it himself?

"Of course not, David. You did nothing wrong. When times

are hard sometimes it's easier to blame someone else. People try to convince themselves that there is a reason for their bad fortune, that it's the fault of someone else. It makes them feel better about themselves, and they don't care what happens to the people they blame."

"Do they blame us, Tateh? Why?"

"I'm afraid they do blame us, Davidle, because we're different from them."

He saw that David absorbed every word and decided to explain further. "Hitler blames the Jews for the hard times that have fallen on this country, and he has the power and authority to force others to think like him. You know, David, it's always easier to follow the crowd rather than to go against it. It's hard to stand up for what's right when you're standing alone. Hitler has a whole army working for him, and he's convinced many people that the Jews are the reason for everything bad in their lives. Instead of questioning Hitler, it's easier and safer to go along with him. What you see all around you is the result of all this hatred."

Leib could see the exhaustion on his son's face. "Come David, let's join Mameh and your sisters under the tree." Leib picked up his child, carried him over to the rest of the family, and lowered him to the grass beside Shoshana.

They spent the night in the park. Hanna and Esther slept intertwined on the bench, and Shoshana and David fell asleep on the grass. Things would be different in the light of day.

Leib did not sleep. He pondered the idea of staying with Marian. He hoped Marian's farm was just far enough out of town to have escaped the inferno.

With the arrival of dawn, Leib gently woke Hanna and the

children, and they made their way to Marian's. He greeted them with open arms. Marian's sister Frania had food and drink ready, as though she'd been expecting them.

While his family was safe at Marian's, Leib immediately went to work on rebuilding the house. When he originally surveyed the damage, he noticed that the main structure was still intact. It wouldn't be hard to rebuild the inside of the house. It was time to call in some favors.

∽

In a few short months, the house was ready for the family's return, but life in Pińczów was not the same as before. The Germans now occupied Poland. Although the soldiers were not stationed in Pińczów, government orders dictated how things would be, and the police were there to enforce those orders.

Regardless of age or sex, no Jew could be seen in the street without a Jewish badge. In Pińczów, this was a white armband with a blue Star of David sewn onto all visible garments. No Jewish business could operate without a sign in the window identifying it as a Jewish establishment.

In October 1939, the first ghetto in Piotrkow Trybunalsi was formed. Ghettos allowed the Germans to herd the Jewish population into small areas like cattle. The ghettos were crowded, isolated, and full of starving, sick citizens.

But the ghettos were only a temporary measure while Hitler deliberated options to realize his goal of the "Final Solution" – his plan to systematically murder all of Europe's Jews.

There was a small silver lining in the destruction of Pińczów.

With its boundaries destroyed, it could not be made into an enclosed ghetto. The Jews of Pińczów still had strict rules and curfews that had to be obeyed, but they could move around more easily and gain access to supplies in a way that those who were trapped in enclosed ghettos could not. They were even able to pray in hiding. The men would secretly assemble in small, designated areas, such as a cellar, where they could conduct services.

Leah, one of Leib's sisters, was trapped with her family in the Lodz ghetto. Leib worked his magic and, through connections, was able to get parcels containing food and clothing to her.

There was no more maid. The tobacco concession was revoked, and Leib had to relinquish its control to a gentile. No Jew was permitted to own any government concession.

Leib did manage to start up a smaller business. He made soap in an upstairs room. Once again, the girls and their mother went to work as best they could. They had to be creative to get supplies. Esther was good at that, and Shoshana and Hanna ran the day-to-day operations of the business and the home. Although times were hard, once again the Golds, like many Jews in Poland, became a little too complacent.

PART TWO
On The Run

CHAPTER 6

Preparing for the Worst
October 4th, 1942

With each passing day, life in Poland became more tense. There were rumors of Jews being beaten, tortured, sent to death camps, and shot.

Now, three years after that awful night when the town was burned, it was time to prepare for the worst. The first thing Leib needed to do was find someone on the outskirts of town that he could pay to help. Worried that they had already used too much of Marian's hospitality, he thought carefully and finally came up with Artur Pilarski. This man had fallen on hard times even before the Nazi invasion. Although they were never really friends, Leib had done business with him for years, and he felt they had a good enough rapport. Pilarski lived modestly and didn't have much room, but maybe he would be willing to at least hide David.

He drove out to see the farmer and to propose the most

important business deal of his life. Pilarski was in the field working. He straightened up when he saw Leib enter the field and walked over to meet his visitor. The two men shook hands. Leib didn't waste any time with small talk. If Pilarski wasn't interested, he would have to find someone else.

"I have a business proposition for you. Can we talk?"

Pilarski sensed Leib's panic. Any proposition Leib Gold had to offer would mean much needed money for him.

"You've heard the Germans are rounding up Jews and taking them from their homes?"

Pilarski didn't speak. Leib continued. "I have a son, David. He's only twelve. He's too young to survive these butchers. I need a safe place for him to hide, and I'm prepared to pay you well for your cooperation."

Pilarski stared at Leib, his eyes narrowed. Leib was clearly desperate, and Pilarski could use that to negotiate a much larger payout. But this was not the time to haggle. They agreed on a price.

A sense of relief washed over Leib as he counted out a large sum of money into Pilarski's hand. He promised that David would bring even more when the time came. David would be spared; at least his only son would be saved.

ᔕ

On the eve of October 4, 1942, the Jewish holiday of *Shemini Atzeret*, the Germans surrounded Pińczów. A decree was issued that any Jew found in the street would be shot on sight. Leib panicked. All the preparations he'd made were useless. There was no way he could get David to Pilarski's place. The family stayed confined within the walls of their home and awaited their fate. They sat together and listened to the gunfire in the distance. The Germans were coming. If he'd only realized how quickly it was all going to happen. He needed more time to save his family. His mind raced searching for a solution. Perhaps he would be able to use some of his high-powered connections. Perhaps he could bribe his way out. But how could he reach anyone now?

They spent an uneventful day in the house. There was the odd scream in the street, and every so often a barrage of trucks thundered by. Gunfire could be heard, but it was still in the distance. The silence in the Gold home was unnatural.

Then Esther sat up in her chair, "Did you hear that?"

"What?" Leib asked.

"It sounded like a faint knock. There! I heard it again."

Leib heard it too. He made his way to the door and peeked through the slats. The sun had set, but in the dark he saw the figure of a man.

"Who is it?" he whispered.

"It's me, Marian," a muffled voice came from behind the door. Relieved, Leib opened the door, and Marian quickly stepped in.

Leib clutched his friend in a warm bear hug.

Marian felt it would be relatively safe for him to walk through the streets, after all the Germans were only hunting Jews, and everyone knew Marian's brother-in-law was Wojtek, the commandant of the Polish police. It was this connection and the identification papers in his pocket that would allow him to accomplish his plan.

With no time to lose, Marian blurted, "I've come for the boy."

David stiffened and took a big step backward. Wide-eyed, he looked at his father and protested. "I don't want to go anywhere. I want to stay here with you and Mameh."

David was no longer a small child and was smart enough to know better than to defy his father, but he instinctively knew what was about to happen. "I'm not going!"

Leib walked over and stood uncomfortably close to his son. He spoke in an inflexible tone. "You are going, and you are going right now."

While this debate took place, Hanna began to remove the white armband with the blue Star of David from her son's coat.

Marian spoke firmly but gently. "David, pay close attention to what I am saying. I will leave first, and you wait at the door. I will make sure no one is watching. When I whistle once, come out. I want you to follow quietly and quickly behind me. Stay at least six meters back. Okay?"

David didn't answer. Leib raised his voice, a rare occurrence, as he was usually in control. "David, do you understand?"

Looking down at the floor, David mumbled, "I understand."

Hanna helped David on with his coat, then his parents walked him to the door. Marian started out, and when he was sure the coast was clear, he whistled. Leib hugged his son tightly, kissed his head, and whispered a hasty prayer as he pushed him out the door. David turned in time to see the door shut in his face. He was on his own.

Once his eyes adjusted to the dark, he spotted Marian in front of him and began to walk. But with every step he took forward, his mind took one step backward. He wanted to be with his sisters and his parents. Why had his father made him do this alone? It wasn't right. He knew he might die, but he wanted to die with his whole family, not alone, not with Marian.

David turned around and with an increased stride made it back to his front door. When he opened it, he came face-to-face with his father. Leib's eyes bulged with rage, and his face flushed. He looked angrier than David had ever seen him before, but he didn't yell. It was much scarier when he spoke in a slow, deep, deliberate voice.

"David, how dare you come back? Don't you realize the chance Marian is willing to take for you? I am not asking you. I am *commanding* you to go to Marian's." Just then Marian walked through the door. He was willing to make one last attempt to save this boy he was so fond of.

Visibly shaken, David was torn between the fear of leaving his family and the chastising he'd received from his father. But it was clear. He had no choice but to go.

Hanna could see the distress in David's eyes. She didn't want him to leave with the bitter memory of this argument replaying in his head. She tried to reassure her son. "Davidle, we're doing this because we love you. It isn't forever. We'll come for you as soon as it's safe. Go *mayn tyreh kind*, my sweet child. Marian will protect you." She hugged him tightly, turned him in the direction of the door, and gave him a nudge to propel him forward. Without another word, David was gone.

Shoshana and Esther stayed quiet, but they both saw their little brother's fear. They went into the other room, where their parents couldn't hear, to discuss David's fate. The more they deliberated, the more they felt David couldn't manage this by himself.

"We have to do something, we can't just let him be alone," Esther whispered to her sister.

"I know. Did you see how he was trembling? He looked so frightened, but what can we do? He's gone," Shoshana replied.

ൾ

Marian and David made it safely to the farm. Once David was back on familiar ground, he felt a little more at ease. Marian had to take precautions in case someone had seen them. By morning, they would know if anyone had followed them.

Frania, aware of her brother's plan, gave David some dinner while Marian talked. She had become very fond of David and his family during an earlier stay. Wojtek, her husband, was gone and would not be back for days. For now, they didn't need to be concerned about him.

"You must stay quiet and still under the straw in the stable until I come to get you," Marian explained. "You're safe here, David, as long as you listen to everything I tell you. No matter what happens around you, do not, under *any* circumstances, come out. The more noise you hear, the quieter and more still you must be, *rozumiesz*?"

David nodded his understanding. They walked out to the stable and entered Bolek's stall. Bolek's ears pricked forward, and his tail brushed back and forth. The two friends were happy to be reunited. Marian told David to lie down in the hollow he had prepared at the back of the stall and covered him in straw.

David felt protected lying behind his four-legged friend. Marian double and triple checked that the boy could not be detected. He was safe.

ꕥ

Back home the girls became more agitated. The thought of David all alone was more than they could bear. They waited for their parents to fall asleep. With the streets dark and empty the two of them planned to find their brother. They knew how to get to Marian's using back streets. They would use buildings as cover along the way. Finally, the house was quiet enough for them to sneak away.

ꕥ

It was only a few hours after Marian had fallen asleep that a rustling outside awakened him. His heart thumped, and he jumped to his feet. He grabbed a fire iron and stepped toward the sound. He heard muffled whispering just loud enough to make out two women's voices. Cautiously, he opened the door, the stoker still firmly in hand and saw Shoshana and Esther.

Briskly, he swept them into the house.

"What are you doing here?" he asked in a loud whisper.

"Where's David?" Esther demanded, "Is he all right?"

"David's fine, he's sleeping. Do you realize what a chance you took coming here? You could've been shot, and now you've put us all in danger," Marian said frantically. "I'm surprised your father permitted this."

The girls looked at each other, and Marian immediately understood. "Your parents have no idea you've come here, do they?" he said. Both girls looked ashamed.

There was no more time to waste. Marian knew that with each passing minute, the risk increased. Now he had to hide the girls too. He went out to rearrange the bales of hay in another couple of stalls. It would be safer to shelter the girls separately. That way there would be no temptation to talk, and if one was discovered, the other might escape detection. He made sure they were far enough away from each other and nowhere near David.

When he returned to the house he spoke quickly and assertively. "David is asleep. I'm not going to wake him to tell him of your arrival, he's had a very trying night."

The sisters nodded.

"I've prepared two areas in the stable for you tonight. You must lie still with no communication until I come to get you. No matter what you hear, stay motionless and silent. Understand?"

The girls understood how crucial Marian's instructions were. They did as they were told and before long, were separately tucked away in the stable. Marian stood back and surveyed the area. He pulled out some loose hay and made sure it was strewn around the bales. He propped a rake up against a stack of hay and stepped back. It looked good. He could go to bed and try to get some sleep. He would need to be well rested in the morning.

ᔓ

Hanna's children were holding out their arms to her, calling for her, but she couldn't reach them. They seemed to be getting smaller and farther away as she tried desperately to get to them. Their voices became more distant and Hanna's panic more intense.

"Hanna, wake up. You're having a nightmare."

Hanna's heart pounded, and she was soaked in sweat. "Oh, my God, it was just a dream!" she exclaimed as she looked around and realized where she was. "Where are the girls?" she asked in an urgent tone.

"They are sleeping, safe in their rooms, and David is with Marian. You need to get some sleep. We have to be strong for whatever tomorrow will bring," Leib answered.

Hanna had to see her daughters for herself. "I'm going to check on the girls, I'll be right back."

There was no point in arguing. Leib lay back and closed his eyes.

A piercing cry came from down the hall, and a moment later, Hanna came flying into the room.

"They're gone!"

"What do you mean?"

"The girls are gone!" she cried in panic.

Leib ran down the hall. Sure enough, their beds were empty. He knew immediately that they had gone after their brother.

He grasped Hanna's shoulders tightly and looked directly into her eyes. "Hanna, the girls went to find their brother, no one has taken them. They'll be fine. Marian will hide them and make sure no harm comes to them. They're much safer at his farm than they are here."

Hanna would not be consoled. All three of her children were gone.

Leib's strong, indomitable wife was crumbling in front of

his eyes. He brought her closer to him, but she regained her composure and pulled away.

"I'm going to find them," she said firmly.

Leib felt the power of her words and knew he could not change her mind; in fact, this might actually be a blessing in disguise. Hanna would be safer with the children, and that would allow him the opportunity to move more freely and work out a plan for their next move. He would know where to find them later.

He told his wife to pack a few things while he disappeared into the spare room. He lifted some loose floorboards and pulled up what looked like a sack of sugar. But instead of sugar, it was stuffed with money. It was filled with zloty and American dollars. In total there was the equivalent of fifty thousand zloty. He grabbed his silver Kiddish cup and Shabbos candlesticks and went back to Hanna.

She took the silver pieces and placed them among the clothing in her bag. Then she took the money sack from Leib and tucked it safely under her dress. Using a large kerchief, Leib secured the heavy sack to his wife's body and then helped her on with her coat.

"Go," Leib said gently. "Your children need you as much as you need them."

Hanna and Leib held each other in a long embrace, their bodies fused together, until Leib finally broke the bond.

"Go, my love, before the sun rises. Be very careful. I'll join you all tomorrow. I still have reliable connections I can use to help us get through this. Don't look back. Your job is to concentrate on moving forward and protecting our family."

Hanna pulled away, looked straight into her husband's face, and said, "Promise me you'll be at Marian's tomorrow."

"I promise," Leib said, but he couldn't return her gaze.

The two of them walked to the door. Leib gently took Hanna's head in his hands and kissed her with an intensity and desperation neither of them had ever experienced before.

Hanna turned and walked out into the night.

CHAPTER 7

Preparations

Marian couldn't sleep. He was worried about the Gold children. Wojtek would be back in a few days, and Marian knew this man would not show any mercy toward them. He'd had a plan to explain David's presence, but he would never be able to come up with a plausible explanation to keep them all.

It was before dawn when Marian heard a faint knock. He was expecting both Leib and Hanna. When he opened the door he was surprised to see Hanna alone. He looked beyond her, to see if Leib was nearby, but there was no sign of him.

"Are my daughters here?" Hanna asked.

As Marian quickly moved her from the doorway into the house, he answered, "They are, and they're safe."

Hanna's body buckled. She collapsed onto a chair and took a deep breath. "And David?" she added.

"David is fine too. They're all well hidden and asleep in the stable. I don't want to wake them yet, Hanna. I still need time to think. Where's Leib?"

She didn't answer immediately, her mind flashed back to the last words he spoke, *I promise.*

"He told me to come alone," she said. "He had important things to put in place, and he promised to catch up with us today."

Hanna saw the blood drain from Marian's face.

"I'll try to go back for him later, when we know more about what's going on out there," he said.

They both knew that would be impossible. The Germans were only a few hours from arriving. Leib was on his own. If he were to survive this, it would be through his own ingenuity.

When the light broke, Marian went out to the stable. David had no idea what had transpired through the night. He'd taken Marian's instructions very seriously and hadn't moved a muscle. He had no idea his sisters were just a few meters away, and none of them could have guessed their mother was there and waiting for them.

It was a tearful reunion when Marian brought them together in the house.

Through all the emotion, Shoshana looked around. "Where's Tateh?"

Before anyone else could speak, Hanna answered. "He had to finalize some important arrangements for us. Don't worry about your tateh. He's a smart, powerful man, and he will find his way back to us somehow. It may take a while, so we have to be strong together. That's what he would expect of us, and we're not going to let him down."

The children were silent. Their father, the man who always made sure everything would be fine, the man who always led the way for them, would not be there to guide them on the most critical journey of their lives.

By nightfall, the Germans had rounded up the Jews of Pińczów. With only the clothes on their backs and one small parcel each, they were marched twenty-five kilometers to the trains in Jędrzejów and transported to Treblinka, one of the six extermination camps in Poland.

Marian took some comfort in knowing he was at least able to keep Leib's family from the fatal death march that night.

The Germans were efficient. By the following morning, most of the Jews were gone. Marian had to think quickly. He had to protect himself and his sister too. There was no way he could keep Hanna and the children for more than a couple of days. Wojtek would be back soon.

Marian suddenly remembered that Leib had told him about the farmer he paid to hide David. Marian knew exactly who he was. He, too, had done business with Pilarski. His farm was in the town of Sobowice. It would take them less than two hours to walk there. They would make preparations, and Marian himself would escort the family to Pilarski's place and make sure they were safe.

He told Hanna of his intentions, and she answered that she would do whatever he thought was best, but even as she said those words she was torn about leaving without her husband. The first thing they had to do was to make sure the money Leib had given Hanna was secure. This would be the only asset they could use to buy their freedom. Their lives depended on keeping the money safe. Frania and Hanna worked together sewing secret compartments in all their clothing. David would carry some inside the lining of his pants. He pulled out the tiny wallet that he carried everywhere.

"I can put some of it in here," he offered. Marian smiled at him and inserted one coin into his wallet.

Both Shoshana and Esther had compartments sewn into their undergarments, and Hanna had sewn a number of hidden pockets throughout her attire. She even hid some of the money under the insoles of her boots.

Once the cash was divided between them, Marian gave them extra clothing to wear on their backs. They each put on an extra shirt and sweater. They had double socks and stockings and two hats, one inside the other. Hanna packed a small bag where she could hide the only two material possessions that meant anything to her: Leib's Kiddish cup and her mother's candlesticks. They were ready. Marian could only hope that the deal Leib struck with Pilarski was solid, and he would honor their agreement. He knew this man was driven by money and hoped that for the right price he would hide the others as well.

Before they left, Frania served them a modest breakfast. Food was already becoming scarce, but she knew this might be the only meal they would eat that day. She gave them each a hard-boiled egg, bread with butter and jam, and an apple. They washed it down with tea.

While they were eating, Marian walked over to David and put his hand on his shoulder. David looked up at him. Marian gestured with his head for David to follow him, and he walked out of the room. After a few seconds, David got up from the table and followed. Standing in the hallway, Marian took something out of his pocket. It was a long, thin piece of black wood about ten centimeters in length. David's eyes widened. He knew exactly what it was. Marian pushed a small metal button, and a long, menacing blade kicked out, turning the harmless wood into a sleek weapon. He showed David how to put the blade back and release it again. He handed over the switchblade and told him to try it. David managed it with no problem.

"Keep this knife up your sleeve or in your sock. When you're alone, practice getting to it quickly and releasing it. If someone attacks you or your family, I want to you use this knife and go directly for your assailant's eye. That will stop him from advancing." David kept releasing and closing the knife as Marian continued educating him on taking down an attacker. "Once you have wounded him, run as fast as you can to safety. Okay?"

Marian got down on one knee. "David, look at me."

David stopped fidgeting with the knife and looked straight at him.

"You are the man of the family now, David. You must take care of the women. Make your father proud of you, my son." With that, Marian drew David into a hug. He released him with a few reassuring pats on the back, and they both returned to the kitchen.

Frania cleared away any evidence of breakfast. She handed them a small bag with some bread, a piece of cheese, and container of water. Hanna thanked Frania for all she had done, and together the Golds, accompanied by Marian, walked out the door.

CHAPTER 8

Discarded and Surrounded
October 7th, 1942

Marian knew the lay of the land and was able to guide them unseen through the mountainous terrain. His own life depended on it as well.

The trek to Pilarski's was uneventful. So much had happened in such a short span they were already losing track of time, but it was still morning on October 7, 1942, when they made it to Pilarski's farm.

"Hanna, you and the children stay there, and remain out of sight," Marian said as he pointed to a wooded area. They all moved quickly into the brush. Hanna watched as Marian walked down the hill toward the lane that led to the farm. From their elevated vantage point, they could see the layout of the property. It was large, with a two-story farmhouse. White horizontal fencing separated the home from the barn and stables. Hanna could see the leftover rows of potatoes that had not yet been harvested from the fields. Pigs roamed in their pens, and a few cows grazed in the distance.

Someone answered the door, but Hanna could not make out who it was. Marian disappeared into the house. It seemed like forever before there was any more movement at the farm, but finally Marian came out. He watched his feet as he climbed back up the hill, avoiding the fallen tree branches.

"Here's the plan," he said when he reached them. "Pilarski is willing to hide you for now, but made no commitment for how long. The deal Leib made with him was for David only, so to hide the rest of you, he wants an additional thousand zloty for each person."

Without hesitation, Hanna agreed. She took three thousand zloty from her boot and handed it to Marian.

Together they all walked down the hill.

Pilarski was feeding the pigs when Marian and the Golds approached. He stopped what he was doing.

"Where's the money?" Pilarski did not make eye contact, or even look in the direction of Hanna and her children. He spoke directly to Marian.

Marian wanted some reassurances before he handed him the cash. "You will hide all of them for this money, correct?"

Pilarski was fixated on Marian's pocket. He knew there was cash in it.

"Yes, yes," Pilarski assured Marian, "you have nothing to worry about. They'll be perfectly safe here."

Marian pulled his hand from his pocket and gave the money to Pilarski. He counted every zloty and then looked up at

Marian. "You go," he said. "Leave the Jews with me."

Hanna didn't like how that sounded, and for that matter, neither did Marian. He turned to Hanna. "You'll be fine here for a while. Take care of the children, and stay safe."

"Thank you for all you've done for us, Marian. Leib would be so grateful to know how you have helped his family. I hope one day in the near future we can enjoy ourselves over dinner like we used to."

Marian felt guilty that he couldn't do more for them. He had no choice but to leave them with Pilarski even though, deep down, he didn't trust the man. He could only hope he had done right by Leib. He felt a pang of guilt recognizing that, in truth, he was relieved to be free of the responsibility and burden of hiding them. He went over to David and crouched down to his height. "You'll be fine here, David. Remember our little talk. Take care of the ladies, my son." He pulled David in for one last hug and turned to leave. He walked back to his home, a load off his mind, but in his heart he feared they would not survive.

ᔕ

Pilarski still had not looked directly at any of them. "Follow me," he said. Behind the stable was an old, battered, wood structure. It was small and smelled like it might have had manure stored in there at one time.

"Get in there," he ordered. They entered, and Pilarski closed the door behind them. Fortunately, there was plenty of light as the wooden slats had so many breaks and holes that the light streamed through every crevice.

Esther, was very good at finding the positive in a bad situation. She had blossomed into a strong, confident young woman.

"Look here," she said. "We can take these bales apart and cover the dirt floor with straw. We'll be fine here for a while, you'll see."

Shoshana and David took their cue and started to pull out the straw from the well-formed bales. David knew it would be easier if he used his switchblade to open the bales but was afraid to reveal it to his mother. She would confiscate it, and he had no intention of letting that happen. David was making decisions by himself now. He had to think what would be best for his family, what his father would do, so he continued to undo the bales by hand and kept the weapon a secret. It took a couple of hours, but they managed to make an acceptable area to rest on. It was getting late, and Hanna still had the bag of food Frania packed. She pulled it out to eat, but decided to ration it, as they had not seen Pilarski since he'd ordered them into the shed.

Pilarski was back at the house rehashing his commitment. What was he thinking, offering to help these Jews?

German propaganda claiming Jews were evil had intensified. Movies and posters depicting them as corrupt, filthy, and lazy circulated. They were shown as people who had taken control of the banks and were blamed for every person's unfortunate situation. The propaganda equated Jews to rats. Comparing Jews to vermin would dehumanize them, making it more acceptable to eliminate them. Drawings were posted, showing Jews with large, hooked noses, warts, and dirty, roach-infested beards. Warnings of typhoid and other diseases were written in red letters, meant to look like blood.

Many Polish people had come to believe this propaganda, and Pilarski was no exception. He'd begun blaming Jews a year ago; around the same time he had trouble putting food on the table. After *Kristallnacht*, the two-day Nazi rampage that started on November 9, 1938, leaving almost a hundred Jews dead and thirty thousand arrested, it was easy to believe Jews were the enemy. It was safer to believe it too.

A few hours later, Hanna heard Pilarski's heavy footsteps. She was hopeful that he was bringing some food. The door opened, and he stood there, once again not looking directly at them. He seemed to be looking past them, over their heads.

"Leave all your things, and get off of my farm," he said in a deep commanding voice.

"What about our deal?" Hanna asked.

"The deal is off. The Germans have invaded the town, and I'm not putting myself in danger for Jews. Get out now." His face was red, and he spat as he spoke.

With a jerk of her head Hanna motioned to the children. They immediately got up, brushed themselves off, picked up their belongings, and prepared to leave.

"Drop everything and go. Now!" he shouted.

With the efficiency of a seasoned thief, Esther hid her mother's sack under her coat as the rest of them put their belongings on the ground and left the shed.

Hanna thought she would try to get their money back. As she walked past him she said, "If the deal is off, then return our money."

"GET OUT!" he bellowed as he picked up a pitchfork.

They fled up the hill, retracing their original path. After

only a few hundred meters they heard a deep voice shouting in Polish, “Hey, Jews!” It was not Pilarski’s voice. This voice was much raspier.

Hanna moved behind David and whispered, “Don’t answer. Keep moving.”

Focused on the forest ahead, they hoped they could lose whoever was calling in the thick brush. They picked up their pace, but did not run.

At that moment David remembered his father’s words when he was being chased by a large dog. “Never look strange dogs in the eye. They will consider it a challenge. If you want to get away, stand tall with your shoulders back, and walk quickly with confidence, but do not run.” David immediately straightened up, put his shoulders back and walked with his head held high.

This time a different voice spoke from behind them. “Hey, Jews! Where you going? We’re not finished with you.”

From the forest two more men appeared. The Golds couldn’t move forward or backward. More people emerged from the left and the right. Carrying shovels, pitchforks, and makeshift weapons, these threatening assailants advanced slowly toward them. One of the men laughed.

He’s enjoying our fear, Hanna thought.

Another man staggered toward them, drinking from a tarnished silver flask. From their clothes, it was clear they were all farm workers.

Hanna and her children backed into a circle, each facing a different direction. Clutching at each other’s coats, they dared not take their eyes off the approaching men. They were surrounded.

Sobowice was a small town, and Pilarski must have put the

word out that he was releasing Jews. These men had come out to harass them, maybe even kill them.

They were growing in numbers, and there was no escape. Then the heckling began.

"Dirty Jews."

"Take your diseases back where you came from."

"Go back to the gutter with the rats that you are."

Hatred spewed as they fed off each other's energy. Waving their weapons and fists in the air, they chanted a common phrase over and over in an awful drone: "Give the Jews to the Germans."

The crowd grew, and now there were at least twenty men. Hanna was sure they were going to be killed.

David recalled the horrible vision of Mr. Zimmerman in pain, holding his stomach, with the blood spewing between his fingers. In that moment David prayed, "Please, *please,* God, let someone shoot me in the head. I don't want to die a slow death like Mr. Zimmerman."

Hanna wanted to at least save David, her youngest child, the only one that could carry on the family name.

"Please, leave us alone," she cried out to them. "Go home. We will leave quickly and not bother you. My son is going up the hill. You can take us if you must, but he is going to leave," she said in an assertive tone.

The farmers could trade these four Jews to the Germans for eight kilos of sugar. They were not letting David go anywhere.

David felt up his sleeve for the knife Marian had given him. He wanted to use it, but there were just too many of them. A few of the men moved in closer. One of them looked directly at him. "Give me your clothes."

David stood tall, as his father had instructed. He did not look the man in the eye, but did not back away, either. As the man moved dangerously close, David braced himself knowing he was about to be struck. It wasn't until a split second before the man's arm made contact that he caught a glimpse of the blade clutched in the fellow's hand. David instinctively raised his own arm to protect his face as the knife came down and plunged into the back of David's hand. The ruffian watched for the boy's reaction, but David did not flinch. He stayed tall and complied with his original command to remove his coat.

The blood dripping from David's hand energized the mob, and their chanting grew louder. Hanna began reciting the *Shema*, a Jewish prayer said when one is ready to die. David watched the blood oozing from his wound and was surprised it didn't hurt. It took a few minutes before the throbbing set in. Esther instinctively placed herself between her brother and his attacker. Without hesitation the farmer pushed hard enough to throw her to the ground.

As the farmers were just about to swarm, an imposing command came from beyond the mad scene.

"STOP!"

Everyone turned to see two burly men walking toward them. The smaller of the two had a gun pointed straight at the crowd.

The two men moved closer. They had the attention of the farmers. The larger of the two spoke in Polish.

"Are you all crazy? What do you think you're doing, have you all lost your minds? Do you have any idea what's going on out there?"

His friend still had the gun drawn, his finger on the trigger.

Surprisingly, the farmers listened as he continued.

"We've just come from Germany; we escaped from a labor camp. The Germans are killing all the Poles as well as Jews. Do you really want to help them? Do you really have to be their instruments and do their dirty work for them? They're coming for you, too. Who will save *you* and *your* families?" He became more enraged as he went on. "Let these people go. They've done nothing to you. You have two choices: either go back to your homes and your families while you still can, or die here." The large man looked over at the gun his friend had pointed at them.

His words actually cut through the collective hatred. Some of the men made disparaging remarks to save face, but they all backed off and dispersed. Hanna breathed a sigh of relief, but unable to control her shaking legs, she grabbed on to Shoshana for support. Esther got up off the ground and moved closer to David to examine his hand. She took off one of her extra socks and wrapped it tightly around his wound to stop the bleeding.

Shoshana steadied her mother and then sprang into action. She could hear her father's voice in her head. *Blue eyes and fine features.* Shoshana was an attractive woman. She was twenty-three and had those intense blue eyes, a small button nose, and a beautiful smile. Her thick, dark hair accentuated her ivory skin and made her appear more Polish than Jewish. She had a sultry demeanor men were drawn to, and she could use it if she had to.

She walked over to the two Poles who had just saved them and with a flirtatious intonation said, "You men were wonderful. How can we ever thank you? I don't want to think what would have happened if you hadn't come along."

While she was talking, she was also analyzing. She needed

their help, but was afraid to trust them. Even though they acted like good people, she was not taking any chances.

As a symbol of respect, one of the men removed the hat he was wearing while Shoshana spoke. "Can you help us find a safe place?" she asked.

Hanna intervened, "Do you know how to get to Działoszyce? We would be very grateful, and we can pay you for your help if you can take us there." Hanna had heard that the Jews in Działoszyce were working in ghettos and had not all been deported to concentration camps. She thought if they could get there, they might buy some time, while they figured out what to do next. Leib's cousin Aaron lived there, and Hanna knew how to find the house if she could only get to Działoszyce. She knew it was about twenty-five kilometers south of Pińczów and figured it would take them the better part of the night to reach it.

At the offer of money, the two men looked at each other, and, once again, the larger man spoke. "We were headed in that direction anyway, so you can come with us."

Shoshana caught the calculating look the two men had given each other, and she didn't want to be robbed. She quickly placed herself between the two of them, and in a playful manner she interlaced her arms through theirs, one on either side of her. "Come boys," she said coyly. "You show us the way." She began to lead with a smiling man on each arm.

CHAPTER 9

Destination Działoszyce

In the middle of nowhere, walking with strange men whom they were afraid to trust, the Golds began the long trek to Działoszyce. The temperature dropped considerably, and the air was chilly. With only a sliver of moon, the stars filled the vast sky like a patterned carpet of twinkling lights. They could only see a few feet in front of them in the dense forest. No one spoke. The wind blowing through the trees, and their shoes crushing leaves and branches were the only sounds. They concentrated on every step to avoid tripping over tree roots, all the while avoiding low branches that impeded their way. It was exhausting, and they hadn't eaten much. The fear of the unknown consumed much of their energy, but at the same time, it propelled them through the forest.

After a few hours of walking, Shoshana rejoined her family.

The two men were now far in the lead. David hurried on ahead so he could keep the two men in his sight, all the while checking back to make sure his mother and sisters weren't falling too far behind. They walked for hours with no rest. The hue of the darkness changed as the first signs of daybreak began to show. David could no longer see the two men. He stood still and whistled for them, hoping they would hear him and come back, but they did not. By then the women had caught up.

"They're gone," David said.

"Gone? What do you mean gone! Were you not following closely behind them?" Esther asked.

"I tried, but they picked up speed, it was like they were trying to lose us on purpose," David explained.

Hanna intervened. "It doesn't matter. We've walked a long way and can't be far from Działoszyce. We need to stop now and rest. As soon as the sun rises, we will have a better idea of where we are, and we'll deal with it then."

There were no arguments from anyone. They all found spots where they could drop and close their eyes, if only for an hour. Hanna took her shoes off and rubbed her tired feet. Shoshana propped herself up against a tree, removed her coat, and used it to cover herself. Within minutes, she was asleep.

All Hanna could think of was Leib. Where was he? Was he alive? Had he found someone to hide him? She remembered his last kiss and for a split second was able to forget where she was. Leib could make her feel so secure and loved with just one look. How she longed to see those tranquil dark eyes now. He was her last thought as she gave in to sleep.

Footsteps walking through a nearby field broke the silence.

They woke to see a Polish farmer making his way toward them. At first they were panic-stricken with memories of the Polish farmers still so fresh, but slowly they relaxed when they saw his non-menacing manner. He was older, dressed in working overalls, and carrying no tools. He called out *"Dzień dobry."*

"Dzień dobry. Good morning," they replied.

As usual, Shoshana spoke. "Can you tell us how far we are from Działoszyce?"

"Działoszyce?" he said. "You're nowhere near Działoszyce. You're closer to Jędrzejów."

The two men who were paid to guide them to Działoszyce had taken them in the complete opposite direction. Esther did a calculation figuring how long they were walking and how far Działoszyce was supposed to be from their starting point.

"We must be at least thirty-five kilometers from Działoszyce," she said, sounding defeated.

It was an unfortunate setback, but they were still alive, and, with the exception of being hungry and thirsty, they were still in good condition. They could make it to Działoszyce, but not without some water and a guide to get them moving in the right direction.

Hanna spoke to the farmer. "Can you get us through these forests and show us our way to Działoszyce? We will pay for your trouble," she offered. "And if you can find us water, we will pay you more," she added.

The farmer thought for a moment. He realized these people were Jews in hiding. He was an old-timer, set in his ways, and tried not to get all caught up in the propaganda around him. He lived alone and had a regular routine managing his farm, which is why he was up so early. He enjoyed a morning stroll before he began his chores. His life was very simple, and he wanted to keep it that way. He was aware of the dangers of helping Jews but did not harbor any hatred, unlike many of his fellow countrymen. He would help these people, if he could do it without putting himself in peril.

Hanna already held money in her outstretched hand. That money would go a long way to help him through these lean times. The farmer took it and stuffed it into the front of his overalls.

"I'll begin walking south," he said in Polish as he pointed in the direction he was about to walk. "Wait here until I'm almost out of your sight, and then follow me. I must stay far ahead of you in case someone sees us. If I'm asked, I will deny knowing you."

"Of course. We just need to find our way to Działoszyce," Hanna answered.

With that the farmer began walking. He picked up a large branch and used it as a walking stick.

"Do you know where we can find water?" Esther asked.

"For now there is dew on the grass. Try to suck on the long strands. There's a stream farther away from here," he answered, "but with no rain the last few weeks, it might have dried up."

David grabbed a handful of grass and shoved it into his mouth. He immediately began to spit it out and cough. He had pulled some of the grass out by the roots, and the dirt tasted horrible in his mouth. He wiped his sleeve across his tongue to get rid of the grit. Shoshana bent down and pulled up a handful more carefully. She gave her first handful to David and then bent down to get more for herself. Esther and Hanna did the same. By now, the slow-moving farmer was far enough away. They followed, bending down every few minutes to pick up more grass to suck on. The sun was rising, and soon the dew would evaporate. They moved on. Their goal was to reach Działoszyce by nightfall.

CHAPTER 10

Aaron's Story

It felt like they had been walking forever. The blue sky was dotted with white clouds, and the hills were carpeted in autumn colors. The view from the hilltops was breathtaking; a majestic landscape covered in a kaleidoscope of golds, reds, and deep greens set against an aqua sky. How ironic that this beautiful day was one of the worst days the Golds had ever endured. They walked in silence, following the directions the old farmer had left them.

Hanna was consumed with thoughts of Leib. She needed to know if he was all right and couldn't focus on anything else. Shoshana made a conscious effort to eliminate the morose images that crept into her mind. She tried very hard to picture herself back in the store where she felt secure, where she was in charge and in control. Esther was focused on a goal. She would reach her destination; find shelter, food, and safety. She was determined not to let this physical and mental beating get the better of her. David's only thoughts were of protection. It was his job to keep his mother and sisters safe. He devised all kinds of unrealistic plans as he drudged on. The only sound that echoed around them was the crunching of fall leaves under their feet. It became almost rhythmic and helped them to keep moving forward.

They were tired and hungry, but nothing came close to the anguish of their extreme thirst. They were not sure how much farther Działoszyce was, but they had been walking for most of the day under the bright sun. It is not unusual for October to be warm in Poland, and this year it was no exception.

Esther saw it first. "Look!" she exclaimed. There it was, like a mirage, a statue of the Holy Maria standing erect and tall right next to a stone well. Propped above the well was a wooden bucket attached to a chain and a crank. Water at last. The well was on the property of a well-manicured farm at the foot of the hill they were standing on.

Shoshana would have to be the spokesperson again. Her linguistic talent would be put to good use.

They walked down the hill with Shoshana in the lead and stood aside while she knocked on the farmhouse door. A large woman answered, but before Shoshana could say anything, the woman yelled, "Jews!"

Shoshana tried to speak over her. "Please, we just need a little water, and we will be on our way. Please have mercy on us," she said through parched, cracked lips. By now they were all disheveled. They had not washed or combed their hair for a few days, nor had they slept much. They were exhausted and hungry, and they looked like vagrants.

"You want water?" the woman shouted in a hate-filled voice. "I'll give you water." With that she bent forward, picked up a handful of stones, and hurled them. Shoshana turned in time to save her face, but the stones hit her shoulder. The four Golds ran up the hill, past the well and the cold water they would never taste. They were relieved to have made a getaway with only a few welts and bruises.

"We can't be that far," Esther said. "You'll see. We'll be in town before you know it, and we'll have lots of water to drink. Come, the sooner we get there, the sooner we can find food and rest." Esther's words motivated them, and they forced themselves to continue their trek.

Like Pińczów, Działoszyce was not a closed ghetto, but Jews were forbidden to leave the town. Aaron Formalski, Leib's cousin, had a house there, and it was their hope to stay with him till they could figure out what to do.

They walked through a dense part of the forest into a clearing. David spotted it first.

The women emerged from the brush and saw it too: Działoszyce. From their vantage point they saw German tanks and trucks patrolling the streets. As night set in, so did the cold. Once darkness blanketed the town and movement came to a halt, it was time to make their move. Hanna knew exactly where Aaron's house was, and they snuck through back alleys, using buildings and trees for cover. Finally the house came into view. They all stayed hidden and watched while Shoshana knocked on the door. There was no answer. She knocked a little harder, still no answer.

David went around to the side of the house. He found a window. The drapes were drawn, so he couldn't see anything inside. David thought for a second about going back to tell his mother of his find, but realized that he didn't need her permission anymore. He pried opened the window just enough so he could move the drapes and peer inside. The room was sparsely furnished, but he could see indentations in the rug were it was obvious that furniture once stood. He looked past the room to an open doorway that led to another room. He couldn't be sure, but he thought he could see what looked like the dark pants of a seated person. He had to go in. He was so thirsty, and there was nowhere else to go. He opened the window very slowly, just wide enough so he could put one leg in and then the other. He was inside. From where he was in the salon, he could clearly see the back of a man sitting at a table. The man was very still. David approached slowly. He could see from the man's clothing that he was not a soldier. David had never met Aaron and hoped this man was him. He walked into the kitchen. The man did not turn to look at David. He seemed to be in a daze.

"Aaron?"

The man turned slowly, toward David's voice, but didn't seem to see him. He turned back to his original position. He was unshaven, his clothes were wrinkled and dirty, and there were crusty dishes on the table and in the sink. Realizing this man was not a threat, David ran through the house and opened the front door. "There's a man inside. He might be Aaron, but I think there's something wrong with him." David led the three women into the kitchen.

The man sat still with his elbows propped on the table, his head balanced on his hands. He looked straight ahead and had not yet acknowledged their presence. Esther quickly got water for all of them. It felt incredible as it slid down their throats and doused the dry, burning pain that had tormented them for the past two days.

Hanna walked over to the man and lifted his head in her hands. She bent down so she was at his eye level and said, "Aaron, do you know who I am?"

Even though Aaron did not move, Hanna could see his eyes had focused on her face. He was back from whatever horror he was reliving.

"Hanna!" he cried as he recognized her. From his seated position he grabbed her hand and held it tightly. "Hanna, they're all dead," he wept. "My wife, my children were all killed."

Hanna put her arms around Aaron, and he sobbed with unbearable sorrow. Shoshana stood watching, unmindful of the tears streaming down her own face. Aaron composed himself and told them how he was separated from his wife, Judith, and their three children. His voice cracked with emotion as he told his story.

"I can still see the terrified look in Judith's eyes when we realized what was happening. We knew this day might come, but now it was actually here. It was just over a month ago, on the morning of September 2. All Jews were ordered to the market square. They told us we could bring a few bags. There were so many of us, Hanna, and the SS and Gestapo were all around us with their guns drawn, ready to shoot anyone who didn't obey. With every passing minute the square became more crowded, and I made sure Judith and the children stayed close beside me.

"I found my brother Shlomo and his family in the square. Without speaking a word between us, we communicated our fear. Both our families stayed huddled close together. Then I saw the horse-drawn carts arrive. The Germans were picking out old people from the crowd and some young children too. They lifted them roughly onto the carts; we saw them toss babies into the wagons as if they were throwing melons. The guard near us had announced that we were going to walk to the station in Miechow. It was a long walk: about twenty-five kilometers away. They were choosing those who were not going to be able to walk that distance. What a fool I was to think the people on the carts were going to be driven to the station. Instead, they were taken out to the cemetery and shot.

"The rest of us formed lines and marched in silence for seven hours to a large field near Miechow. Judith and my three children walked in front of me, and Shlomo and his family followed. On the way we heard weeping and the steady sound of gunfire. We knew people were being killed, so we were very careful not to do anything to draw attention to ourselves. Even my youngest, Shmuly, who was only six, did not cry or misbehave. When we arrived we joined hundreds of other people who were already there."

Aaron was no longer looking at Hanna; he gazed past her, as he relived every last agonizing second in his mind. He continued speaking. "With expert precision, the Germans selected who would go where. It was done so quickly, it was only a few minutes till it was our turn. One of the SS soldiers looked at us, and with the flick of his finger he sent my brother and me to the left and our wives and children to the right. We did not even have a chance to say good-bye. They rushed them away so quickly, but I could hear Shmuly calling "Tateh, Tateh!" It broke my heart.

Judith blew me a kiss before she was whisked onto a train along with the rest of the women and children. That's the last image I have of my beautiful family. We found out after we arrived at our destination that they were taken to the crematoriums of Belzec extermination camp."

Reliving this fresh memory was taking its toll on Aaron's already fragile soul. Hanna spoke. "Aaron, you don't have to continue, you can finish telling us later. Why don't you rest now?"

Aaron's voice hardened. He ignored Hanna as though she hadn't spoken and continued his story. But now, instead of sorrow, there was anger in his voice. "Shlomo and I were crowded into a cattle car along with all the able-bodied men who were selected. It was an hour or so before the train stopped in Plaszow."

While Aaron continued his story, Esther and Shoshana prepared some food they found in the kitchen cupboards.

"How did you get back here Aaron?" Hanna asked.

"The camp was still being established. The barracks were not finished, and the lights and sewers were still in the process of being built. There were factories being erected as well. More and more people poured into the camp. Every few hours another transport would arrive. There were Jews, Poles, men, women. All were separated accordingly and sent in different directions. Shlomo and I were assigned to the same barrack. It was overcrowded, and we slept in bunks that were three rows high. Our 'mattress' was a wooden board. It was amazing how we looked forward to arriving back to those stinking barracks after the fourteen-hour days of digging and smashing rocks. At least we were temporarily sheltered from the elements and, to some degree, from the lash of the guards."

Aaron paused, trying to find the strength to continue. When he was ready, he resumed his tale, while David sat wide-eyed on the floor with Shoshana, and Hanna stayed close to Leib's cousin.

"Shlomo and I were lucky. They chose us to work outside of the camp borders. We prepared land for the municipal gasworks so light and gas could be carried inside the walls of the camp. Our morning started at four a.m. We were marched in single file with armed guards all around us to the outskirts of the camp. We spent all day digging up earth, shoveling coal, and breaking up rocks. We were given so little to eat, a piece of bread and some watered-down soup, but it was not enough to sustain us while doing hard labor. Shlomo and I knew our days were numbered if we did not get out of there. We had nothing to lose, our families were gone, and our lives would be too. We had a choice to live for a short while in these conditions, or take our chances and make an escape. We chose the latter.

"One morning, after the routine roll call and the long march to the road outside the camp, we decided to make our move. We knew the routine by then. When we arrived at our work site, some of the prisoners were designated to unload the tools from the trucks. That was the only time we were not in an organized line. It was the *only* time we could make our escape. The sun was just starting to rise, and it was very gray – harder to see.

"While the guards were busy lashing out at the prisoners unloading the trucks, we snuck behind one of the parked vehicles. We hid there for a short time, and when we noticed that the guards' backs were turned, we ran into the forest. We camouflaged ourselves with dirt and old leaves and stayed still till nightfall. We could not chance running in daylight. We would be too easy to spot, and our feet would make too much noise on the dry leaves and branches. No one would discover we were missing until they returned to the barracks and did another roll call.

"I stayed under those leaves, but my body shivered. I was not sure if it was from the cold or because I was so terrified. I prayed that my shaking would not betray me. I needed to be perfectly still so the debris I was covered with would stay still as well. My prayers were answered as I fell asleep. When I woke, it took a few seconds for reality to set in. Everything was dark and silent. I was afraid to move. Finally I heard Shlomo whisper my name. We both stood and surveyed the forest. We were alone. We began our journey using the moon and then the sun as our guide. We were cold and hungry, and it took us much longer than it should have to walk the fifty-five kilometers back home.

Shlomo and I split up when we reached Działoszyce. He went to his house, and I came here. When I arrived, less than a week ago, I thought I would be happy to be back, but there is nothing for me here, nothing but the ghosts inside these walls." His frail and broken voice weakened with his last statement. Hanna held on to him and let him cry.

CHAPTER 11

The Działoszyce Ghetto

Shoshana held her brother throughout Aaron's story. David was unnerved by the horrifying events Aaron recounted. She broke the flow of the conversation and redirected it to the present. "Aaron, we have to find a safe place to hide. Can you help us? Is there a cellar or a crawl space where we can stay for now?"

Aaron's house had two floors. An apartment upstairs and one downstairs. Besides the usual attic at the top of the building, there was also a second attic between the two floors. It was not very high, but it spanned the entire length of the house, and it was large enough for the four of them to hide in.

After having something to eat, they washed off the filth that had accumulated in the last few days. Bathing served as an emotional cleansing as well. They felt a little more human when they entered the closet to climb the ladder to the attic. At least for now they would be safe and warm. David entered first and crawled on hands and knees in the tight space to the other side, giving his mother and sisters enough room to enter and find a spot they could stretch out in. Within minutes they were all asleep.

Hanna was the first one down in the morning. She felt stronger than she had in days. With food in her belly and her body well rested, she was strong enough to start thinking of their next step.

Aaron was already up and dressed. He was going out to survey what was new in the town. Every day there was word of someone else being abducted or shot. Hanna wanted to join him. She wanted to familiarize herself with her new surroundings. She needed to know where she could buy food, whom she could trust, who was running this ghetto.

"Aaron and I are going out for a while, you stay here and remain out of sight." She instructed her children.

The two of them stepped outside. Hanna borrowed one of Judith's overcoats complete with the mandated armband for Jews. The sun was already high in the sky. The air was crisp, and it felt good to be walking in the streets of a town again. It seemed almost normal. People were out, talking with each other, shopping, conducting their daily lives. The Jews were identifiable by the armbands on their sleeves, and for some strange reason Hanna thought everything would be fine now. She went to the grocery store, bought sugar, flour, milk, bread, and other staples. The prices were hugely inflated, but she still had plenty of money. She saw uniformed police all around, and Aaron explained they were the *Judenrat* of the town, the Jewish police, established at the command of the Germans, to serve as liaison between the controlling German authorities and the Jewish communities. There was a Judenrat in most towns to run the day-to-day city operations, such as hospitals, schools, and all municipal requirements. They were forced to choose between giving up their fellow Jews, or paying with their own lives. This type of power created two types of men. The ones who got carried away with their authority and fed off the violence they witnessed from the Nazis, and the ones who were torn by the task of betrayal.

"They may be Jewish police, but don't fool yourself into thinking they are any better than the Germans. They've been rounding up young boys, beating them, jailing them, and forcing them to work in labor gangs along the roads. They are no better than the Germans they work for," Aaron told Hanna.

Hanna pretended to pick out potatoes as she listened to Aaron and watched two members of the Działoszyce Judenrat walking and swinging their batons in authoritative rhythm. They were laughing and talking to each other, but their eyes were fixed on the streets, searching for victims.

In a few days, the Golds settled into a routine at Aaron's house. They relaxed a little and stopped hiding all the time. The girls and David were getting restless and needed to get out. Not wanting to travel the streets when they were the busiest in the middle of the day, they tried going out at dawn. Curfews prohibited Jews from being out after dark, so mornings worked out well, or so they thought. Times were corrupt, and people looked for any way they could make money and to win favor of the Judenrat or Polish police. Snitching was common practice, and neighbors noticed the new people in town. It didn't take long before the Jewish police crashed through Aaron's door.

It was evening, and the Golds were just about to make their

way up to the attic, when four policemen stood in the entranceway, batons in hand. One of them yelled, "Everyone here out, now!"

The family exchanged horrified looks. For a fleeting moment Hanna's thought was to run, but there was no escape. Once the police knew of their existence, there would be no place for them to hide. One by one they walked into view.

These Jewish policemen didn't care that they were torturing their own people. They had to prove their worthiness to the Germans, or they, too, would be dispensable. But did they have to enjoy the intense fear they could see on the faces of their victims?

Pandemonium erupted. The largest of the men grabbed David. Batons swung wildly and struck the women repeatedly as they tried to free David, but it all happened so fast. Two of the men dragged David from the house as he tried to resist. Hanna and the girls screamed. David was gone.

Aaron came out of hiding and tried to calm the hysterical women.

"They won't kill him," he said. "They need him. As long as he is useful, David will live."

Aaron's words were of little comfort. Hanna was furious that Aaron had stayed hidden while the police took her son away, but she said nothing. She needed this man more now and was not about to anger him, but she never felt the same about Aaron after that day.

David was taken to the jailhouse where he came face-to-face with Samolski, the commandant of the Jewish police. *How ugly he is,* David thought, as he saw Samolski's pockmarked face and large jowls. The man seemed to enjoy watching this frightened boy.

"I'm just doing my job, you know," Samolski said to David. "Now you get to work with other boys just like you. Isn't that better than sitting around doing nothing?" He laughed as he walked out, scraping his baton along the bars.

David was not alone in that dark room. There were other terrified boys there too. He dared not speak. He was paralyzed, not knowing what they had planned for him and barely slept at all. *Am I going to be shot? Are they going to deport me to one of the extermination camps?* Every time he tried to close his eyes his thoughts became louder, but eventually his body gave in to exhaustion.

In the morning, the inmates were given some watered-down coffee and a piece of bread with some kind of fat spread and jam. David ate his. Then the doors were unlocked, and the boys were all gathered together outside. A man in uniform appeared and spoke to them.

"You are all working men now. You will march quietly and in an orderly way through the fields to the roads outside the borders of the town. Once you reach your destination, you will receive your orders. When you are finished working, you will be marched back to town, and then you may go home."

You may go home, David repeated in his mind. Had he heard that correctly?

The officer continued. "You will report to this station at five every morning to begin your work day. Anyone who disobeys or makes the slightest bit of trouble will be shot."

Other guards soon appeared. They were dressed in blue uniforms and looked different from the Jewish police. These were the *Junakies*, the Polish auxiliary guards used by the Germans to keep the labor gangs working. They carried no guns but were expert at using their clubs as weapons.

Dawn was breaking when they filed out of the station and began walking. David was functioning on nervous energy. They walked for almost two hours through the fields in the direction of Skalbmeirz. By the time they reached their destination, the sun had risen. David heard one of the guards talking in Polish. He said something about making better time tomorrow, and that it shouldn't have taken this long to walk ten kilometers. Now David knew how far out of town he was.

A wagon stood at the side of the road loaded with sledgehammers and shovels. "Grab a shovel or a mallet and begin clearing the road. You will have a short break for lunch, but if we see anyone resting before that, there will be hell to pay." The guard picked up one of the heavy hammers and threw it at the boy standing beside David. He was not prepared and didn't catch it. It hit his leg, and he bent over in pain. A baton came down hard on his back. "Stand up, you weak Jew. Take that hammer, and get to work."

ഗ

Pulling on Judith's coat, Hanna left the house. The stores were not yet open, but a few people were walking in the streets. These days Hanna didn't make friends easily. It was very hard to trust anyone, and she preferred to keep to herself. But today was different. She needed to speak to people and ask questions. She needed to figure out where her son was without raising suspicion or causing a ruckus. She saw an unkempt man wearing a dirty cap and overalls.

His lack of an armband and his working attire gave him away as a Polish farmer. His open market stall had straw spread all around, and he sat in the middle on a wooden box with large cartons of eggs stacked in front of him. Hanna watched as he cracked the eggs one by one and with a quick jerk of his head guzzled their contents into his mouth like shots of whiskey.

Hanna approached "Dzień dobry, good morning."

The farmer raised his head and looked at Hanna. She was rattled by his empty eye socket, which had once housed a brown eye to match his other one. She tried not to let her revulsion show.

"Dzień dobry," the man replied.

He looked around to see if anyone was watching and then offered Hanna the opportunity to buy some of his eggs at a very inflated price. Jews were not permitted to buy eggs, but Hanna paid his price and took the carton, which she hid under her coat.

"Have you seen a boy, twelve years old, with black, curly hair? The police took him last night, and I have to find him. He is my son," she added with desperation in her voice.

"If they took him, then he's long gone from here," the man answered.

Hanna thought she was going to faint.

The man continued. "They left a long time ago, they go every morning out to work on the roads."

A glimmer of hope returned, and Hanna regained her composure. "Work? Work where?" she asked.

"The guards take them south of town every morning to work on the highways, and they return in the evening," he said matter-of-factly.

"Do you know when in the evening they will be back?" She asked.

Before he had a chance to answer, they both spotted two men in the distance walking slowly in their direction.

"Here comes the swine that probably snitched on your son." He pointed. "There. See that tall man with the high black boots? Not the one in the uniform. The other one?"

Hanna nodded.

"That's Bialobrodah. He's a Jewish pig. He walks, laughing with the SS guard and the two big dogs, like he's better than everyone else. The Germans use him as their informant to capture Jews. He is a disgusting, ruthless human being. You'd better get out of here while you still can."

Hanna thanked the man who had given her the hope she needed and left quickly. She snuck down a street, out of sight of the two approaching men and walked briskly toward the house.

ↀ

Shoshana woke up and decided to familiarize herself with the kitchen. Searching to see what Aaron had stocked on the shelves and where he kept his pots and dishes for cooking, she opened the cupboard under the sink and bent down to find a good-sized soup pot. When she took it out, something moved. She screeched, and the pot clanged loudly as it hit the floor. A little gray mouse presented itself at the edge of the cupboard. It stopped for a second, wriggled its tiny nose, and jumped down onto the floor. It hugged the wall as it scampered to the other end of the room toward the salon doorway and then turned the corner and was gone.

Shoshana sat on the chair, her heart pounding. All of a sudden she started to laugh uncontrollably. She couldn't catch her breath and tears flowed down her cheeks. Esther heard all the commotion from the other room and came quickly to see what had happened. At first she thought Shoshana was crying, but when she got closer and moved her sister's hands from her face, she realized it was laughter.

"Shosh, what is it?" Esther asked.

Shoshana tried to speak but could barely get the words out. *Mouse* was the only discernable word Esther could hear. The laughter became contagious, and Esther joined in, slowly at first, but by then the two girls were caught up in the mouse story and how ridiculous it was to be so frightened of the tiny creature after all they had been through. Shoshana held her stomach, and Esther wiped her eyes. Their jovial outbursts filled the room as Hanna entered the kitchen.

She was shocked to see her two daughters laughing. She just stood there quietly taking in the scene. She was devastated at the thought of losing David, but at the same time she hadn't heard laughter, especially from her girls, in such a long time. She didn't really cry, at least not audibly, but tears rolled down her cheeks as she watched.

It took a few minutes before the girls noticed their mother standing at the doorway of the kitchen. Their laughter ceased immediately, and the mood in the room turned serious. Esther noticed that her mother, who only a couple of weeks ago had been strong and forceful, now looked small and haggard. She no longer stood tall as if she owned the world. Her shoulders were rounded, and her demeanor was insecure and meek, which was very unnerving.

Shoshana stood and, with her sleeve, wiped the remaining moisture from her eyes. She approached her mother, uncertain of what kind of reaction to expect. She held out her arms and brought Hanna close in a warm embrace. Hanna let herself go for the first time since she'd left Leib and cried into her daughter's shoulder. Esther walked over and rubbed her mother's back in a consoling gesture, and all three surrendered to the emotion that had been suppressed for so long.

The day dragged on. The women worked quietly organizing Judith's kitchen and going through her clothes. After discussing it Aaron agreed there was no reason for everything to go to waste. Judith would never return from the Belzec death camp. Judith was smaller than the Gold women, so Hanna spent the day ripping seams and altering Judith's warmest coats, sweaters, and dresses to fit them. Hanna made sure the armband with the Star of David was securely fastened to the sleeve of any outer garment. Not wearing the armband meant instant death.

The project helped to pass the day. It was three o'clock when Esther went into the kitchen to start dinner. She wanted to prepare a soup and found enough onions, potatoes, and carrots to make a hearty broth to accompany the eggs Hanna had bought. But no one was going to eat until they laid eyes on David. Hanna told the girls what the one-eyed man had said to her; that David would return in the evening. She kept repeating it under her breath, over and over.

The sun set before five, and they all sat in the dimly lit salon waiting. Each minute that ticked by felt like an hour. Esther told the story of how David had snuck into their tobacco store one morning when she was unloading boxes and hid under the counter, only to jump out at her when her arms were filled with tobacco pouches. She was so startled, she hurled the pouches into the air, and some of them landed on the open shelves near the top of the ceiling. The girls looked over at their mother for a reaction, but she was barely listening. Shoshana also tried to take her mother's mind off the waiting and added to the story, "Remember how mad you were, Esther? You came home and told Tateh if David was not forbidden to set foot in that store you would take matters into your own hands. And you wouldn't be responsible for what might happen to him."

Esther smiled and said, "Yes, and Tateh just looked at me and laughed. He thought the whole thing was very funny." The memory of their father caused the girls to join Hanna in silence, as each of them reminisced.

CHAPTER 12

Life in the Labor Gang

It was just after seven when they heard the front door open. He looked horrible. This once-vibrant, twelve-year-old boy was now filthy, covered in blood-soaked clothes, and wincing in pain.

David tried to hide his condition as he walked through the door, but it was impossible. Hanna jumped up to hug her son, but David jumped back.

"Don't touch me!" he yelled, the desperation evident in his voice.

She immediately backed up. Something was terribly wrong. Shoshana and Esther stared at their brother in silence.

David walked over to the kitchen, grabbed the top of a chair, and dragged it across the floor into the salon. He turned the chair so its back was facing his family. He put one leg over the seat, straddling it backwards. Then he crossed his arms along the top of the chair, creating a soft spot to rest his head.

"I spent the night in jail. I was really scared, but there were other boys my age there too. There was a Jewish policeman they called Samolski. He was so mean, and he spoke like a big shot. He acted like one of those Nazis, not like one of us. God's gonna punish him one day, I know he will. He said we were going to work on the roads, and he threatened to kill us if we didn't obey his orders. He was so ugly, Mameh. He smelled and spit when he spoke. It made me sick to watch him. He told us we have to come every morning at five and do this all over again." David's voice cracked.

While he continued his story, Shoshana got up and ladled soup into a bowl and handed it to her brother. David stopped talking and guzzled it down. He handed the empty bowl to Shoshana for a refill.

"Samolski made us line up and gave orders to police in blue uniforms. We all walked out of town through so many fields, and I had no idea where I was going, or how long I would have to walk. It was hard to see my feet, and I kept tripping on rocks and holes in the ground, but I kept my balance so I wouldn't draw attention to myself. A few of the boys fell and were beaten with clubs till they stood up."

David was silent for a moment. He got through this initial march by imagining his father walking behind him. He remembered vividly how Leib had walked behind him when the Germans burnt down his town. He remembered that walk to the churchyard, when he saw the mutilated horse and how his father's words and gentle push kept him from being afraid. He felt his father's hand on his shoulder today while he marched through those fields. He didn't share that part of the story with his family.

"After walking forever, we finally stopped. There was a wagon full of shovels and mallets beside a rocky, muddy path that was so long, I couldn't see the end of it. Then one of the Junakies blurted out our orders. The entire time he spoke, he kept hitting the palm of his hand with his club, just daring one of us to speak or make a mistake. I had a heavy mallet. At first I wasn't even sure I could lift it, but I watched the way the others were using theirs to smash huge rocks, and I copied exactly what they did. Most of the rocks split with the first strike, and I could feel the vibrations run up my arms. It kind of felt good when I saw those rocks smashing. I played a game in my head and pretended each rock was Samolski's head. I did okay for the whole morning, and then we stopped for lunch. They let us sit on the ground. They gave us bread and cold soup with something in it. I'm not sure what it was, because it turned to mush, but I was so hungry, I didn't care.

"I don't know how much time we had to rest, but it wasn't very long, maybe fifteen or twenty minutes before they yelled at us to get back to work. When I tried to stand I was very stiff. It was hard for me to lift the giant hammer after resting, but I ignored my aching muscles and began to crush the rocks again. That's when I made a big mistake, Mameh. I took a split second to stop and straighten up. It was only a second, Mameh, I swear, but it didn't matter. One of the Junakies came over to me and started yelling, 'You filthy Jew! I'll teach you not to be lazy.' He picked up a large, thick tree branch from the ground and hit me over and over with it. I thought every bone in my body would break. He wanted me to continue crushing the rocks while the blows kept coming. Everyone watched, but no one helped. They were too afraid that it would happen to them too, so they kept quiet and kept on working. Finally, Mameh, finally the branch broke in half, over my back. The Junakie couldn't be bothered to find another one, and he was probably tired from striking me repeatedly. He said, 'Don't let me see you slacking again! Next time I won't be so gentle,' and he walked away. It was over, and I was still standing, Mameh.

"At the end of the day, the orders came to put our tools in the wagon and line up. Finally, I knew I was going home. There was a guy, Mameh, his name was Adeck. Do you remember him? He had a brother named Lieleck. They lived near us and went to my school when I was little. You never let me play with them, Mameh. They weren't good enough, you said. They were the sons of a tailor and not good enough to be my friends. Do you remember that?"

David had a hint of sarcasm in his voice, his tone almost disrespectful when he said, "While we were walking back, Adeck was behind me. When the Junakies were not near us he said, 'So David, how does it feel to be one of us? You're no better than anyone here. Now we are all the same, my friend.' I was ashamed, Mameh. I was ashamed."

Hanna listened intently to every word her son spoke, but the part about Adeck didn't seem to faze her. She was much more concerned about her son's condition. She walked over to him slowly. "I have to look at your back, David. I promise I'll be very gentle."

It was clear now why David had not let his mother hug him when he came into the house and why David was sitting backwards on the kitchen chair. The girls stood too, and watched from the side as Hanna helped David off with his coat and shirt. David winced with every movement. Not only had the blood dried to his clothing, but his muscles were sore, and sitting had caused them to stiffen up again.

Aaron was already in the kitchen boiling water. He found some iodine and tore up a white undershirt so Hanna could clean the wounds. Once David's shirt was off, the gasps came in unison. The girls said nothing, but the horror in their eyes could not be disguised. Hanna was more composed. She remained calm and in control.

"It isn't so bad, David, we will fix you up like new *tataleh*," she told him with a comforting smile. David felt relieved and comforted knowing he was safe and surrounded by people who loved him. He finally relaxed. David put his head down on his hands, and closed his eyes as his mother went to work.

She soaked the white cloth in soapy water and carefully washed David's wounds. There were many, but they were not deep. She knew they would heal quickly. She had to keep them clean so there would be no infection. The bruising was already visible. Hanna topped off the cleaning by smearing his entire back with iodine. Even though it stung, it was a good pain. David was covered in the red antiseptic.

Shoshana suddenly had a flashback to when David was a little boy, and he dropped the bottle of iodine all over the floor. He was painted in red back then too, but then it was funny. She was not laughing this time.

David slept in a real bed that night. There was no need to hide in the attic any longer. His existence was known now, and he would have to be back in a few hours to start work all over again. He lay on his stomach all night with no nightshirt, giving his wounds the chance to dry up and heal in the cold air.

At five a.m. sharp, David was up and ready. His waking nightmare was about to begin anew.

CHAPTER 13

The Dream
November 7, 1942

The days settled into a routine in Działoszyce. The women went out daily to buy food. Esther was best at finding people who would sell meat and vegetables on the black market. It was expensive, but they had no choice. They had to eat, and there were plenty of Poles in town who were more than happy to exchange their produce for money.

David continued working on the labor gang every day with the exception of Saturdays. The daily routine worked to harden both his body and soul. He would come home in the late evening and over supper tell stories of how the farmers would come out as they were walking through the fields and attack them with pitchforks and stones. The Junakies followed behind and laughed. They thought this was great fun. Many of the boys were hurt during these walks home, but their wounds were dressed, and by the morning they were ready for a repeat of the day before. This constant abuse became almost normal. David eventually stopped telling about his grueling days of forced labor, and his mother and sisters stopped asking.

On Saturdays David went to a *shtiebel* to pray. There were no open synagogues, so Jews created these little shtiebels in back rooms of houses where they could congregate for services. It was on one of those Saturdays, on *Rosh Chodesh*, the beginning of the month, when David was approached by a Rebbe. David didn't know this man, but he looked wise and had a gentle way about him.

"*Gut Shabbos*," the Rebbe said to David.

"Gut Shabbos."

"So, my son, where are you from?"

"Pińczów."

"Ahh, Pińczów. I knew many Jews from Pińczów. What's your name, my son?"

"David Gold," he replied.

The Rebbe put his hand on David's shoulder and looked into his face intently. "David, I want you to know that you will survive this war. There are miracles happening all the time, and you, David, are one of those miracles."

The Rebbe spoke like he knew something no one else was privy to, like he had a direct line to God. Those words stayed with David like a cloak of armor. They gave him hope and strength, and he believed with all his heart that these words were not spoken from the mouth of a mere mortal; they were a prophecy. From that Saturday on, David walked and talked as if he had grown up overnight. This twelve-year-old boy was every bit the man his father had raised him to become.

The weeks passed, and the cold rains of late autumn set in. The trek to the road became more treacherous. As word spread that there was no permanent German police station in Działoszyce, more and more people arrived. The district authorities were in nearby Miechow. As a result, the watchful eyes of the Nazis were not as attentive in Działoszyce, and life was more bearable than in many of the other towns.

Some of the local residents who had been in hiding began to return, and many refugees, like the Golds, made temporary homes there. Before long the crowding was oppressive, and local housing conditions became deplorable. Aaron left his home and went to live with his brother. The Golds never saw him again. One day they heard that Aaron and his brother had been shot while rushing home to make curfew.

Conditions were desperate. Food was scarce, sanitation nonexistent, and disease was spreading rapidly. There were rumors that the Germans were making their way to town to deal with the remaining Jews of Działoszyce.

It was now the beginning of November 1942. Hanna understood that they had to leave, but didn't know where to go. Dense forests surrounded the town, and her family would have to flee and hide in the protective cover of the trees and brush.

On the night of November 7, 1942, they gathered for a family meeting.

"Tomorrow before daybreak we're leaving," she began. Her children listened. "The Germans are almost here, and we won't be able to escape once they've surrounded the town. We're going to run north to the forest. Hopefully we'll find some other Jews in hiding to join up with. It's the only choice we have, and at least we'll all be together. Get a good night's rest. Then we'll pack what we can carry and be ready to leave at daybreak."

Shoshana, Esther, and David packed bags with the salvageable food they had, water, and extra clothing. They still had their original money sewn safely into their undergarments, and David had the knife Marian had given him.

Hanna went to sleep. She would need strength for the journey ahead. But it wasn't long before she had one of her vivid dreams. She was at the kitchen table with her mother, back home in Wislica. She was not a child in the dream. She was the forty-five-year-old woman of today, sitting with her mother, who had not aged at all.

Her mother spoke to her as if she was still a little girl. "Listen to me carefully, Hanna. You will not leave in the morning. Stay exactly where you are, and someone will come to rescue you." In the dream Hanna did not speak. Her mother's words kept repeating in her head. "Stay exactly where you are, and someone will come to rescue you."

It was very cold in the house, there was no more wood or coal for heating, but Hanna woke covered in sweat. She sat up in the dark and tried to recall her dream. It seemed so real: not like a dream at all. She knew what she had to do. They were staying put. They would not run to the forest. She had no doubt about her decision, but was not sure Shoshana, Esther, and David would feel the same.

CHAPTER 14

The Savior

They all woke early, ready to leave. Everyone's nerves were on edge. The day ahead would be dangerous, and the fear of the unknown was overwhelming. Esther noticed a dim light coming from the kitchen. She went in to find her mother sitting at the kitchen table, drinking tea. The room was lit by a single candle in the Shabbos candleholder. Hanna was not rushing around, preparing to leave like she should have been. From where Esther watched in the doorway, she could see that something in her mother's face had changed. Hanna was strangely calm. How could she be so relaxed when their fate was so precarious?

Esther broke the silence. "Mameh, are you okay?"

Hanna looked at her daughter and then at her other two children, who had joined Esther at the doorway.

"Come here and sit down, *mayn tyreh kindeh*," she said. The three of them exchanged bewildered looks as they took a seat around the table.

Hanna spoke quietly and with an even tone. "We're going to be all right," she said to her children, who were anything but calm. "We're not going to escape to the forest today. We are going to stay here and wait for someone to come and get us."

Had she lost her mind in the night? She was perfectly normal when they'd gone to bed.

Esther rested her hand over her mother's and spoke carefully, trying not to break the delicate state she thought her mother was in. "Who's coming to get us, Mameh?"

"I don't know," she answered, "but today we will be rescued by a kind stranger."

They looked at each other. Perhaps the stress had finally broken her.

Hanna took a sip of her tea and gazed at her children. The hard expression on her face told them their mother was back from whatever fantasy she had escaped to. She was definitely in control.

Hanna started to explain their change of plan. "Your grandmother came to me last night."

Shoshana interrupted. "This is all about one of your dreams, Mameh? We don't have time for that now. We have to go."

"No, Shoshanaleh, this was much more than a dream. Your grandmother spoke directly to me, and she was very clear. I could see past her eyes, into her soul. I could even feel her warm skin and her moist breath as she spoke to me. She took my hand and told me we had to stay here until someone comes for us, and that is exactly what we're going to do."

This wouldn't be the first time the family had acted on one

of their mother's premonitions. They quickly came to terms with the change of plan. It wasn't like they had much of an alternative.

"Leave your bags packed," Hanna added. "One way or another, we will leave this place today. Go and get ready," she said. "It shouldn't be long now."

Hanna's three children rose slowly from the table and huddled together in the bedroom. Shoshana whispered to her siblings, "Do you think we should be going along with this?"

"Mameh has always had this unusual gift," Esther replied. "We have to listen to her, Shosh. You can see how strongly she feels about it. We must have faith too."

"It's not as if running into the forest and hiding is a much better idea anyway," David added. "We might as well go with Mameh's vision; maybe God has a better plan for us."

The dark sky began to show signs of a new day that Sunday morning of November 8, 1942. The four of them all sat at the kitchen table and waited for their mystery "savior" to arrive. This would be the first Sunday since his arrival in Działoszyce that David would not be reporting to work. He hoped this person his mother was counting on would arrive before the Jewish police did, or he would be beaten mercilessly for not reporting to work.

As time ticked on, the feeling of impending doom grew stronger, and their fate grew more precarious. The rumbling of the tanks and trucks became louder, and gunshots echoed in the distance.

It was just before ten o'clock in the morning when Esther finally spoke. "If we're going to stay here, we had better hide in the attic. Can't you hear the Germans coming? We can't just sit here in full view."

Esther was right. Hanna was starting to doubt the strength of her premonition when they heard a faint knock on a side windowpane. All eyes turned to the sound.

They went into the salon, and David slowly moved the curtain just enough that he could peek out without being seen. He was looking at a woman wearing a black kerchief on her head and a dark coat. David moved the curtains slightly more, and Hanna motioned for him to open the window. He nudged it open slightly, just enough to be able to hear what the woman wanted.

"Are you the Gold family?" the stranger asked.

"Yes, we are," Hanna said.

"Please let me in, I need to talk to you."

David looked at his mother, who nodded. Once the stranger was standing in the salon, they could see that she wasn't very old, maybe in her mid twenties, a little older than Shoshana. She didn't look Polish or German. She had dark wavy hair, dark brown eyes, and a round face. Hanna suspected she was Jewish, but she wasn't wearing an armband, so she couldn't be sure. The woman was clearly nervous and spoke quickly.

"You have money?" she asked.

"Who are you?" Hanna blurted out.

Shoshana was not at all happy with the way this stranger started the conversation. What did she mean asking if they had money?

"My name is Nessa, and I've come to help you, to take you away from here."

When she heard the woman's name, Hanna knew she was the person they were waiting for. Nessa is a Jewish name, derived from the Hebrew word *ness*, which means miracle. This was the someone of her mother's dream.

Nessa saw the suspicious looks on their faces and spoke quickly. "I was sent here to find a family by the name of Rapaport. They were supposed to come with me to a farm outside of town where a man, a Polish farmer, is taking care of some of the wealthier families – for a price. I work for him too. He pays me to bring him well-off Jews. When I arrived, I found the Rapaport family had already gone, and I don't want to return to the farm without another family. I asked around, and someone told me to come to this house and ask for you. They said you had money."

Nessa waited a split second for a reaction but got none. "So are you coming?" she continued. "You have no choice, you know. The Germans have arrived, and you only have a few hours to live if you stay. They will shoot you or take you to a concentration camp. Either you follow me right now, or I leave."

Shoshana was uncomfortable with what had transpired in the last few seconds. Here was a Jewish woman being paid by a Polish farmer to bring him wealthy Jewish families. No good could come of this, but she could see that her mother was set on going. It was all part of the vision she was so sure was meant for them.

"Go get our bags." Hanna told her children.

Esther and David were also apprehensive, but the three of them obeyed. They all put sweaters and overcoats over their double layer of clothing. David slid the knife Marian had given him up high inside his sleeve.

They left through the back door. David went first and scouted out the road. He turned and gave them the all clear to follow. Nessa took the lead.

"Stay close behind, and move quickly," she commanded.

They walked along a back road for a couple of blocks till they reached an area strewn with discarded wooden boxes. Nessa stopped at the debris and began to move it with her hands. David helped, and together they revealed a heavy manhole cover, which partially covered a sewer hole. David looked down and saw an iron ladder attached to the wall. His strength had improved greatly after working in the labor gang for the past month. He managed to move the heavy cover enough that they could all fit through the hole. As he slid the heavy metal disk to the side, he wondered how Nessa had moved it enough to crawl out of the hole in the first place. One by one they lowered themselves into the sewer. Nessa first, followed by Shoshana, Esther, Hanna, and finally David, who had the job of sealing the opening before he disappeared into the smelly tunnels under the town.

With the manhole cover in place, the light was almost completely shut out. The ladder felt cold and only reached halfway down the side. As the dark enveloped them, they helped each other down, jumping from the last rung into the ankle-deep ice water. A wave of suffocating stink hit them, and they needed time to adjust to their surroundings. Ahead, light streamed into the dark tunnel through grates in the road at regular intervals, lending an eerie glow to the river of filth before them.

Nessa moved forward and stopped just a few meters ahead. She bent down to dig at something near the bottom of the of the brick wall. She removed the stuffing from a hole in the side of the culvert and pulled out a flashlight. She switched it on and shone the beam ahead of them. "We have to hurry," she said. "Stay close, and watch your step." The current of sludgy water moved in the same direction they were traveling. The height of the sewer restricted them from standing upright, and the slippery bottom, with its hidden crevices and debris, made walking difficult. They could not move as fast as Nessa would have liked. Having done this many times before, she moved effortlessly through the tunnel.

Sounds echoed, and they heard voices. They couldn't make out where the voices were coming from, but the noise confirmed they were not alone in the bowels of this town. Others knew of this escape route as well, but the Golds were fortunate enough to have a guide. The overpowering stench in the sewer caused Shoshana to continually gag. She concentrated on breathing through her mouth, but she could taste the foul odor. Every slimy, wet rat that slithered past caused her to recoil. Nothing seemed to affect Nessa; she trudged on, only looking back once in a while to check that they were all still following.

They came to a joint in the sewer system with three branches. The connection where the three tunnels met was small, and they had to crouch down to get through. David took the bags and then helped the women, one by one, till they were all heading down the next tunnel.

This went on for what seemed like an eternity. Finally Nessa spoke. "We're almost there." What a relief to hear those words. It was tiring, balancing and lifting their legs through the heavy waters. They were cold and wet, and their bags had become very heavy. Up ahead, Nessa stopped. She turned and pointed the flashlight at them. When they caught up to her they saw an iron ladder just like the one they used to enter the sewers.

Nessa climbed it and used the back of her flashlight to bang on the underside of the manhole cover.

CHAPTER 15

Jozef & Nessa

In a secluded area outside of Działoszyce, a horse hitched to a hay wagon and its driver waited patiently. The driver, a disheveled, burly man, sat reading what was left of a torn, wet newspaper. He had been parked there overnight on the outskirts of town near the river. The noon sun felt good on his cold face after a long night of wind and freezing rain.

Finally, he heard a faint metallic rap coming from underneath the wagon. He looked around, saw no one, and, with two clucking sounds, cued the horse to move forward. As soon as the wagon cleared the spot it had been parked on, the man jumped down and brushed away some dirt and gravel, revealing a manhole cover. He quickly moved it aside and crouched down to help his wife emerge from the sewer.

Nessa spoke quickly. "The Rapaports were gone when I got

there," she said nervously. "I asked around and found another family."

The Golds were waiting at the bottom of the ladder as instructed. Looking up, Shoshana was surprised to see Nessa talking to a man. Her active imagination took her to lurid places. She hadn't trusted Nessa from the moment she laid eyes on her.

"Did you check them out? Do they have as much money as the Rapaports were supposed to be carrying?" Jozef asked.

"I didn't have time to check. The Germans were closing in, and if we hadn't left quickly, we would never have made it out. I was told they were wealthy, and when I asked them straight out, they confirmed it. So I took my chances," Nessa explained.

Jozef was not happy with this change of plan, and Nessa didn't like the look on his face. She had seen it many times before and had taken the brunt of his temper in the past.

"Let's get them out of there and be on our way. Hanosz is waiting, and he's expecting us to supply him with a rich Jewish family. They had better come through with their money, or we're going to pay with our lives," he grumbled to his wife. "Hurry up, it's going to take longer to get there with the wagon full."

Although it was faint, Shoshana could hear the arguing above. Something was wrong. Nessa knelt down and motioned for the Golds to make their way up the ladder. Hanna climbed first, followed by Esther, Shoshana, and finally David. It felt good to be able to stand up straight and smell the fresh air, even though the sewer stench still permeated their clothing. Hanna looked around to get her bearings and saw the town behind them and a dirt road leading to a forest ahead of them.

All six of them stood for a moment to take in the sight of the German trucks and tanks surrounding the town in the distance.

Shoshana made her way straight over to Nessa, who was visibly shaken. She put her hand on Nessa's shoulder. "Thank you, Nessa, for your help. I don't know what we would have done without you."

She's planning something, Esther thought, as she watched her sister attempt to befriend this woman.

Shoshana's instincts told her they were being set up as pawns in a much bigger plan. She needed some answers, starting with who this rough, ornery man was. "Nessa, are you going to introduce us to this gentleman?" she asked.

"This is Jozef, my husband," Nessa answered. Jozef didn't turn or acknowledge Shoshana. He continued to prepare the horse for the trek.

"Oh, you're married," Shoshana said. "And what's your family name?" she asked.

"Lanski," Nessa answered. "Why?"

"Since we're close in age, I just wondered if we had any friends in common, but I don't know anybody by that name. So, where are we going?" Shoshana asked.

Nessa answered curtly, "Do you hear all that gunfire? We have no time for your questions; our lives are at stake too. Get in the wagon, or we'll leave here without you."

Shoshana realized she had her work cut out for her. Nessa was not going to let her guard down easily. She stopped talking. At least she knew from their surname that Nessa and Jozef were probably Jewish. Shoshana disliked this man and was uncomfortable with the way he spoke to his wife.

The wagon was old but large enough for all of them. It had huge metal-spoked wheels. The sides were about a meter high, and it was easily three or four meters long, piled high with hay. There was a wooden area at the top where Jozef sat holding the reins and waiting for everyone to climb up. Nessa went first and mounted effortlessly. David followed, and Esther tossed their bags up to him. Once he'd hidden them under the hay, David reached out his arm to help his mother and two sisters into the wagon. Shoshana climbed in last. She waited for Nessa to find her seat near the back of the wagon, and then she sat right next to her. The rest of them dug holes to the bottom of the hay so they could sit low. This way they could quickly cover themselves up if necessary.

Jozef grabbed the reins, and the horse started to walk. He steered it off the road and into the forest where it plodded along a semi-groomed path just wide enough for the wagon.

Shoshana didn't waste any time resuming her conversation with Nessa.

"Nessa, we would have surely died in that house if you hadn't shown up when you did. You and your husband have done a great *mitzvah*. I know God will repay you one day. You are Jewish right? You know what *mitzvah* means?" Shoshana didn't wait for Nessa to answer. "It means a good deed, one that God commands us to do."

"I know exactly what a mitzvah is." Nessa sounded annoyed.

With that statement, Nessa confirmed that she and her husband were, indeed, Jewish. At least they had that in common, and Shoshana would work it as best she could.

Nessa didn't add to the conversation. She looked back at the town that had once been her home and watched it being destroyed. She tried desperately to avoid Shoshana. Nessa had a job to do and needed to stay focused.

ᔓᔕ

Nessa and Jozef were cattle farmers before the Germans occupied Poland. At thirty-seven, Jozef was quite a bit older than his wife. His family was in the cattle business, and he learned everything he knew from his father, who had died when Jozef was only nineteen. Jozef took over the family business and, as a result, had dealings with all the farmers in Kolkow and the surrounding towns. He knew every one of them very well.

Nessa had grown up in Działoszyce, the eldest of four children. She had two brothers, and her sister, Sara, was the youngest. Her father was a butcher and worked in his own shop. Jozef met Nessa when he came into town to sell his wares to her father. Nessa loved people and was wonderful with the customers, another thing she and Shoshana had in common. She worked with her father in the shop almost every day. Jozef was smitten with Nessa from the moment he first spoke to her. He loved the sparkle in her eyes and the passion she had for everything she did. She wasn't afraid of adventure or hard work. She was smart, and she made him smile every time they were together. He had fallen in love with this dark-haired beauty and thought she would be quite an asset to his business. The couple courted for almost a year before they married in 1935.

After their wedding, Nessa moved to Jozef's farm in Kolkow, about twenty kilometers from her hometown. She was able to see her family at least once every couple of weeks. She would routinely ride her bicycle to town, stay overnight, and ride back to the farm the next day. She missed them so much and was worried how her father would manage the business without her. In the end, it didn't really matter. By 1939, the Germans made it almost impossible to run a Jewish business, and Nessa's father was forced to close down his shop. He still managed to make some money selling meat from his home but on a much smaller scale.

It was on September 2, 1942, when everything changed. On that day the Germans entered Działoszyce, rounded up all the Jews, and marched them to Miechow. Nessa's family was among them. She would find out about their fate when it was too late. That was the day Nessa used the town's sewers for the first time. She had to get to her family. The Germans were everywhere, and she couldn't access the town any other way. Nessa and Jozef had no flashlight that time and had to feel their way along. They had no idea where the tunnels would lead and had to peek out of manhole covers to find their way. Eventually, after spending almost two days in the sewers, they surfaced close to Nessa's home. The streets were empty. They quickly made their way to the house, only to find it deserted.

Nessa panicked. She didn't know what to do first. Jozef had never seen his wife so confused and incoherent. She broke down. "Where are they Jozef? Where have those Nazi bastards taken them?" Jozef let her get the immediate grief out of her system before he would slap her back into a productive mode. The reality was, that for every second they stayed, their lives were in more danger.

"I'm not leaving without finding out what happened to them," she told Jozef.

"Fine, we'll ask if someone's seen them." Knowing her husband wasn't going to fight her, Nessa calmed down considerably. Questioning anyone who would talk, she finally found Janek, an elderly Polish neighbor, who'd often frequented her father's shop.

Janek was coming out of the back of his apartment when Nessa called out to him. "Janek where's my family? Have you seen them? Do you know what happened to them?" Janek couldn't look at her. Jozef read the grief on his face. He tried to pull Nessa gently by her arm, but she jerked away from him and gave him a look he had never seen before.

She was screaming now. "Where are they?"

Janek spoke quietly, "You know about the round-up, Nessa. Your family was among the Jews taken to the transports in Miechow." Nessa's body went limp. She'd known from the beginning, but it wasn't real until she heard the words come from Janek's mouth. The sparkle, the hope in Nessa's eyes died that day. She left Działoszyce a different person than when she had come only hours earlier. With the exception of her husband, nothing and no one mattered.

There was no reason for them to stay any longer. By the next evening, they were back at their farm. The Germans were coming, and it was time for them to try to save themselves.

The Germans were beginning to branch out to the farms, looking for Jews who owned property. Hanosz, a Polish farmer with whom Jozef had done business, approached him with a proposition. Hanosz would not have been Jozef's first choice to rely on, but with the Germans so close he didn't have any option but to listen to his proposal. Hanosz promised Nessa and Jozef he would take care of them and make sure they had food and shelter as long as they worked for him. They made an agreement and signed over their property to Hanosz.

What Jozef and Nessa didn't realize was what kind of work Hanosz had in mind. Jozef was strong and could do any farm job that was required, and Nessa was a wonderful cook. But Hanosz did not want to use those skills. He wanted their skills as Jews. He wanted them to find rich Jews from nearby towns and lure these wealthy families in with the promise of saving their lives. Instead, he would rob them of all their money and valuables. He would give ten percent of the money to Nessa and Jozef as an incentive and then kill the Jews himself, or throw them out, knowing full well they would be either shot or captured.

The Golds were their next victims.

CHAPTER 16

Befriending the Enemy

Shoshana continued trying and befriend Nessa and to glean more information about the situation her family was in.

"So Nessa, where are you taking us?" she asked.

Nessa, still not looking at Shoshana, answered, "We're going to a farm in Kolkow."

Shoshana's mind raced, trying to figure out exactly how much time she had. She knew of Kolkow, but had never visited there. It was a small farming village about ten kilometers from Pińczów, their hometown, but now they were approaching from the south side, from Działoszyce.

"Is it your farm?" Shoshana asked.

"We don't have a farm anymore," Nessa answered. "I told you before we left I was taking you to a Polish farmer. You will pay him to hide you. Now stop talking." Nessa didn't want Jozef to hear them conversing in the back. He wouldn't approve, and she didn't want his temper to flare.

Shoshana stayed quiet for a few minutes, but she had to find out more. She knew that the man driving the wagon was dangerous, just from the way he treated his wife. There was no telling what he would do to them.

She decided to make small talk. "We originally came from Pińczów," she said. "My parents ran a grocery store and tobacco concession there. I worked there every day and helped my mother in the grocery store. My sister, Esther, ran our tobacco concession. Our brother, David, went to school and worked on the farm of a family friend. His name is Marian Wicinski."

Shoshana spoke to the back of Nessa's head the entire time, but she had no doubt Nessa was listening. Nessa wasn't sure, but she thought the name Marian Wicinski sounded familiar. Jozef may have had dealings with him. Maybe she'd written his name in her books when she was doing the accounting.

Shoshana continued, "It was horrible when the Nazis first attacked three years ago. They came in and rounded us all up. We thought we were going to die for sure. Those animals separated my father and brother from the rest of us and pushed us to join the rest of the women in a churchyard. We watched, as they burned down our homes, businesses, schools – everything we loved."

Nessa had heard about that incident in Pińczów, when so many were killed, and the whole town was burned to the ground.

"But nothing was as horrible as the night, just a few months ago, when the Germans took over Pińczów, and we were secretly hidden by a friend. That was the last time I saw my father, Nessa.

He sent his children and wife to a safe place and said he would join us the next day, but he never came, and we had to leave. We're all so worried about him." Shoshana's voice cracked, partly on purpose, as she spoke of her father. "His name is Leibus Gold. Is it possible, since you live so close to Pińczów, you may have known him? He was very well known in Pińczów, he was one of the city councilors. We are so desperate to hear where he is and if he's alive."

Shoshana's voice drilled into Nessa's head. As hard as she tried to ignore her, Shoshana's words penetrated. The story she was telling brought out feelings that Nessa had managed to suppress for a long time. She was afraid to allow herself to think of her own family, and what had happened to them when they were taken to Miechow. Nessa was a master at controlling her emotions. She'd built an impermeable wall around herself, so no German would ever get close to those memories she had locked deep inside. So deep, in fact, that often she couldn't reach them herself. Shoshana was bringing everything to the surface.

Nessa turned to face the girl who couldn't seem to keep quiet. "Shut up!" she said, louder than she meant to. For the first time since the wagon ride began, Jozef turned his head and looked back at her, his thick brows furrowed in anger.

Shoshana had hit a nerve. She stayed silent for a couple of minutes, but then resumed the one-sided conversation.

"I'm sorry if I said something that sparked a painful memory for you," she said. "I keep forgetting that we Jews all have loved ones we are separated from. I should never have told you about our father." She spoke quietly so that Jozef would not overhear.

Hanna, Esther, and David looked away from the two

women, not wanting to interfere in any way. They tried to listen in, but the squeaky, grinding sounds of the old crotchety wagon drowned out Shoshana's soft voice. She was purposely speaking quietly so the man driving the wagon would not overhear.

Shoshana's sensitive nature worked for her. Not only was she probing for information, but also she was genuinely concerned for this woman, and her kindness penetrated Nessa's hardened shell. Shoshana continued, "I didn't stop to think that you too, must have family missing, Nessa. Are you from Działoszyce?" From the way Nessa had moved through the town's streets and sewers, Shoshana thought she had to be. If this was the case, then Nessa's loved ones had likely been deported to the camps, just like Aaron's.

"We were staying with the Formalski family; Aaron Formalski was my father's cousin. Did you know them?"

Nessa knew Judith Formalski. Judith used to shop in her father's store, and Nessa had served Judith personally many times in the past. She also knew that Judith and her children had been sent to Belzec extermination camp along with her own mother and sister.

They had been riding for quite a while, and Shoshana had spoken most of the way. She was determined to force Nessa to view her mother and siblings as real people who had suffered, just like her. If Shoshana could succeed in that, perhaps Nessa would break down and divulge what lay ahead. It would be easier for Nessa to betray her husband and the farmer, Hanosz, if she could relate to the Golds as human beings who had been victimized just like her. Shoshana needed to exploit Nessa's guilt.

"Nessa," she said, her voice dropping to a whisper. "I know

you have something planned for us," she hesitated. "From your silence, I can only assume it's not good. The first words out of your mouth were *Do you have money.* It can't be money alone that you want, or you would have robbed us and left us by now. I know someone else must be directing this, Nessa. Is it the farmer you mentioned? What will happen to us when we get there? Tell me what this man has planned for us. Nessa, why can't you look at me?"

A burning sensation gnawed in the pit of Shoshana's stomach. Everything pointed to danger. The closer they got to their destination, the more desperate she felt. Away from the others in their corner of the wagon, she alone had to wear Nessa down.

"You are Jewish, just like us. You don't make life selections like the Germans do. They've perfected that task, using our own people against us, but only God has the right to decide who lives and who dies. *Please* trust me enough to tell me what we're walking into."

It was time for Shoshana to play her trump card. "If this man you're taking us to *is* dangerous, you can be sure he will turn on you too. Maybe not today, but he won't hesitate to betray you as soon as you are no longer useful to him. Never forget, Nessa, you and your husband are Jews before you are anything else. How many rich Jewish families can be left for you to find? Together we can come up with a plan, Nessa, one that will use our money to save you and your husband from whoever is controlling you."

Nessa did not react, but she absorbed everything. She drew parallels between their lives. They'd both been through so much. They were even connected by people they both knew. But the biggest thing they had in common was the loss of family. Where were their loved ones now? Would they ever see them again? The words *You don't make life selections like the Germans do* sparked a flame within her. She and Jozef were no better than those murderers who made selections that sent her family to the death camp.

What am I doing? she wondered. Nessa was back to a place where she was able to feel again, but she needed Shoshana to stop talking. How would she bring Jozef to alter the original plan? He was strong and determined, but Nessa was much smarter. They had almost reached Hanosz's farm, and Nessa needed time to think.

"I'm not going to tell you again," Nessa whispered. "You have to stop talking."

There was something different about the way she said it this time. Shoshana noticed her moist eyes when she turned to scold her. Her tone was different too. There was no anger in her voice now, but there was some concern. Shoshana stayed quiet for the rest of the journey.

Nessa looked up to see where they were. She knew they didn't have much longer, and she had to talk to her husband before they reached the farm. She could see the forest clearing up ahead where the path reached the dirt road. It was now or never.

She let out a short, sharp whistle. Jozef abruptly stopped the wagon. The Golds all looked at each other. Shoshana raised her finger to her lips, signaling the others to stay quiet.

Nessa and Jozef jumped down from the wagon and moved out of earshot. Jozef, taking no chance that the Golds would run, never took his eyes off the wagon.

Shoshana filled the others in on what had transpired between her and Nessa. "I think I got through to her," she said.

"I hope you did," Esther muttered, "because this man is evil, I don't trust him, and I am scared to think where they're taking us."

"She told me we are going to a farmer in Kolkow. She wouldn't say anything else. I think she's trying to get through to her husband, now. I think we can trust her far more than we can trust him. Anyway, we have no option, we're at their mercy. Shhh…we can't let them hear us talking," Shoshana said.

"I think we should run," David said in a voice just louder than a whisper.

"David, we can't run. There are Germans in every town now," Hanna said. They were nearer to Pińczów, and thoughts of her husband flooded her mind. She was so close and yet, so dangerously far from being able to reach him.

Meanwhile, Nessa spoke to Jozef. She wanted to appeal to his sense of decency, but she hadn't seen that side of him in such a long time, she wasn't even sure it still existed. So, she spoke the language he understood. Money.

"The woman who was sitting next to me, her name is Shoshana, she told me they are from Pińczów. They are friends with Marian Wicinski." She watched Jozef's face for a sign of recognition, and she got what she was looking for.

"Yes," Jozef said, "I did business with him. He lives with his sister and her husband. He was a decent man, sat on the Pińczów town council I think. What does this have to do with anything?" he blurted out.

"This man, Marian Wicinski, was close to Shoshana's father. His name was Leibus Gold. He, too, was on the town council. This family has much more money than what they are carrying. We can send them back to Pińczów to get more, and they must have property too. I know they are very wealthy and Pińczów is so close." She could see Jozef contemplating this information, so she continued. "You know we will not be able to go back to Działoszyce anymore. Now that the Germans have completely taken over the town, there will be no more Jews for us to bring to Hanosz. What do you think he will do with us when we are of no use to him?" She gave Jozef a minute to ponder what she had just said.

"Jozef, we have taken two families to Hanosz before, and we never saw them again. We both know what their fate was."

Jozef grabbed his wife by her shoulders. Even through her heavy coat she could feel the pain of his fingers digging into her. "Their fate is not our business! We were paid well to do a job, and we did it. We need that money. Hanosz has taken all we have, and this is our only chance of survival. Once we have enough money we will leave, and I will find us a safer place to hide, but for now, bringing him this family will give us ten percent of everything they have."

As Nessa tried to peel his hands off her shoulders, he realized how hard he was holding her and let go.

"What if we change the plan?" she suggested. "Let's go back and tell Hanosz he should wait a few days before he does anything with these people. We will tell him they have a lot more money in Pińczów, and we will find a way to get it. Jozef, with the money the Golds have and the connections you have, we can find a different farmer, a more honest one who will hide all of us. The woman in the wagon has already offered to use her money to help us. I believe we can trust her. These are good people. We don't need to have their blood on our hands too."

Jozef considered everything his wife had said. Even though he didn't treat her well, he respected her intelligence and courage. She was right. The Golds were their chance to get away from Hanosz. Nessa had a way of seeing what would come next. He had never thought of what would happen once they were no longer useful to Hanosz. His mind raced, contemplating which farmers he could approach for help. With the Gold's money, he could bribe any number of them.

Jozef finally spoke. "Maybe your plan can work. We can't tell this family what Hanosz has done in the past. It will panic them, and they might run. We have to be smart and only reveal what they must know to get us to the next step. I need a few days to set up a new hiding place; I know exactly who I'm going to approach. You're sure these people can be trusted?"

"Yes, I can tell Shoshana is a good person. She and her family have been through a lot. They have made it this far and are still together. This means they're smart and determined. I didn't speak to the others, but I'm sure they will go along with whatever we decide," Nessa answered.

"I don't know if they are smart or just lucky," Jozef said, "but we'll go back and fill them in on everything. We must all have the same story and the same goal before we get to Hanosz. Our plan has to be perfect. If Hanosz has any suspicions, he won't hesitate to get rid of all of us. Let me do the talking."

Nessa let out a deep sigh. She was relieved that she'd gotten through to her husband. Even though he was a stubborn man, he too, realized the danger they were in.

CHAPTER 17

A New Plan

It started to snow, and the wind picked up. Nessa crossed her arms in front of her body, tucking her freezing hands into the folds of her coat, as she watched her husband approach the wagon.

Shoshana observed every move as Jozef walked up to the side of the wagon where she was sitting. He looked at her and began to speak. It was the first time this man actually looked at any of them.

"We are taking you to a farm. The farmer's name is Hanosz, and his wife is Marta. Hanosz was going to keep you for money, but we don't know how long he will allow you to stay. He's a dangerous man and is becoming more unpredictable as the Germans close in. Nessa tells me you're willing to use your money and pay for our safety too. Is that true?"

Shoshana nodded.

"How do I know I can trust you?" Jozef said.

Before Shoshana had a chance to answer, Hanna spoke up. "You can trust us because we have no choice. What's our alternative? This is your town, and you know the people. If we betray you, it will be like signing our own death warrants. We are both crucial to the plan. Our money is useless without your connections, and your connections are useless without our money. Don't you see? Separately, we cannot accomplish anything, but together, we are a strong partnership. We have no choice but to trust each other."

Jozef stared at this older woman. *She's managed to stay alive and keep her children together till now. Her words are true, we each have something the other needs.* Jozef was convinced.

"Listen carefully. We must all keep to the same story. If Hanosz smells even a hint of deceit, we will all pay with our lives. Do you understand?" He turned his gaze to David when he spoke these words. He was obviously afraid, because of his age, that David would be the one to trip up. Hanosz was a cunning man, very capable of tricking a young boy into saying something he shouldn't.

"We *all* understand," David answered, looking directly at Jozef. The rest of them nodded in agreement.

"When we arrive, I will have some explaining to do. You are not the family Hanosz is expecting. You are only here because the Rapaports were already gone. I will tell Hanosz we checked you out, and rather than coming back empty-handed you were our only choice. We will tell him that you have money, and you will give him 5,000 zloty to prove it. However, we are also going to tell him you have much more cash, gold, and silver hidden in Pińczów along with the deed to your property. We have to make him believe that if he just holds out for a few days it will be very worth his while. I'll tell him I need a little time to figure out how we're going to get to the money. You, old woman, you're going to offer Hanosz all of it, and in exchange he will hide you."

Hanna interrupted. "My name is Hanna," she said.

Jozef continued, "Remember, he is evil and smart – a dangerous combination. Do not let him divert our plan by making you a better offer or by tricking you in any way. We have seen what this man is capable of." Jozef wanted to put fear into the Golds. He wasn't going to take a chance that anything Hanosz might tell them would change their minds.

"We are honorable people," Hanna said. "Your wife saved us just in time. We owe you. We're in this together and will not change from the plan, no matter what Hanosz says. I promise you can trust us, Jozef." It was the first time Hanna spoke his name. She hoped saying his name would bond them in some small way.

Nessa stood over to the side shivering and listening to the exchange. She was comfortable with this new plan. Jozef motioned to his wife to get back in the wagon. They took their places: Nessa in the back next to Shoshana and Jozef in the driver's seat.

He turned and faced the five people in the wagon. "Ready?"

They were all in agreement. Jozef prompted the horse to start the last leg of the journey. He wanted to get back to the stable. He had pushed the animal harder than normal, and it needed to eat and rest.

ᔓ

The remainder of the ride went silently. The anxiety level was high, with all of them lost in their own thoughts and fears. When they reached the edge of the forest, Jozef pulled back on the reins and stopped. The sun was low in the sky. The sun set early this time of year, and it would be dark around four o'clock. This left Jozef just enough time to make his way in the dim light to the other side of the farm.

"Cover yourselves with the hay. Nessa, make sure they're well hidden, and come sit up here where you usually do."

They did as they were told. Jozef steered the wagon past the farm and into an open field, which led to the other side of the property. The snowfall was thick, and the howling wind, with nothing to stop it, sounded like a moaning ghost in the open field. The Golds were sheltered from the snow, but Jozef and Nessa were exposed to its lash. Finally Jozef stopped the wagon near the back of the farmhouse. He dismounted, as did Nessa, and turned to speak to what looked like an empty wagon. "Wait here, and don't move. We will be back for you after I've prepared Hanosz."

Hanosz met the couple at the back door of the farmhouse. The warm air instantly melted the snow on Nessa's face. The farmer had waited all day for Jozef's return and was not surprised to see the "empty" wagon. This was how Jozef had brought the other Jews as well.

Hanosz's wife, Marta, was in the kitchen. Jozef and Nessa were cold and hungry, and she had prepared a steaming bowl of soup for each of them.

"Sit, sit, Jozef," Hanosz said in a jovial voice. "Have some soup and warm up." He did not even acknowledge Nessa's presence, but she was used to that.

They both sat and devoured the soup and bread that Marta placed before them.

"So Jozef, you have brought me the Rapaports' money?" he asked.

Jozef put down his spoon, looked straight at Hanosz and said, "No, by the time Nessa reached their meeting place, the Rapaports were gone."

Hanosz's eyes narrowed, but before he could unleash his anger, Jozef said, "But we did not come back empty-handed. We have brought Jews who have much more than we could have imagined getting from the Rapaports." Hanosz's facial expression went from angry to pleasantly surprised.

"Ahh, I should have known you would come back with something. Tell me who these people are and how much they have."

Jozef stood, reached his hand into the right front pocket of his pants, and took out a thick wad of bills. He slapped the wad on the table in front of Hanosz and said, "This is just the beginning."

Hanosz licked his lower lip as he picked up the bills and flipped his thumb over one end to reveal they were all hundred-zloty bank notes. "How much is here?" he asked.

"Five thousand," Jozef answered. "This is just a pittance to these people, they have much more," he added.

Hanosz was intrigued. "I'm listening."

"Their name is Gold. How's that for an omen?" Jozef snickered. "They are from Pińczów. They told me about all the silver, gold, and jewelry they left hidden back home, along with a lot of

American dollars. If you're smart and patient, you will be richer than you could have ever dreamed of being with the Rapaports." Jozef watched Hanosz carefully for signs of acceptance.

"What do you propose?"

"We keep them here for a few days, maybe even a week, just until I have time to get to Pińczów, find the location, and bring back the whole treasure. It will be worth your while to hide and feed these people for a short time. I need to be very careful. Germans are everywhere now. They are shooting people on the spot and rounding them up for the camps. They are just as merciless with Poles as they are with Jews. We have to be very smart if this is going to work, Hanosz," Jozef explained.

Hanosz had his hand on his face rubbing his stubble up and down from his cheek to his chin. It was a sign. Hanosz always did this when he was deep in thought. Jozef was getting through to him.

"This farmhouse has an attic. I can prepare it for the four of them to stay there until we are done. No one will know they are up there," Jozef said.

Both Nessa and Marta were listened intently as Jozef spoke. Hanosz was ruthless and unpredictable. Marta wasn't sure her husband would go for a plan that meant hiding Jews for so many days.

Hanosz spoke. "There are four of them? Why so many? I expected only a husband and wife. I don't want to keep four Jews here," he said indignantly.

"There's a mother and three children. They are not young children, they are teenagers, and I believe the oldest girl is over twenty. These people have been through much together, they've already lost the man of the family and have become very protective of each other. They won't be separated. If we try to divide or isolate them, the plan will fail. They will die together before being apart. Keeping them hidden together is a small price to pay for the bounty you'll receive at the end. Then you can do what you like with them," Jozef added.

Hanosz was silent while he continued to stroke his face. It took only a moment for his greed to win out. He stood abruptly and said, "Okay, Jozef, there will be a nice bonus in this for you, my friend. Bring in the Golds. It's time to meet these Jews."

Jozef couldn't help feel a little amused listening to Hanosz call him his friend. Hanosz would shoot his own mother if it meant more money in his pocket. Jozef and Nessa exchanged a quick glance. Without another word, he went out to get the Golds.

Outside, the temperature had dropped, and the wind had stiffened. The Golds were all shivering. Snow that had piled on the wagon had fallen through the loose hay. It was a welcome relief when they heard the back door open and the footsteps crunching in the fresh snow.

"We're ready," Jozef said. "Leave your bags buried in the wagon. We will need whatever you have in there for our next hiding place. No matter what Hanosz says, or how pleasant he makes himself, do not let him separate you. Insist at all times that you must stay together."

After that long trek through the sewers and then the cold wagon ride, Hanna had stiffened up. Dismounting wasn't easy, but David helped the women to the edge of the wagon, and Jozef lifted them down.

"Come," Jozef said. All four followed him and entered the farmhouse.

It felt so good to be inside. They followed Jozef into the kitchen where Hanosz sat at the table, waiting. Nessa and Marta stood quietly near the stove. Hanna noticed the slightest nod of Nessa's head as she blinked at Hanna in a sign of solidarity.

"So, you are the Golds," Hanosz said in a friendly tone. "Welcome to my home," he added in a deep bellowing voice, his arm extended, moving around him in a slow welcoming gesture toward the kitchen table.

Jozef had heard this ritual before. Hanosz was nice to all the Jews before he disposed of them. It was like a game to him. Jozef hoped this time would be different. Other than telling him there would be a bonus for him, Hanosz never actually acknowledged he was willing to wait the days Jozef needed to find a new farmer to hide them. He could only assume the money would be enough of an incentive for Hanosz to hold out. It would mean he would have to house and feed four Jews. That was something Jozef was not sure Hanosz was capable of.

"Marta, give our guests some soup, they must be cold and hungry," Hanosz said.

They were all hungry, but David especially was starving. He was a growing, teenaged boy, and it was rare that he was not hungry. His mother was always amazed at how much this boy could eat and then ask for more.

"Jozef, while your friends eat, why don't you prepare a comfortable sleeping place in the attic for them."

The large farmhouse had an equally large attic. Jozef threw two bundles of straw up through the trap door in the ceiling.

He used a ladder to get through the hole to the attic, where he immediately opened the bales and spread the straw on the center of the floor. The roof of the farmhouse was high enough in the middle that Jozef could actually stand upright. At the sides, where the roof sloped down, there was less space, and it was far more cramped. Jozef put a large metal pail at the side where they could relieve themselves. They would be here for the next few days. It was cold in the attic, but if they stayed close to the floor, the heat from the farmhouse below would keep them warm enough. Jozef didn't know if Hanosz would offer them a blanket, but at least they had heavy outerwear. At this point, Jozef's only concern was keeping them alive. The Golds were his ticket out of there, and he was going to make no mistakes.

Marta ladled soup into four bowls and set them on the kitchen table.

"Please, eat," Hanosz said. He got up from the table and left the room. It was bad enough these Jews were eating his food and sitting in his kitchen, he didn't need to share a table with them. He kept telling himself it would all be worth it. Once he left, Marta gave each of them bread to go along with the soup. David was famished. The soup had carrots, potatoes, and a little meat. It was hot and salty and felt good going down.

"Finish quickly," Nessa said. "We can't take any chances. We must get you into the attic soon. You never know who's watching. You can take the bread with you into the attic and keep it for later."

Hanna stood up from the table, and the others followed. Jozef walked them over to the ladder in the hallway. "David, you go first, and then you can help the women in," he said.

Rubbish, Esther thought. She certainly did not need David's help to climb a ladder and get through a hole, but she kept quiet. This was bigger than Aaron's attic. They could easily stay here. They had room to sit up, stretch their legs, and if they took turns, stand in the peak.

"We'll be fine here," Hanna said to Jozef, whose head was sticking up through the trap door. "Thank you for all that you've done," she whispered.

"Stay quiet, and don't move more than you have to. Keep your ears open, and listen for any sound of someone coming in or out of the house. There are neighboring farms all around, and other farmers visit all the time. They must not hear anything coming from this attic. You know what Hanosz will do to you if you are in the way. First thing tomorrow, I will start my search for a new place." Jozef did not wait for a response. His head disappeared, and he shut the trap door behind him.

Hanna, Shoshana, Esther, and David were comfortable for now. Knowing they could not speak, Esther took her mother's hand on one side and her sister's on the other. Shoshana joined her hand with David's, and he completed the circle by grasping his mother's. They sat like that for a long while, the energy they shared through touch radiating through their bodies. As they warmed up, the exhaustion from the trek through the sewers, the wagon ride, and the overwhelming tension and fear caught up with them. They arranged themselves close together on the straw. It only took seconds before they fell into a deep sleep.

CHAPTER 18

Tricking Hanosz

The following morning Jozef and Hanosz met at the kitchen table. The snow had stopped, leaving the fields and trees covered in a pure white blanket.

"So Jozef, are you going to Pińczów today?" Hanosz asked impatiently.

"I'll go out this morning and see what news I can find. I need to know what the conditions are like in Pińczów since the deportations. We need to be very careful, Hanosz. If we make any mistakes, we'll blow this opportunity."

Only a couple of weeks earlier, at the end of October 1942, the SS soldiers had surrounded Pińczów in their second attempt to rid the town of Jews, just as they had in Działoszyce. The Germans were well into *Aktion Reinhard,* the code name given to the operation to kill all Polish Jews. It was all part of the Final

Solution. Any Jew who had escaped death earlier was deported to a concentration or labor camp where the objective was to kill each and every one. All towns were to become *Judenrein,* free of Jews.

Hanosz stroked his coarse beard. "After you eat, go see Kowalski. He always has the latest news. He'll tell you what's going on there and how best to get in and out quickly."

Kowalski was a man with connections. He owned one of the larger farms in Kolkow, and his brother had close ties with the Polish National Army. For the past few months, Kowalski had been supplying the farmers with information of when and where the Nazis were attacking.

Jozef hated Kowalski. He was a huge, filthy man, who smelled like he hadn't seen water in weeks. His belly hid the entire top of his pants, and his calloused fingers were tobacco-stained from smoking. He was disgusting, and Jozef was sickened by him.

Jozef could see that after only one night of having the Jews in his house, Hanosz was itching to get rid of them. Hanosz was a bully and also a coward. He was afraid of being caught hiding Jews. Jozef and Nessa had forged Polish identification papers, so the threat of the Germans finding them was not a problem for Hanosz. They had a story prepared just in case. They would say that Nessa and Hanosz were cousins. This would account for the different family names on the identification papers. Jozef did not dare tell Hanosz that the Golds were carrying their *kennkarte* papers. These were identification papers issued by the Third Reich. Everyone was to carry them. The color of a kennkarte was based on ethnicity. Poles had gray ones; Jews had yellow, Russians and other non-Poles had blue. The name Sara was added as a middle name on all the Jewish women's identification papers, and the name Israel was added to the men's papers.

Jozef was under tremendous pressure. He hoped he could trust his own instincts because the hatred of Jews was infectious. Some of the farmers, whom he'd thought were good people, were now more than happy to turn them in. They felt the Germans would look favorably on them for cooperating.

What fools they all are, Jozef thought. He had been up most of the night weighing his options. He kept coming back to one farmer by the name of Wiktor Stanczyk. He was a hard-working, simple man, married with three children. Jozef used to enjoy his business meetings with Stanczyk. They would often sit and talk for a while, laughing and drinking. They had built a strong relationship over the years. It had been a while since Jozef had seen or spoken to Stanczyk, and he didn't know if the propaganda had brainwashed him, like it had many of his neighbors. Luckily, Stanczyk stayed pretty much to himself, and Jozef hoped that hadn't changed. With the exception of his brother Max, who was part of the Polish National Army, Stanczyk didn't concern himself much with anything outside of his farm or family. The other stroke of luck was that the farm wasn't far from Hanosz. Jozef needed to get to Stanczyk's farm, and the most direct way should have been straight through the fields, but with the new snow on the ground Jozef didn't want his footprints to give him away. He would have to take a roundabout route and go through the forest to get there because Kowalski's farm was in the opposite direction.

He put on his coat and boots and turned to Hanosz, who was eating bread and porridge. Without lifting his head, Hanosz waived him off. Nessa and Marta were already in the kitchen but hadn't said a word. They were both waiting for Hanosz to finish his meal and start his routine. He would go out and tend to the animals and spend much of the day working outside.

ం

Hanna opened her eyes and could hear the men talking below. She was lying right over the kitchen. The heat from the stove made it the warmest part of the attic. Hanna looked at her children, still fast asleep. The day before had exhausted them. Her bladder was full, but she could not move until she was sure Hanosz was gone. She didn't want to make any noise that would remind him of their presence.

After breakfast, Hanosz left. The women watched as he made his way to the outhouse.

"Can you make some more porridge for the Jews?" Nessa asked. Marta nodded and went to work. She was a very simple woman. Uneducated and raised in an abusive home, Marta had watched her father constantly beat and mistreat her mother. She had learned from her mother that if she always stayed quiet, her life would be easier. As a result, Marta didn't say much, but she listened to everything. Nessa went down the hallway, removed the ladder from the nearby closet and propped it up to the trap door. She quickly climbed up and pushed open the door. She peeked in and saw Hanna lying on the floor awake. At the sound of the trap door opening, the girls started to stir.

Nessa whispered, "He's gone, you can move now. If you hear me whistling a song, stop moving. It means he is coming back. I'll bring you something to eat."

"I heard Jozef leave this morning," Hanna said quickly before Nessa disappeared. She wanted confirmation that he was out searching for a new place. Hanna had a very bad feeling about this farmhouse. She knew they would not survive here much longer.

Nessa simply nodded. She did not want Marta to hear her conversing with the Jews in the attic. They needed to be so careful. One wrong word or gesture, and they would all perish.

Hanna quickly got up to use the pail that Jozef had left for them. Both Shoshana and Esther had heard the instructions too. "Let your brother sleep till she brings up the food," Hanna told them.

It wasn't long before Nessa was back at the attic door. Marta stood underneath her at the bottom of the ladder holding a large bowl half-filled with porridge. Marta handed Nessa a spoon and the bowl. Nessa put it through the hole in the ceiling, and Esther took it from her hands. The sides of the bowl were warm, and the smell was heavenly. The porridge was followed by half a loaf of bread, which had been cut horizontally and smeared with butter. There were also two apples and a jug of water. Esther thanked Nessa and Marta for their kindness, and the door was closed.

The smell of the porridge immediately woke David. They took turns eating. Each one took a couple of spoonfuls and passed the bowl over the next person until it was all gone. Not knowing if they would get anything else to eat, they decided to save the bread and apples for later.

David spoke first. "Did she tell you anything, Mameh?"

Hanna put her index finger to her lips. "Shhh," she whispered softly. "If you must speak, be so quiet that sitting right next to each other we can barely hear you. I was up early and heard

Jozef talking to the farmer," she continued. "Their voices were muffled, and I didn't hear what they said, but I do know that Jozef left, and the farmer is outside working."

"I really hope we don't have to stay here much longer," David added. "I don't like this place. I think we're in big danger."

Esther passed the bowl to Shoshana and spoke. "We've made it this far, we'll make it to the next place, David. Remember, Jozef and Nessa have as much to lose as we do. He will get the job done, have faith."

Esther always made sense. She managed to bring perspective into the worst situations.

She is right, David thought as he put the bowl over his whole face and licked what was left off the sides.

ꕥ

Jozef made his way to Kowalski's first. He had to make an appearance there in case Kowalski and Hanosz met up for a visit. Jozef wanted to cover every eventuality; he was not going to make any mistakes.

Kowalski was in the stable with the horses when Jozef approached. A cigarette dangled from the side of his mouth, and he looked and smelled as unkempt as ever. Jozef made small talk with him and then asked if he had any information about where the Germans were and in which direction they were headed. Kowalski informed Jozef that the Germans were in all the surrounding towns, and they would surely make their way to Kolkow eventually. Because of its light population and vast farmland, Kolkow was not a priority for them. They wanted to gather the

Jews in the largely populated towns before they bothered with smaller pockets in the surrounding areas.

Jozef thought how well that information could work into his plan. Once he established a new hiding place, he would tell Hanosz that the Germans were coming, and to be safe, Jozef should take the Golds out of the house and return them after the Germans finished their sweep of Kolkow. Hanosz would never fight him on that. He was too much of a coward to take any kind of risk. The pieces were falling into place. If Jozef could persuade Stanczyk to go along with him, it would all be set.

Jozef continued talking to Kowalski, pretending not to be in a rush. He said he had work to do with Hanosz and would see him around. They said their good-byes, and Jozef went on his way. He walked back toward Hanosz's farm and then veered into the trees.

Before long, he was in the forest that ran along the side of Stanczyk's farm. Stanczyk, too, was outside tending to his chores. He was startled to see a man emerge from the trees and went for the rifle propped up against the barn. Before he could pick it up, Jozef yelled out to him.

"Stanczyk, my friend, it's been a long time."

CHAPTER 19

A New Farmer

Stanczyk was shocked to see Jozef. He hadn't seen or heard a word of him for a long time and assumed he was dead. They walked toward each other, shook hands, and then moved in a little closer to pat each other on the back.

"How've you been Wiktor?" Jozef asked.

"Lanski, we thought you were dead."

"As you can see, Wiktor, I'm very much alive," Jozef said as he stood back, opened his arms wide, and did a full turn on the spot.

Stanczyk laughed. He was quite happy to see Jozef. "Come to the house, my friend. Let's get out of the cold." Stanczyk put his arm over Jozef's shoulder, and they walked side by side toward the farmhouse.

Lujia, Wiktor's wife, was kneading bread on the kitchen

table, when she looked to see her husband and a man enter the house. It took her a few seconds to realize who it was. She, too, was happy to see Jozef, but she didn't approach him.

Jozef's presence reminded the Stanczyks of better times, when they were all able to move through the countryside freely. Whenever Jozef came, he would often stay for dinner, and by the time he left, they had purchased either cattle or meat from him. It was a time when food was abundant, and fear was not part of their lives. Theirs was a good relationship, and they had grown close over the years. Both Wiktor and Lujia knew Jozef was Jewish, but it didn't seem to make any difference. They didn't recoil in fear or revulsion at the sight of a Jew on their property, like so many of the other farmers would have.

Jozef looked around, "Where are the children?" he asked.

"Kassia and Gita are washing the clothes, and I don't know where Fredek has gone off to." Lujia looked at her husband as she spoke, hoping he might fill in where their seven-year-old son might be.

"I left him in the barn; he was tying the bundles of wheat. He's probably still in there," Wiktor answered.

The Stanczyk's farmhouse was tiny and run-down. The kitchen had a dirt floor and the cupboards and stove were old and worn. Jozef wasn't sure how they managed with the little they had. With the war limiting purchases of food, clothing, and necessities how would they survive? *Their poverty could work well into my plan,* Jozef thought. He hoped his offer would be enough motivation for Wiktor to agree to put his whole family at risk. Jozef surveyed the farmhouse and quickly realized there was no place to hide six people here. The only place that would work was the old barn that was near the road. Jozef had been in there a couple of times in the past, but wanted to see it again to assess the feasibility of hiding six people in there.

"I haven't seen Fredek in so long," Jozef said, "Let's take a walk out to the barn and have a look at your young man."

Wiktor was happy to comply. He was proud of his son and delighted to show him off. Fredek was a hard-working, obedient child. Wiktor couldn't have been prouder of him. They put their coats and hats back on and went out.

Jozef surveyed the small barn carefully from the outside. It was about the size of a cattle boxcar on a train. One end faced the dirt road and the other end butted up to the trees. There were two entrances on either side of the barn. Jozef didn't think the roadside entrance was used much. The main entrance to the barn faced the farmhouse. It was a large double door, which swung out into the yard. It was secured from the outside by an iron bar. The most attractive feature was the built-on addition of a small tool shed that extended out and completely covered the view of the doors from the road. *A little added insurance,* Jozef thought. There was also an iron gate attached to a wooden fence, protecting the property from intruders. It wouldn't be the most comfortable place, as the walls of the barn were made of wooden boards that had warped and weathered over the years. Jozef knew it would be cold and drafty in there, but the alternative was death. *We could manage just fine in here,* he thought. He needed to go inside to see the layout.

One of the doors was already open, and they both entered the barn. Fredek turned to see Jozef and his father enter. "Fredek!" Jozef said. "Do you remember me?"

Fredek looked at his smiling father and relaxed.

"I sure remember you," Jozef continued. "Remember the last time I was here I brought you and your sisters big red lollipops?"

A sheepish smile covered Fredek's face. He nodded to Jozef that he remembered, and he walked over to his father, who put his arm around the boy.

"How about if you go inside and ask your mama to make us some coffee? Would you do that for us?" Jozef asked.

Stanczyk knew something was up. As soon as Fredek was out of earshot, he spoke.

"So Lanski, what brings you to see me now?"

"I have a proposition for you, Wiktor. I bring you an opportunity to make a lot of money and at the same time save both my wife and me. Interested?" Jozef asked.

"Go on," Stanczyk answered.

"You probably don't know this, but Nessa and I have been living with Hanosz. It's not a good situation there. He's unpredictable, and as long as we're with him our lives are in danger." Jozef went on and explained in detail what the arrangement had been between him and Hanosz. Stanczyk didn't look all that shocked at hearing some of the horrors that went on at that farm. Even when times were good, Hanosz was a crooked businessman and an opportunist. Stanczyk could easily believe he was capitalizing on the suffering of others.

Jozef continued, "On one of our journeys to bring back Jews for Hanosz, we met up with a family. A mother with two grown daughters and a young son, just like your family, Wiktor. Their name is Gold. They were very wealthy in Pińczów, and they've brought much money with them." Jozef watched Stanczyk very carefully for a reaction, but so far he was still listening intently.

"The Germans will make it to Kolkow any time now. Wiktor, you know at the first sign of danger Hanosz will not hesitate to turn us over. I'm asking you, my friend, to hide Nessa and me and the Golds. They will pay you very handsomely for your kindness, and in turn, you will have money to eat and survive as well." There. He'd said it all. Jozef waited for a response, and it was a very long minute before Stanczyk spoke.

"How much?" he asked.

Jozef knew Hanna had both zloty and American dollars. The two men haggled back and forth and ended up with a price of seven thousand zloty a month, or the equivalent of eight hundred American dollars. He wasn't sure the exact amount the Golds were carrying, but knew they had enough for many months. Without a word Stanczyk turned to leave the barn. Jozef watched as Stanczyk entered his house and closed the door behind him.

He waited for what seemed like an eternity. It was taking much too long for him to return. *This is not good,* Jozef thought.

An hour had passed when the door to the farmhouse opened. Stanczyk came out and approached Jozef in the barn. *It is a good sign that he is looking at me,* Jozef thought.

Stanczyk stretched his arm out and shook Jozef's hand. "Lanski, we have a deal," he said.

Jozef's muscles finally relaxed. "Wonderful!" he answered, clasping Stanczyk's hand with both of his and shaking vigorously.

"We only have one problem," Stanczyk said. "Lujia is not happy with my decision. She's going along with it because she has no choice. She knows we need the money, but the thought of hiding Jews on our property has made her very anxious. She won't make any trouble or tell anyone, but I thought you should know she's not happy about this arrangement." Stanczyk explained.

"I can't blame her, Wiktor, and I wouldn't ask, but the situation is desperate for us. You know the Germans are killing Jews without a second thought, and they're not doing much better with you Poles. These animals don't take much time to distinguish between races. If you're not one of them, your death papers are as good as sealed. Working together is our only chance at survival. In time, Lujia will come to understand. When the money you are paid puts food in her children's stomachs, she will know she's doing the right thing," Jozef said.

Stanczyk nodded, and Jozef continued speaking. "While you were in the house, I looked around to see where we might hide six people." Jozef walked over to the structure that was used to hold hay. It was just over a meter high and four meters long. It took up half the length of the barn. "If we continue to build this right down the whole length of the barn, we can all fit in. Four people will lie lengthwise, and two people will lie widthwise. It can work Wiktor, but we have to build it quickly, and it can't look like a new addition."

"Come with me," Stanczyk said, as he led Jozef out of the barn to the back of his chicken house. A stack of old wooden boards was piled behind it, more than enough to extend the enclosure. Without a word, the two men grabbed a bunch of boards and carried them into the barn. Stanczyk went into the tool shed and came out with two hammers, a saw, and a large box of nails. He dropped the equipment beside the boards and walked back to close the barn doors. The two men immediately began sorting, measuring, and sawing, wood. They figured it would take a few of days to get it ready. Jozef had little time to work on it because he had to get back to Hanosz's farm with a good story. He had to stall Hanosz for at least three days and make sure the Golds were kept alive.

He watched the time and set out on his way back through the forest. He walked past Hanosz's farm and came out on the road so it looked like he was returning from Kowalski's farm. As he walked through the forest, there was evidence that others besides him walked through this path earlier. There were many sets of footprints, and he would have to be extra careful now. He didn't know whose footprints they were, but they weren't made by German boots.

CHAPTER 20

Preparations

The sun was low in the sky as Jozef approached the farm. He walked through the front door, stomping his feet to remove the snow from his boots then wiping them on the straw mat. Hanosz was in his easy chair, smoking and reading a newspaper.

"Did you meet with Kowalski?" were his first words.

Jozef sat down and explained to Hanosz it would take a few days and possibly a week to get to Pińczów. It was too dangerous to head into the town now, the Germans were in the process of removing the last of the Jews, and they were shooting Poles, Jews, and anyone who looked at them the wrong way.

"Give me a few days to set up connections. You know I have many people in Pińczów who would be happy to help for a fee. The problem is, I have no idea where they are now, or what their situation might be," Jozef explained. "I need more time to set up a plan that will work. In the meantime, you have a strong, able-bodied boy in your attic. Use him to help you with the chores around the farm. The women can help Marta cook and mend the winter clothes. They don't have to leave the attic to sew; I can bring them whatever they need," Jozef said, praying that Hanosz would approve.

Hanosz continued to puff on his cigarette without looking up from his newspaper. Jozef thought he'd better continue trying to persuade Hanosz to go along with his fake plan to get the money from Pińczów.

"Remember Hanosz, you have much to gain in exchange for a little patience. There's gold, silver, and cash just waiting for someone to retrieve it. I'm going to be that person, I'll get it all and bring it here to you. You know I need my ten percent payment, so you can be sure I won't let you down."

With that Hanosz put down his cigarette and spoke to Jozef. "I'm counting on you, Jozef. You better do this fast. I can't promise how long I can hold out feeding and living with Jews. If there is one sign of a German truck coming through this town, I'll put all of you out for the Germans to enjoy. That includes you and your lovely wife, too."

It was the first time Hanosz had actually threatened him and Nessa. Jozef couldn't wait to be out of his grasp. With every rumor Hanosz heard of the horrors happening to the Jews, he became more arrogant and dangerous. *This stupid man thinks his life will be spared because he's not a Jew? He's going to learn the hard way,* Jozef thought to himself.

ᔓ

Nessa and Marta worked in the kitchen, but both listened carefully to the men talking in the other room. Nessa was relieved to hear her husband was able to buy them some time, but she wasn't sure if he'd found a place for them to go. She would have to be patient and wait for the right time to exchange information with her husband. Jozef got up from the chair and walked into the kitchen. He acknowledged Nessa with a nod of his head, a sign to her that he was, indeed, successful.

"When you have something for me to take up to the attic, give it to me. I have instructions to give them," Jozef said. "Marta, the women will help you with whatever you need. If you want them out of the way, you can give them things to do in the attic, like sewing. If you need help cooking or washing, they can come down for a while. Starting tomorrow morning, the boy will work with Hanosz outside." Jozef explained to the women, "It's going to take about a week for me to get what we need from Pińczów. By then the Germans will have finished their operations. With my Polish papers, I know I can get past them without a problem."

An hour or so went by. Hanosz and Jozef ate, and so did their wives. After supper Jozef put on his coat and made his way to the outhouse, but before he walked out the door, he took a detour to the back room where he and Nessa slept to pick up a pencil and a piece of paper. Once in the outhouse, he began writing: *I found a farm, it will take time to set up, go along with whatever I say.* He came back in with the note tucked into the cuff of his sleeve.

It was time to take some food up to the attic and fill the Golds in on their fate. Jozef took the large bowl of soup from Marta and headed down the hallway. He flipped open the door in the ceiling then he went up an extra step on the ladder so he was waist high in the attic. He passed the bowl to David. They all stared at Jozef, hungrier for information than for food.

Jozef spoke loudly. "Eat. Tomorrow you will work." Before he stepped down, he removed the note from his cuff and left it on the floor. The hatch closed behind him, and he made his way straight into the back room where he and Nessa slept.

Hanna motioned for her children to be quiet. She slid over to the note, picked it up, read it, and passed it along so each one of them could read it. When the note made its way back to her, she tore it into tiny pieces and added it to the soup. They ate it. There could be no sign of treason if this was going to work. They clutched each other's hands in an affirmation of hope and took turns with the soup.

ᔕ

The November sun rose later and later. It was almost seven a.m. before it was light. The Golds had been awake for a while, anticipating the changes this day would bring.

Jozef and Nessa had barely slept after he explained his plan to her. They both tossed through the night, lost in their own thoughts and fears of what the next few days might bring. Hanosz was already violent and unstable. Adding fear and doubt into the mix would surely send him over the edge, so Nessa had to work her magic while Jozef spent his days with Stanczyk, preparing their new shelter.

Jozef was the first one in the kitchen. He went to retrieve David but gave the boy only the details he needed to know.

With half his body in the attic Jozef motioned for David

to come close. He whispered in his ear. "You're going to work with Hanosz until we are out of here. It will be at least a few days, maybe longer. Don't let him trick you into doing or saying anything. You stick with the story, and no matter what he offers, stay true to the plan." David agreed with a nod. Jozef then spoke out loud, "David, come with me, time to put you to work."

As Jozef made his way down the ladder, Hanosz came out of his room scratching his belly. Marta returned from the outhouse and began putting wood into the stove. David followed Jozef down the ladder.

I can do this, he thought. *I'm going to do whatever it takes to get us through this. Tateh will be proud when I tell him how I survived all these torments and kept my word to be the man of the family.* It was this promise that he'd given his father, along with the premonition of the old Rebbe in Działoszyce who told him he would survive this war, that kept the twelve-year-old boy going.

Hanosz took one look at David and turned away in disgust. "Show him where the wood is. Let him start chopping," Hanosz told Jozef. Hanosz spoke as if David was not in the room. Jozef could see Hanosz was not in the best mood and got David out of there quickly. He took him out to the woodpile behind one of the barns and told him to stay quiet and chop until he received further instructions.

"Don't worry about me," David said. "Just make sure my mother and sisters are safe."

Jozef came back in, ate some breakfast, and told Hanosz he was going to see if he could find what happened to some of his old connections who would help him get in and out of Pińczów. While Hanosz began his morning routine, Marta took some hot cereal out to David. He put down his ax, ate quickly, and thanked her. She gave him a hunk of bread to keep with him. There was something about this woman that David couldn't quite understand. He had yet to hear her voice, but she seemed to be able to communicate with simple expressions. She didn't appear to be as hard as her husband.

When Marta returned inside, Nessa asked what she would like the women to help with. "Washing, mending, and drawing water from the well," she answered. Marta didn't trust them near the food; she would continue to prepare all the meals herself. Nessa took charge and showed them where everything was. They would rotate the chores. This way they had the opportunity to exercise a bit and break the monotony of living in the attic.

ೞ

Using the same route he'd used the day before, Jozef made his way to Stanczyk's farm. Once again, in the forest he saw evidence of human traffic. Besides the many footprints, he found a piece of a shoelace, an apple core, and wood shavings, as if someone had whittled a stick, possibly to use as a weapon. By the time he reached the farm, Stanczyk was already in the barn working. The boards were laid out, and the two men immediately continued building the shelter.

Days of the same routine passed. The only difference was in Jozef's daily report to Hanosz. He would say where the Germans were and how they were closing in on Kolkow. He had to balance his story perfectly. On the one hand, he wanted to make Hanosz nervous enough to allow Jozef to take the Jews into the forest for a short time while the Germans made their way through the town, but not so nervous that he would simply take care of the problem by shooting them.

It was the morning of November 20, 1942, that Jozef would complete the last phase of this plan. By the end of the day, Wiktor Stanczyk's barn would be ready to house the six of them. That morning Jozef took the hay wagon instead of traveling on foot. He told Hanosz he was finally going to attempt the trip into Pińczów. If questioned, he would say he was a farmer selling food to the few local shops that were still being operated by Poles. He used the opportunity to take the bags the Golds had hidden in the hay wagon to Stanczyk's farm. Jozef had no idea what was in those bags, but knew it either had to valuables or items necessary for survival.

After the long day of hard work, Hanosz instructed David to get back up to the attic. He always stayed outside after David finished so he could have a smoke and check that David had done his chores correctly. David entered the house with his cheeks bright red from the cold. Marta turned to look at him, and then she poured him a hot cup of weak tea.

Marta looked into the eyes of this young boy and spoke for the first time. "I feel sorry for you Jews," she said. Nessa was stunned by the rare sound of Marta's voice and stopped what she was doing to listen from the back room.

Marta continued, "We have no choice, you know. You must die. It's the way it must be. All of you Jews must die."

David looked at her in horror as she spoke these words in a soft, matter-of-fact tone of voice. She spoke with such quiet conviction that it terrified him. David's hands shook as he put his tea down on the table and quickly made his way up to the attic. He sat down, pulled his knees up to his chest, and began to rock. Hanna and her daughters watched, disturbed. Even though David looked fine physically, they knew something horrifying had happened. Through everything he had been through, David had never shown this kind of despair. Without speaking, his mother and sisters gathered around him, and for the first time since he'd left home, David allowed his silent tears to drop onto his mother's hands.

PART THREE
The Barn

CHAPTER 21

Moving in
November 21, 1942

It was time. *All the planning and lying will be over tonight,* thought Jozef, as he made his way back to Hanosz's farm. He would have to act panicky and frantic, which was not going to be hard, if he was to convince Hanosz to let the Jews go. He arrived back, but left the horse and hay wagon in the middle of the field so he could run through it and storm into the house, breathless. It was an extremely dark night, the air was biting cold, and it had snowed again, but he would have no trouble leading them all to their new hiding place. Jozef rushed into the house yelling, "The Germans are coming, they're on their way."

Hanosz and Marta stood paralyzed, staring at him.

"Quick, Hanosz! We must get the Jews out of here. They can't be found here!" The plan worked. Jozef's hysteria was contagious, and he managed to plant the fear of God into Hanosz, but his job was not over. He knew Hanosz's first reaction would be to shoot them all and throw their bodies into the woods.

Jozef spoke without giving Hanosz a chance to think. "I'm going to take the Jews and hide in the woods. I'll bring them back only when it's safe, after the soldiers leave. Once the Germans pass through Kolkow, they will head west to finish their sweep of the towns. Pińczów will be empty, and I'll finally be able to collect the money. Then you can do what you want with the Golds."

Hanosz stroked his chin. He quickly determined Jozef was right. It would take too long to dispose of the Jews his way. Besides, if he killed them now, it would mean he'd endured living with them for nothing. It would be better to let them go with Jozef. After all, Jozef was as desperate for their money as he was.

"Go," Hanosz said as he fell back into his chair. Nessa had already packed a few things and was ready to leave. As soon as she heard Hanosz's approval, she was up the ladder. "Hurry," she said to the Golds. "We have to leave, the Germans are on their way." It took only seconds for the Golds to make their way down. The whole thing was going better than expected. *What a fool that stupid Hanosz is,* Jozef chortled to himself.

ᔕ

Once again the Golds were on the move. With Jozef in the lead, they walked quickly through the field and into the forest. The trees served as a protective barricade from the wind and prying eyes. It wasn't until they were a safe distance from Hanosz's farm that Hanna spoke.

"Stop!" she said in an authoritative tone. They all turned to look at her. "Where are we going, Jozef?" Hanna asked. Jozef, caught up in making this plan work, had completely forgotten to divulge any information to the Golds.

"To another farmer," he said. "Wiktor Stanczyk. He has a barn where he will hide us for seven thousand zloty a month, and for that he will feed all of us, provide shelter, and conceal us."

"Seven thousand zloty?" Hanna said in alarm. "That's a fortune! That price will only buy us six or maybe seven months."

Jozef's face contorted as his temper surfaced. He approached Hanna and got very close. In a low, angry voice he said, "Do you have a better idea? What do you think I've been doing all this time, lying to Hanosz and trying to keep you all alive, while I snuck out every day to build us a shelter in that barn? Maybe I should have let Hanosz shoot all of you. Would you have been happier paying that price?"

Nessa moved in closer. She knew her husband's body language well and was afraid he was about to strike Hanna.

Hanna realized she had unleashed his temper and tried to diffuse the situation. "I'm sorry, Jozef. I appreciate all you've done. It was just a shock to hear how much it would cost. Please, let's keep going."

Nessa took her husband's arm and said, "Come, Jozef. They're tired and hungry and haven't had a chance to process this information. Hanna's a smart woman. She knows there is no price too big to save six lives. We all owe you our lives, and we are grateful for the skillful job you did, finding someone to keep us all alive."

The stroking of his ego and Hanna's apology doused Jozef's

anger, and he reverted to the man who'd been in control just moments before.

"It's not far," he said as he turned and resumed walking. They followed silently, in single file, for about thirty minutes before Jozef stopped.

"We're here," he said pointing through the trees. "See that barn? This is where I've been spending my days building a shelter." It was dark, and they could barely see the barn, but they spotted a light coming from the farmhouse beside it.

"Stanczyk has a wife and three children, they're all in the farmhouse, and I don't know what they've been told, so stay quiet and follow my lead."

They followed Jozef out of the forest and onto the property of Wiktor Stanczyk. Jozef motioned for them to stay back. The place looked deserted. He walked over to the barn. The iron bar, which held the doors together was on the ground. He knocked faintly on the barn door, and Stanczyk opened it. Jozef whistled, and they all moved toward the barn, each one assessing the landscape before them.

Four structures were in close proximity to each other. The farmhouse faced one side of the barn, a stable stood near the back of it, and what looked like another animal shelter was beside the stable. All the buildings were old and run-down. They walked into the barn where they met their new host for the first time. He had an oval-shaped, weathered face. His sallow skin was filled with deep lines, and he was unshaven. He wore a fur-lined hat, and he was wrapped in a thick feather quilt.

Jozef broke the silence. "These are the Golds," he said. Stanczyk held up his kerosene lantern to see their faces. Then he noticed Nessa, standing behind the boy. He had met her a number of times in the past.

"Pani Lanski," he addressed her with respect. "Good to see you again."

Nessa bowed her head, "Good to see you too, Pan Stanczyk." He shone the lamp across each of them and stopped when he got to Shoshana. The light illuminated her blue eyes. "*Dobry wieczór*, good evening," he said directly to her.

"Dobry wieczór, thank you for taking us in," she answered. Stanczyk immediately noticed her perfect Polish. No hint of that Yiddish accent that so many Jews had. He acknowledged her statement with a single affirmative nod and moved on to the others. He wanted to get a good look at each of them.

David was not paying attention when Stanczyk shone the light on him. He was busy exploring the barn, trying to imagine where they were going to hide in this place. On top of the wheat that was piled high on the ledges on either side? *No. We could not hide there,* he thought. Maybe in the small external overhang he saw as they walked into the barn? He kept searching for answers as his eyes skimmed each corner. He was standing on a large concrete pad in the center of the barn, which was used to thrash the wheat. He searched for an opening in the concrete leading to a cellar, but there was none.

"What are you looking for boy?" Stanczyk asked. David was so involved in his search, Stanczyk's question startled him.

Trying to recover, David replied, "I was looking for where we are going to hide, sir." Jozef and Stanczyk looked at each other with relief. *If the boy can't see the enclosure, then no one else can, either,* Jozef thought.

"Turn around," Stanczyk said. They all turned in the direction he pointed, but still saw nothing. Stanczyk moved between them over to the structure, which was about one and a half meters high and now spanned the length of the barn. David didn't notice it because it looked like nothing more than an enclosed shelf piled high with hay from one end to the other. There was an identical structure on the other side of the barn as well. Stanczyk removed two old vertical boards to reveal a sort of cave. They all bent down to see inside. Stanczyk moved the lantern in to light up the space. The dirt floor was carpeted with a thick layer of straw. One end butted up to the outside boards of the barn, and the other end had a partition, which was visible from the inside only. From the outside, it all looked like one long enclosure. There were vertical pieces of wood inside, supporting the top of this tiny nest.

Jozef took over. "The four of you will lie lengthwise side by side." He demonstrated with his hand as he spoke. "Nessa and I will sleep across the end. It will be tight, but we will be well hidden."

Jozef walked over to Hanna, took her by the arm and led her away from the rest of them. The others all crouched down examining this tiny crawl space, but didn't step in. It was like they were waiting for a formal invitation to enter their new home.

"I need seven thousand zloty now, the first payment," he whispered to her. Without hesitation, she took off her boots, counted out the money, and handed it to Jozef. They returned to the rest of the group, and without exchanging words Jozef handed the money to Stanczyk. He quickly stuffed the cash into his front pocket. There would be plenty of time to count it inside with Lujia. Maybe when his wife actually saw and held the money in her own hands, she would come around to the idea of hiding Jews on her property.

David was the first one in. Bending forward, he made his way to the far end and sat down. Hanna followed, then his sisters. They sat side by side, along the back wall. Jozef shook Stanczyk's hand and thanked him once again. Stanczyk took the thick blanket from around his shoulders and handed it to Jozef who passed the blanket inside to the Golds. Nessa and Jozef retreated to the enclosure, but before sealing himself in, Jozef accepted the large metal milking bucket that Stanczyk gave him. They would use it as their toilet. From the inside, Jozef replaced the two boards with expertise, blocking the entrance. He had practiced doing this a number of times when he created this hiding space. He built a small lip where the boards could balance and lock in place. It would blend perfectly with the rest of the vertical boards. From the outside it was undetectable. Stanczyk made sure the opening was completely invisible to any Nazi who might come in searching for Jews. He smiled to himself as he surveyed the barn. It was perfect. He lit a cigarette and walked out into the cold. From the outside, he placed the iron bar across the doors and sealed them in. It was November 21, 1942, when the Golds and Lanskis spent their first night in the new "home" built especially for them.

CHAPTER 22

The Stanczyks

The protective darkness prevented everyone from feeling claustrophobic. When Jozef closed off the entrance to the enclosure, and Stanczyk left the barn, lamp in hand, the blackness became complete. David probed his tiny space, but his hand landed right on top his mother's face. Hanna took his hand in hers and petted it slowly. It soothed him, and he stopped trembling. As Hanna lay there holding her son's hand, the noise inside her head blared louder than the rumbling in her stomach. With only her terrifying thoughts to keep her occupied, she was the last of the six to fall asleep.

ᔕ

Lujia was still up and puttering in the kitchen when her husband entered. It was after nine p.m., and she was usually in bed by now, but tonight she was too nervous to sleep. She was harboring six Jews in the barn a short distance from her front door. Her children had already gone to bed, and the couple was alone in the kitchen. Wiktor sat down in front of the tea and small piece of cake Lujia served him. She joined him at the table.

Without a word, Wiktor leaned back in his chair and reached down into his front pocket. He removed the wad of bills and slapped it down in front of his wife. A small gasp escaped her lips as she stared at the money. She had never seen so many bills at one time. Wiktor didn't take his eyes off his wife as she gathered the money into her hands and counted it. It was all there – seven thousand zloty.

Wiktor and Lujia were modest people used to a hard life. This money would buy them extra food and clothing. Their children would have books and toys, and they would even have enough to buy better equipment for the farm. Of course, they would have to spend some of it to buy food for the extra six people they sheltered, but Lujia was experienced at making supplies last a long time. Her reaction pleased Wiktor. Maybe now she would accept the decision he had made. But it only took a few seconds before Lujia's expression turned from elation to stone. She stood and abruptly took her husband's hand. He watched in amazement as she placed the money back in his palm and wrapped his fingers around the wad.

"This is your blood money," she said. "It will cost us our lives. When the Germans find those Jews hiding on our property, they will kill them. Then they will murder our children, and after we have watched them die, the Nazis will kill us. If you feel seven thousand zloty a month is a good price in exchange for our lives, then enjoy your money alone."

She retreated to her room, leaving Wiktor alone to think over her words. He sat for a long while agonizing over his decision. He knew he was putting his family at risk, but besides the money, it was the right thing to do. How could he have turned away his friend when Jozef had come to him for help? He knew about the death camps, the shootings, and torturing. His brother, Max, kept him informed of everything.

Max was a member of the Polish National Army. He believed strongly that Poland belonged to the Poles, not the Germans or the Russians, and he fought to stand up for those beliefs. Max joined in the sport of hunting Jews. Although Wiktor would hear stories of these hunting expeditions, he was half convinced his brother was just talking up a good story. It would go a long way to prove to his fellow party members that he was not a coward. Many members of the NSZ were responsible for killing Jews, but there were also those members who were credited with saving countless Jewish lives. Wiktor was sure his brother was nothing but a big talker. It had crossed his mind that Max would not approve of his harboring Jews, but he knew his brother would never turn him in, especially since Wiktor had every intention of sharing some of the money with him. A little extra insurance couldn't hurt.

Wiktor continued to rationalize why his decision was sound. The opportunity to make this amount of money did not present itself every day, and he was not going to let his wife's fears stand in the way. *Lujia's a good woman,* he thought. *Eventually she will come around.*

ᔓᔕ

Lujia was up early the next morning. Whether she liked it or not, she had six additional mouths to feed, and she had to start cooking. The first thing she baked was a large, black bread. She figured if she could make one loaf every couple of weeks the Jews could ration it amongst themselves to supplement their meals. Oats, wheat, and buckwheat were in abundance on the farm. She prepared a large portion of buckwheat, also known as *kasza* to the Poles. It was a staple in their home, and Lujia served it almost every morning as a breakfast cereal with milk. Finally, she filled a large jug with water and left everything out on the table for her husband to deliver.

Wiktor woke to the smell of baking bread. He smiled to himself, realizing his wife was preparing food for the Jews. He knew she would come around. Even through all her protests, she accepted his decision to harbor these people.

"Dzień dobry," he said as he walked into the kitchen. Lujia turned to look at him and pointed at the food on the table.

"This is for them," she said.

"Aren't you going to take it out to them? You know Jozef and Nessa, but you should meet the mother and her three children, too," Wiktor said to his wife.

"Wiktor, don't mistake my preparing this meal as an acceptance of your decision. I'm still against this dangerous arrangement you've made, but I'm not going to let six people starve in our barn. Please, please just take the food. I'm not going out to meet anyone."

As she finished speaking, their youngest child, Fredek, came into the kitchen rubbing his eyes. She took her son's hand and walked him back to his bedroom. She didn't want her children to hear the arguing. The children didn't know about Wiktor's new guests. Their parents had planned to tell them at breakfast.

Wiktor juggled the warm bread, the pot of cereal, and jug of water and walked out to the barn. It was still dark, but the sky was beginning to show signs of the day ahead. Wiktor put everything down as he removed the iron bar from the barn doors. Inside, he placed the food on the concrete pad and closed the door behind him. He crouched down in front of the two boards and lifted them out. All of the "guests" were awake, lying there in silence.

"Dzień dobry," Wiktor said to Shoshana.

"Dzień dobry," she answered as she attempted to comb her hair with her fingers. Aware of how disheveled she must look, she was embarrassed to have a stranger see her like that. They all sat up ready for something to eat and drink. Not even a sip of water had passed their lips since they left Hanosz's farm the day before. "*Dziękuję*, thank you," Shoshana said as she accepted the items one by one. Wiktor put his hand into his pocket, pulled out a few spoons and handed them to her.

"Ration the bread," he said. "You will only get one loaf every couple of weeks. I'll be back later this morning with some other things to help you pass the time. When you finish eating, leave the pot inside with you."

"Thank you for your kindness, Pan Stanczyk. God bless you," Shoshana whispered.

He gave her a quick nod, replaced the boards, and left.

Jozef took charge of the food. He began eating with such speed that it was clear he would be consuming more than his equal share. The rest of them watched but didn't say anything as he devoured far more than he should have. Jozef was not used to being hungry. He had eaten quite well when he lived with Hanosz and Marta. The rest of them exchanged looks as Jozef ripped off a piece of black bread and wiped the pot clean. Esther reached over and took the remainder of the bread and the jug of water, offering to hold it for later. Completely satiated, Jozef did not argue.

Shoshana had her eye on the bucket. By now they were used to using a bucket as a toilet, but not in such close quarters and certainly not in front of strangers, and certainly not in front of a man. She tried to wait. Jozef, on the other hand, did not hesitate to use the bucket. They all turned away to give him privacy. After he was done, the rest of them took turns. It was awkward and embarrassing to carry out something so private in such tight quarters. David waited till the rest were finished, and when he was done, added straw to the bucket in an attempt to smother the odor. The open slats of the wooden barn were a blessing, as the cold air helped to dissipate the strong odor. With their stomachs reasonably full, they rearranged themselves back in their spots and tried to sleep again.

Back in the house, Stanczyk decided to look through the Golds' bags. He felt completely justified. If he was going to hide these people, he was surely entitled to their belongings. He found clothing, paper, a pencil, gold jewelry, silver candlesticks, and a silver Kiddish cup, which he knew Jews used for blessing wine on the Sabbath. He put the paper and pencil aside, put the rest back into the bags, and slid them under his bed. He would find a better place to hide them later.

The sun brightened the cold day. The Stanczyks all sat down

for breakfast and Wiktor began to explain about a very dangerous creature he was now keeping in the barn. Keeping the details vague, he wanted to make it sound as menacing as possible. He discussed the dangers of mauling and disease and tried his best to instill terror in his children. Besides the scary picture he created of what he was harboring in the barn, he frightened them even more by telling them what he would do if he ever saw one of them near the barn. By the time he was done, the children had no idea what was out there, but they knew they had better stay away. Lujia didn't contribute to the conversation. She was as uncomfortable lying to her children as she was hiding Jews.

After breakfast, Kassia, the oldest daughter, went out to milk the cow as she did every morning. Gita, the middle daughter, helped her mother in the kitchen. Fredek was on his knees in the salon, making sound effects as he crashed his toy tractor into his truck and waited for his father to come get him. Wiktor and Fredek worked together every day on the farm, feeding the animals, baling hay, and chopping wood. Although Stanczyk's farm was very small, there was never a lull in the work. At busy times Wiktor would enlist the help of the girls to work in the fields, help with the harvest, and store the grains, potatoes, and cabbage. Stanczyk's farm produced only enough to meet their needs with a little left over for commercial sale.

David rolled over to face the open slat between two warped boards. Squinting one eye, he pressed the other against the opening. Outside, the fresh snow sparkled like diamonds in the bright sunlight. The pines just beyond the back of the barn were covered in snow. It all looked deceptively pretty and peaceful. The front of the barn was so close to the road that David could feel the vibrations of a truck as it drove past. He wondered if the vehicle belonged to a farmer or a German soldier. In the dark, they hadn't realized how close they were to the road. This added to the danger of being caught, so they would have to be extra careful.

Stanczyk came out, carrying a book and the paper and pencil he'd found in the bags. He had a few books in the house and thought this would help them pass the time. *Żyd Wieczny Tułacz*, which translated meant *Jew the Eternal Wanderer*, was written in 1927 by Aleksander Wat. It was a well-known book, and they were all happy to read and reread it. There was enough light during the daylight hours to read comfortably. Reading and writing were safe activities that did not produce sound.

Hanna recognized the paper and pencil and knew Stanczyk had been through their bags. Her only thought was of her mother's silver candlesticks and Leib's Kiddish cup. It was all Hanna had left of them. She chose to stay quiet, rationalizing that she and Leib would shop for new ones when the war was over. Thoughts of her husband were all she had to keep her going. He kept her company through the night, and if she closed her eyes she could fall asleep next to him, smelling his cologne and feeling his warmth.

CHAPTER 23

Life in Confinement
Winter, 1943

The months passed slowly and the days grew colder. They each took turns with the books Wiktor would bring. Reading or sleeping was the only escape from their tight jail. David claimed the paper and pencil and wrote daily lists of everything he ate. The Stanczyks made sure to feed them regularly. Although the menu was the same most days, there was enough food to keep them comfortable. It varied with milk, bread, cheese, cabbage, potatoes, and groats, in different combinations. They longed for a piece of meat or an egg, but at least their stomachs were not empty. They were not expending many calories, and most of their energy was used just to stay warm.

Sometimes they had unwelcome visitors in the night. Field mice, desperate to find warmth, joined them in their cramped quarters. One morning Hanna woke to find a mouse tangled in her long hair. Unnerved, she almost screamed, but Jozef hooked his hand over her mouth just in time. He looked into her terrified eyes, willing her to compose herself. "Shhh," he whispered. With Jozef's hand firmly across Hanna's mouth, David attempted to untangle the squirming, screeching rodent from his mother's hair.

"Kill it," Jozef demanded. But David couldn't bring himself to kill the small creature. He released it onto the floor, hoping it would escape through the slats. As the tiny rodent jumped to freedom, a large boot stomped the life out of it.

"We'll never see him again," Jozef said, laughing.

But the tiny visitor had many friends, and sharing their accommodations with the field mice would be something they would have to accept. Hanna tied her hair in a bun making it a lot less convenient for the mice to use it as a nest.

David hated to see his mother lose control. She was his rock, and to watch her crumble because of a mouse made him realize he had to rely on himself to get through these torturous days. He could no longer lean on his mother; she was doing all she could to keep herself together. Even Esther, who was always the cheerleader of the group, stopped encouraging them. The loss of freedom and dignity was taking its toll on everyone. Living in filth, rarely washing, eliminating in front of each other, and being totally reliant on others for survival chipped away at their morale.

The one hope they clung to was that the war would end, and they would be reunited with Leib. How much longer could it go on? As much as food, they hungered for news, but Stanczyk was not forthcoming with reports. For some reason, he chose not to offer information to his boarders, even knowing how vital it was to them.

Shoshana could tell Wiktor was enamored of her. She couldn't understand why. She was filthy and smelled so bad she could hardly stand herself, and yet, this man seemed to enjoy talking with her. Sometimes, when Lujia and the kids were all in the house, he would let Shoshana out of the crawl space, so she could stand on the concrete pad talking with him. They discussed different topics such as books, weather, or his family. Shoshana asked Wiktor questions about his life and massaged his ego. It had been a long time since someone made him feel important. During this small talk, she would steer the conversation to the war and hope to gather some information. Shoshana was clever enough to bide her time and use the bond they established to her advantage.

ᔕ

Kolkow, a small farming community of less than a thousand people, had its own town council. Max Stanczyk was the town *soltys*, a position similar to that of the village councilor. His brother Wiktor was the elected *agronom*, the man in charge of agriculture. The town council would have meetings at Max's house, which was marked with a red plaque engraved with the word *SOLTYS* on the front door. During the war, the discussions were always more about politics than town affairs, and Max would share information from his meetings with the NSZ. He had access to the British Broadcasting Corporation or BBC reports, and he and his comrades met often to smoke, drink, and discuss military and political issues. German news was unreliable and mainly consisted of propaganda.

On February 2, 1943, the BBC made the following announcement:

> "The Soviet Government has announced the final defeat of the German Sixth Army at the port of Stalingrad, in southern Russia.
>
> A statement late this evening said: 'Our forces have now completed the liquidation of the German Fascist troops encircled in the area of Stalingrad.' The last center of enemy resistance in the Stalingrad area has thus been crushed. The declaration brings to an end five months of heavy fighting for the city. The battle has been described as among the most terrible of the war so far."

The German defeat at Stalingrad was a turning point in the war. Stalingrad marked the first time that the Nazis publicly acknowledged a failure. Max couldn't wait to spread the news. This was the ray of hope everyone was waiting for. The Russians were going to defeat the German army. Max hoped the two armies would kill each other off, and Poland would be returned to the Polish people. By evening he made it to his brother's home.

"Just in time to eat with us," Wiktor said when his brother arrived. Lujia turned to acknowledge Max and proceeded to put another place setting down at the table. "Fredek, go get a chair for Uncle Max," she instructed.

From the look on Max's face, Wiktor knew something big had happened. It was not often he saw his brother in such good spirits. "You have something to tell us Max?" Wiktor asked with a smile. Max's mood was highly contagious, and his presence immediately put everyone in a good mood.

"Lujia, go get some glasses, we're going to drink a toast to the defeat of the Germans in Stalingrad," Max finally announced. A split second of silence was followed by hugging, cheering, and a celebration that lasted late into the night.

ഗ

"Something big is happening in there," Shoshana whispered to Esther. "Listen to them. They're laughing and singing." It was faint, but they could hear jovial sounds coming from the farmhouse.

"There are two men. I can hear two different voices," Esther said.

"Maybe it's good news about the war," Shoshana speculated.

"We could use some good news," Jozef said.

"There's no point in guessing, we won't find out anything till morning," Hanna added.

They lay down in their designated spots and concentrated on the sounds coming from the farmhouse. Not another word was spoken between them.

Shoshana didn't get much sleep. The wind played a melodic tune and she was back in her salon playing the mandolin with the warm sun beaming through the picture window. She was lost in her music for most of the night, and it was close to daybreak when she finally fell asleep.

An hour or two later, she heard the familiar sounds of someone bringing breakfast. She hoped it was Wiktor. Lately, Lujia had been bringing food too, but she would set it down and leave as quickly as possible without a word to anyone. Peeking through the slats, Shoshana recognized Wiktor's boots as he entered the barn. She waited for him to close the doors and then whispered, "Pan Stanczyk."

He barely heard her faint voice, but crouched down to remove the two vertical boards. As he did, he released the repulsive odor that permeated the crawl space. It was Jozef's job to empty the bucket. Every other night Stanczyk placed the bar just halfway through the doors, so it only appeared to be closed. Jozef would open the door and walk outside, where he could breathe fresh air, see the stars, and touch the snow. His job was to empty the bucket on top of the animals' manure pile behind the stable. Using a shovel kept in the overhang of the barn, he would cover his tracks and bring the empty bucket back into the enclosure. From the odor this morning, Wiktor surmised last night had been Jozef's off night.

Stanczyk helped Shoshana out of the hole. She stood upright, stretched her body, and straightened her skirt and coat.

"We heard you having a wonderful time last night, Pan Stanczyk. It's so long since I've heard laughter like that. It was really delightful," she said in Polish.

Wiktor was a little hung over, but still excited about the news, and he wanted to give Shoshana something to be happy about, too. She was gentle and refined, it didn't seem right that she was in this hopeless circumstance. He knew he could fix that temporarily with the information he was about to tell her.

Wiktor lit a cigarette, took a deep drag, and said, "The Germans were defeated in Stalingrad!" Exhaling, he smiled revealing his two broken front teeth. He watched Shoshana carefully for her reaction. It was news they all needed to hear. Inside the crawl space they clasped hands and hugged. Outside, Shoshana jumped straight up in the air, surprising herself with such a reaction. For the first time she touched her landlord. Clasping both her hands around one of his, she shook it frantically.

Stanczyk left the barn smiling, knowing he had given them hope. The war was far from over, but this turn of events gave the entire country a reason for optimism.

The news of Stalingrad changed the mood in the barn. Esther was immediately her old self. "You know what that means, don't you? Liberation is just around the corner," she declared. "We're going to make it. We're going to go home and see Tateh!"

At the sound of her daughter's words, Hanna's genuine smile turned into a forced one. Esther was so sure she would see her father again, but Hanna was afraid to hope that Leib was alive. She would never forget her husband's promise to meet them at Marian's farm. It was the last conversation they ever had, and that broken promise haunted her dreams every night.

Sunday mornings were their favorite time. The Stanczyks would put on their best clothes and walk with neighbors to Gory, a small town just west of Kolkow. They would gather at the church for prayer services. Since all the Polish farmers in Kolkow were devout Christians, the town completely emptied out. David propped himself in front of the open slats to watch as each family made their way down the road, past the barn. By the time David eyed the stragglers, the rest of them stepped out of the crawl space into the middle of the barn. This was their opportunity to stand up, to jump, and to talk above a whisper. No one was there to hear. It was like a vacation. The women took this opportunity to use the old cloths and melted snow Lujia provided to clean themselves. They would disappear behind the bales of straw and wash as best they could. This small act made a made a big difference to their comfort and dignity.

Esther had the task of removing lice from each of her roommates. She positioned herself near the warped plank, which allowed for a wide beam of light to stream in. She would slide the menacing insects along strands of hair and pop them, one at a time, between her fingers. Sometimes she would pretend each one was a Nazi, and the more she killed, the sooner she would be home. She became skilled at her job and was able to delouse everyone with speed and accuracy, ensuring they would all be less itchy for a few hours.

But the days turned into weeks, and news of liberation never came. The Russian advancement was slow, and time seemed to stand still. The elation they all felt just a short while ago, once again turned to despair.

CHAPTER 24

Close Call

While Lujia stirred the porridge for breakfast, a shot echoed through the air. She jumped and dropped her spoon. As she bent to pick it up, the second blast rocked the morning silence. Then a third – and a fourth. Heart racing, she hung on to the sink to steady herself. Dark thoughts rushed through her mind. *The Nazis! They're here. They're going to find the Jews and kill us all!* Not sure what to do first, she ran to find her children.

She pushed open the outside door that led to the kitchen and saw them standing with their father. "Come inside now," she shouted. She saw them staring in the direction of the shots. Wiktor grabbed Fredek's hand and herded the children into the house.

"What was that, Mama?" Fredek asked.

"Maybe one of the farmers shot a wolf," she answered.

Fredek shrugged and retreated to the salon to play with his toys.

"Go to the salon with your brother," Lujia told the girls. "Breakfast will be ready soon."

Lujia didn't realize how much her hands were shaking till she saw her eldest daughter Kassia focused on them. She immediately hid them under her apron. Quivering as the gentle touch of her husband's arms enveloped her stiff body, she whispered, "It's the Nazis. They're here. Who did they shoot, Wiktor? What are we going to do? We're next!"

Wiktor gripped his wife's shoulders and looked into her face. "Calm down Lujia, we do nothing. We go about our morning like we always do. If they come here, they will be watching our every move to see how nervous we are. Our lives depend on how well we perform," he explained.

She nodded her head, acknowledging his words and proceeded to set the table.

As she set the plates down, she thought how smart Wiktor was not to tell the children what, or who, was in the barn.

The Stanczyks ate breakfast but the tension in the room was thick. When they heard the faint sound of an approaching vehicle in the distance, their meal came to a halt. The engine stopped outside their window. Lujia leapt to her feet. Her only thought was to save her children.

"Get up! Hurry! Go to your room, and don't move, no matter what you hear. Stay quiet," she ordered.

Kassia grabbed the hands of her brother and sister and hurried them into the back bedroom.

Wiktor rushed to remove the children's plates and threw

them into a cupboard, leaving only his and Lujia's breakfast dishes on the table.

He and his wife sat pretending to eat as two German SS officers pushed open the iron gate and let themselves onto the property.

As they appeared at the doorway, Wiktor stood, wiped his mouth, and said, "Guten Morgen, officers. Can I help you?"

In a polite manner, one of the men spoke, while the other scanned the area with his eyes. "We're sorry to interrupt your breakfast Pan…"

"Stanczyk," Wiktor filled in.

"Pan Stanczyk, we're conducting a search for runaway, or hidden, Jews," he announced.

Wiktor swallowed hard, his pointy Adam's apple sliding up and down his neck. "Why here? There are no Jews here," he said.

"We are going from farm to farm, Pan Stanczyk. We'll check your house first, then your cellar, your barn, your stable, and chicken coop. If we find nothing, we'll be on our way," the soldier answered.

The barn, Lujia thought. The blood drained from her face while the porridge she'd just eaten rose in the back of her throat.

Wiktor snickered, trying to cover his tension, "You won't find any Jews here," he repeated. "You're wasting your time."

"Enough talk. We have many farms to get to," the soldier said. He motioned for his comrade to begin. The soldier pushed past Lujia and stomped toward the children's room.

She ran after him. "Please, my children are back there."

"We're not after your children," the officer said.

Lujia followed the soldier as he looked through every room

and closet. He pushed open the door to the bedroom. The three children sat huddled together on the bed. He walked past them and opened the closet. Using his rifle to push the clothes and boxes aside, he looked up for an attic door. Lujia spotted Hanna's bag. She knew the Judaica was still in it. She held her breath as the soldier pushed it aside. She expected him to turn and put a bullet right through her, but he closed the door and walked past her instead.

The soldier marched back to the kitchen and signaled to his partner that the house was clean.

"Where is your cellar?" the officer demanded. Wiktor felt his heart beating like a hammer in every vein. He led them outside past the dilapidated chicken coop, to an old wooden door raised above the ground. He lifted the door, and both men peered down into the small pit filled with burlap potato sacks. One of the men plunged his bayonet into the hole over and over, goring each sack.

"Now your barn."

Wiktor's unstable legs barely carried him to the barn. He removed the iron bar slowly, opened the door, and said, "You won't find any Jews in here."

The hidden Jews were already on high alert after hearing the shots. With the exception of Shoshana's tremors, there was absolute stillness under the hayloft. She listened to the heavy trample of their boots as they made their way to the back of the barn where a few crates of cabbages still remained from the winter. She could hear the crisp sound of cabbage being cut as one of the soldiers stabbed through each crate. Then came the thud of hay bales hitting the concrete floor. *They're looking for a hidden door,* she thought.

Shoshana's body stiffened when she realized they were stabbing at the bundles of grain piled on top of their enclosure. *They're coming closer, they're going to find us. We're going to die!* she screamed in her head. Her hands tightly covered her mouth.

She looked over to her mother, searching desperately for reassurance. Hanna stared back at her daughter, then shut her eyes. *She can't even look at me,* Shoshana thought, trying desperately to control her terror.

Suddenly, a sharp steel blade thrust through the slats, entering her space. She held her breath at the sight of the shiny metal hovering above her feet. She exhaled slowly as the blade retreated. A moment later, the blade cut through again, this time just above Shoshana's neck. She willed herself to stay still, her breathing quick and shallow. Her eyes wide and fixed on the menacing point of the weapon, Shoshana prayed hard for a quick death. *Please God, I don't want to suffer. Let me die without pain.*

"Let's move on," one of the SS officers said to the other.

Is it over? Did we make it? Shoshana turned her head and saw David peek through the cracks and watch as black boots retreated from the barn. The clang of the iron bar securing the door was the most beautiful music they could imagine.

No one spoke, no one moved. Many hours passed before the tension left their bodies.

The entire search only lasted a few minutes, but it took years off their lives. Lujia didn't speak to her husband for days, and in the barn no one slept soundly for a week. Hanna had prepared herself to die and was surprised that she wasn't as frightened as she thought she would be. The six of them didn't move or speak for the rest of the day, or the entire night. No one needed to use the pail, nor were any of them hungry.

By the end of the day, the Germans had pulled out of Kolkow, and the town was returned to its original state. It wasn't till the next morning that Stanczyk came in to report the details.

He brought food with him and set it down as he removed the two slats. Shoshana was the one that would step out. She was the one he always spoke to. He lit a cigarette, leaned against the boards on the other side, and spoke very calmly as the rest listened on.

"They found four Jews in Pankow's stable. The SS beat them – a mother, a father, a ten-year-old boy, and an eight-year-old girl. After the beating, the SS made them dig a grave, ordered them to step into it, and shot the children in their heads as their parents watched. Then they shot the mother and father. They took Pankow and hanged him in his orchard in front of his wife and son."

Shoshana couldn't stand it any longer. She wanted to die too. She didn't notice Esther step out of the enclosure and come toward her. "Shoshana, it's not us. We're alive. You're okay Shoshana, you're safe," Esther said, as she guided her shaky sister gently back inside.

For a moment, Stanczyk felt guilty for telling her what had happened. Maybe he shouldn't have, but he wanted them all to know what their fate would be if they were caught. He had to instill the same fear in them that he felt himself.

David listened to every word Stanczyk spoke. David's only thought was how lucky those other Jews were. *One quick shot to the head and it was all over for them. They're free now.*

It took a long time for the memory of that day to dissipate. Neither the Stanczyks nor the Jews ever spoke of it again.

ᔕ

By March 1943, food had become scarce. Crops stored over the winter dwindled, and Stanczyk made fewer trips to town for supplies. The lineups were long to get government-issued flour and sugar, and sometimes, even after standing for a full day, he would leave empty-handed. Food in Poland was running out, and the little bit available went to the German army first. Max had access to black market supplies. Using the monthly money Wiktor received from the Golds, he was able to give Max enough to buy flour, sugar, and fat. Meat was harder to come by, and occasionally he'd show up with a half kilo, which was never shared with the Jews in the barn.

As the days grew noticeably longer and the nights less cold, the Golds became more restless. They ran out of books to read, and, since the food they ate was exactly the same every day, David stopped keeping his food log. Being thirteen, he had plenty of energy and nowhere to spend it. David and boredom were not a good combination. His sisters tried to keep him busy with word games and stories.

"Remember the time we almost drowned?" Shoshana asked David.

An instant smile appeared on his face. "I thought that was the end for me," he answered.

Hanna looked bewildered. She didn't remember hearing about her children almost drowning. "When was this?" she asked, sitting up, her legs crossed under the blanket.

David and Shoshana exchanged a united look. *It is too late to get into trouble now,* Shoshana thought, as she began telling the story.

"I was walking in the park along the river, and David was playing behind me. I saw Adam up ahead, and I wanted to go and talk with him. Remember Adam, Mameh? He was that really nice Jewish policeman who used to walk me home sometimes and carry my bags."

"Go on," Hanna said in a suspicious tone.

"He was happy to see us, and it was a very hot day. Adam was preparing to go out for a ride in his kayak, and he invited me to join him. I told David to wait for me, that I wouldn't be long. But you know David. He started to whine and cry that he wanted to come too."

"I did not," David interjected.

Shoshana lowered her head, furled her brow, and stared at David without saying a word.

"Okay, so maybe I whined a little," he confessed.

Esther got a kick out of watching her siblings squirm telling this story, which under normal circumstances would have landed them with a huge punishment.

"David wouldn't let us leave without him, so Adam helped me in the front compartment of the kayak, and I sat far back enough that David could just fit in the same hole with me. Then Adam got into the back compartment, leaned over to take the oar, when David turned quickly and said 'I want to paddle.' He turned so abruptly that he threw the kayak out of balance, and it rolled upside down into the water."

Without realizing it, Hanna splayed her right hand over her chest and her left one across her mouth.

"It's fine, Mameh," Esther said, grinning. "They're here. Nothing happened to them."

Hanna was fuming. "I want to hear the rest."

"Adam slid out of his compartment with ease, and he came over to pry us loose. We were wedged in pretty tight. Since my arms were the first things he reached, he pulled me hard. I kicked my legs and was able to free myself from the kayak and stand up. David panicked, and I could see he was taking in water. With me out of the boat, it was easy for Adam to free him. Adam put his hand over David's mouth and nose to prevent him from breathing in. By the time David came up to the surface he was coughing and spitting water. It was scary, Mameh, because he couldn't seem to get air, but with his last sputter of water, his coughing turned to an intense cry. I was so happy to hear him wail like that."

"She grabbed me," David interjected, "and made it even harder for me to breathe."

Shoshana continued, "Adam felt horrible. He helped us both out of the water, and we tried to calm David, who was screeching by then. People were looking at us. Eventually David's cries turned to whimpers, and we both calmed down. We knew we had to think of a way to cover up the disaster."

"Tateh would have killed us if he'd known what we did," David said and continued with the end of the story. "So Shosh said we had to stay in the park and wait for our clothes to dry before we went home. Shoshana and I swore to each other we would never tell anyone, but then she went and told Esther."

Nessa and Jozef listened to the story and didn't really see what the big deal was.

Hanna, on the other hand, was shocked. How could she have been unaware of such an important event when two of her children could have lost their lives? It was fun for David and Shoshana to relive the event. The memory took them out of the barn for a short while, and they enjoyed the break.

David lived for the moments he could be outside the enclosure. Although his calorie intake was severely cut, he was still growing. David often talked about going toe-to-toe with "those murdering Nazis." But deep down Hanna knew her son was putting on a brave front. She watched him fall asleep every night and mumble a prayer for God to keep him and his family safe. Sometimes she saw David squeeze his eyes shut to hold in his tears like he used to do at home after having a bad dream.

Whenever David had the opportunity, he worked hard on his project. Using the knife Marian had given him, he carved words into the wooden planks of the barn. *I'm not going to die here with no one knowing of my existence,* he thought. Slowly and methodically, over the period of a couple of months, he managed to carve the words *Hanna, Shoshana, Esther, and David Gold from Pińczów hid here from the Nazis – 1943.*

CHAPTER 25

Warsaw Ghetto Uprising
Spring, 1943

Spring arrived. They no longer needed the heavy feather blanket they'd used all winter, so they took turns sleeping on it, instead. They were able to peel off one layer of clothing, which freed them up and gave them a little more elbowroom in the enclosure. They used those extra clothes to pad their sleeping areas.

There was much work to be done on the farm to prepare for the spring planting. The soil needed tilling, and the clean-up from the winter began. The extra chores kept Stanczyk and his family very busy. He visited the barn less and less. Lujia would put the little bit of food they received on the floor just inside the barn doors and leave without ever saying a word. The Golds were desperate for news, but Wiktor and his whole family were so busy, they had almost forgotten about their guests.

With the townspeople in full working mode, it was more

important than ever to stay quiet in the barn. Many people traveled the road very close to the barn. After the long winter, everyone was anxious to get outside. Voices of children playing could be heard, and friends dropped in for visits. David lived next to his favorite slat, propped against it, listening to conversations of people passing by. Often the talk centered on the war, and it was essential for him to pick up any information he could. Since food rations were dwindling, the farmers would have to be self-sufficient and survive on their own harvests. Along with their one horse, one cow, one rooster, six hens, and two pigs, Stanczyk's farm had enough land to grow what they would need. Anything extra would be sold or traded on the black market in exchange for meat, sugar, and butter.

The weather cooperated through the spring, and Stanczyk managed to sow the cabbage, potatoes, oats, and other crops in record time. He had planted the wheat in the fall just before the first frost, and already, signs of its growth were apparent.

It was a cool evening in the middle of May when Stanczyk arrived with their usual dinner. They all noticed how uncoordinated he was, spilling soup from the large pot, as he attempted to close the door.

"He must be drunk," Shoshana whispered.

He spoke louder than he should have when he blurted out, "Some of you Jews have more guts than brains."

Hanna nudged Shoshana to get out and quiet him down. She opened the two boards and stepped out of the crawl space.

Shoshana greeted Wiktor with a big smile. "Here, let me help you with that," she said, taking the pot from his hands. Every bit he spilled was that much less they had to eat. She bent down and handed the pot to David before she turned her attention back to Stanczyk.

With her finger up against her lips she said in a soft voice, "Come, let's move from here and have a little chat." She took his hand and led him to the corner of the barn farthest from the farmhouse and the road. He followed willingly.

"Now, then," she said, "you can't just make a statement like that without an explanation."

Waving his arms about, he replied, "How could you think you could possibly win?"

"I'm sorry, Pan Stanczyk, but I'm not following you. Did something happen?"

He became boisterous again and said, "Now they're all going to die."

"Who's going to die?" Shoshana asked.

"In Warsaw. The Jews in the Warsaw ghetto," he said, as though she should know what he was referring to.

With patience and persistence she finally got the story out of him.

Jewish rebels in the Warsaw ghetto had gotten together to fight back. They smuggled in weapons, and the Polish Home Army helped them obtain pistols and grenades. On the night of April 19, the beginning of Passover, the SS entered the ghetto. They were going to send all the remaining Jews to the Treblinka extermination camp.

"They gave them a good fight," Stanczyk said. "I'll give them that much. But the Nazis burned down every house on every block. Most of the Jews were killed, many of them burnt alive, and the rest were sent to Treblinka to die."

Shoshana's face turned ashen. She was able to turn away in time to vomit on a pile of straw behind her.

Stanczyk didn't realize the effect this news would have on Shoshana, and for a moment he sobered up. "I'm very sorry," he said sheepishly, as he pulled out a cloth from his back pocket and handed it to her.

Shoshana was light-headed and needed to go back to lie down. Wiktor led her over to the enclosure, where the rest of them waited to help her in. They had all heard the conversation, and each of them reacted differently.

"Good for those men who fought back. At least they took some of those bastard Nazis with them to their graves," Jozef said.

Hanna, on the other hand, held her visibly shaken daughter closely and rocked as she quietly recited *Kaddish,* the Jewish prayer for the dead.

CHAPTER 26

No More Money

It was a Sunday morning at the end of May. David watched through the slats as people went to church. Jozef, Nessa, and Shoshana stood outside the enclosure talking, but Hanna chose to stay inside with Esther.

Esther, lying on her side, her head propped up on her hand, watched as her mother counted money. Hanna counted out the seven thousand zloty she had to give to Stanczyk for June. With a jolt, she realized she didn't have enough money left to pay for July.

"What's wrong, Mameh?" Esther asked, as she saw her mother grow pale.

"Nothing, Esther. Everything's fine."

"Mameh, please don't lie to me, I can see by your face something's wrong. Tell me. Maybe I can help."

There was no point in lying to Esther. "This is the last month we can pay for our keep. There will only be three thousand zloty left for July. That's not enough for Wiktor to keep us here. I don't know what will happen to us," she said.

Esther sat up and took her mother's hand. "We've managed to stay together this far, and we will accept whatever fate God has planned for us. He's looked after us up to now, hasn't he, Mameh?"

Hanna was proud of her daughter's response, but she knew the reality of the situation. With the Allies fighting and the Russians (now aligned with Britain and the U.S.) infiltrating Poland, the Nazis were more desperate than ever to eliminate every Jew. The Final Solution was within reach, and they were accelerating their goal to cleanse the world of the Jewish race. Without the shelter of this barn, the Golds would have to rely on the protection of the forest. They would be exposed to the elements and would have to forage for their food and water. Even though their meals were sparse, at least they were eating and drinking enough to stay alive.

"We're going to have to tell the others, Esther. Let's go out. At least we can talk standing together outside this hole."

Hanna put the money away in the hidden compartment of her coat, and they both crawled out of the enclosure. Shoshana was alarmed by the serious looks on the faces of her mother and sister.

"Come," Shoshana said to Jozef and Nessa. "They have something to tell us." They all gathered around the two women. David, who was still looking through the slats, turned to see the group huddle and joined in.

"What's wrong, Mameh?" Shoshana asked.

At that moment Hanna recalled the argument she'd had with Jozef in the forest when they first left Hanosz's farm. When he informed her of her how much they would have to pay, she told him right then that they would only have enough for seven months. *This should not come as a surprise to him,* she thought. Still, there was no easy way to say it.

"We're out of money," she said, watching for their reactions.

No one spoke. There was nothing to say. The reality of Hanna's disclosure set in slowly.

For some reason, they collectively turned and looked at Jozef.

"What are you looking at me for?" he snapped. "You're lucky I got you this far."

Hanna spoke in a reasonable tone. "Nobody's expecting you to get us out of this, Jozef. We all turned to you because you were the one that found this place. We don't know this area, or the people. You do. Don't be so angry. Together, we'll come up with an idea. There's enough for this month, so Stanczyk will not throw us out tomorrow."

"Don't breathe a word of this to him; he doesn't know how much money we have," Jozef said.

"Let's not forget the silver that was in Mameh's sack," Esther said.

"Yes, that should be payment enough for at least another month," Hanna acknowledged.

Jozef's anger subsided when he realized he was not being blamed. But the Golds knew he was out for himself only. The only reason they'd made it this far with him was because they had money. Hanna knew very well, if it weren't for that, Jozef would have been fine leaving them to die at the hands of Hanosz. Almost anything could set off his volatile temper, and it was a delicate balancing act, keeping him in check. Nessa bore the brunt of his abuse without complaint. She was too afraid to do otherwise.

ᔕ

On the last Sunday in June Hanna decided to finalize the discussion they'd started almost a month earlier. Since her revelation about the depletion of their money, no one had spoken aloud of their impending fate, but it was all each one thought about.

Stanczyk was due to come in looking for his July payment any time now.

It was time to confront Jozef. They had survived this long, and Hanna was not about to let her family be thrown to the Germans. She didn't trust Jozef. For all she knew, he had a plan that didn't include them. This spineless, bullying coward would not be the cause of her family's demise.

By mid-morning, when the townspeople were all in church, Hanna faced Jozef. She was not afraid of him. She knew he would never strike her, like he did his wife. He was the only one who really knew Wiktor Stanczyk. He also knew the lay of the land and where they were in relation to any nearby towns. Jozef was their best chance to get out of this situation alive.

Looking straight at him she said, "Stanczyk is going to come for his next payment in a few days. Have you thought of a plan?" Blood rose to his face. He was getting that look in his eye, the one he displayed every time he was confronted.

Before he had a chance to speak, Hanna bellowed, "Don't you *dare* lose your temper with me, Jozef Lanski. Your connections and *our money* got us this far. Get past your ego and come up with a concrete plan, so we can survive the rest of this detestable war."

Silence fell over the barn as everyone watched this petite, demure woman take on the bully. To their amazement, her words didn't anger him. In fact, they had the opposite effect. She was right, it was up to him to come up with a plan. He had been thinking of one, but he was afraid Hanna would never go along with his idea.

"I do have an idea," Jozef said in a surprisingly calm voice.

"Well," David interjected, "are you going to share it, or do we have to guess?"

Hanna pinched David's arm hard. "Be quiet David, and don't be disrespectful," she said.

David retreated to sit on a bale of hay and listen from a distance.

"We're out of money right? And we all know where there might be more money."

Hanna clued in on where he was headed and didn't like it one bit.

"In Pińczów," he continued. "You have hidden money and valuables in Pińczów!"

The fleeting moment of hope Esther and Shoshana had felt as his plan was revealed, quickly faded when they realized how ridiculous it was.

"What kind of a plan is that? We're nowhere near Pińczów," Hanna said.

"Ah, but that's where you're wrong. We're actually very close to Pińczów. One of you could walk there in a matter of hours, retrieve the treasures, and return," Jozef said.

"No problem," Esther said. "One of us will just stroll down the country road, past the German tanks and SS guards, mosey into Pińczów, stuff the gold coins into a sac, and walk back here with them. Are you crazy? Have you lost your mind?"

"Esther, hold your tongue," her mother demanded. "Go on Jozef. Let's hear the whole plan, and then as a group, we'll decide how feasible it is."

Shoshana felt the blood drain from her face. Her hands and feet became cold and clammy, and her head began to spin. If anyone were going to go to Pińczów, it would have to be her. She continued to listen as Jozef's plan became her nightmare. She leaned back on a bale of hay to steady herself.

Hanna eyed her daughter and knew exactly what was going through her mind, but she made no move to comfort her. She didn't want to give any credence to the thoughts going through her daughter's head – at least not yet.

"Pińczów is a lot closer than you think, and the forest runs all the way there. It is probably ten kilometers away. It shouldn't take more than three hours to walk there. You could walk through the forest, come out on the road near the town, go to your house, get the money, and come back the same way," Jozef said.

"As easy as that?" Hanna said sarcastically. She felt her breathing become labored. What a dangerous scheme he'd cooked up. No wonder he didn't want to share it.

Jozef watched Hanna's reaction carefully. If she rejected his idea, they would be back to square one and, in all likelihood, be out wandering in that forest, trying to survive. He had to convince Hanna it was possible to accomplish this and return safely. She would never go along with his plan if there weren't a reasonable chance it would work. From the closeness he'd witnessed of this family, he was sure they would rather die together than sacrifice one to save the others.

David tried with all his might to keep his mouth shut, but it was more than he could bear. He stood abruptly, pointed his finger at Jozef, and said, "If it's such a great idea, then *you* go get the money. Let's see what a great plan it is if *you* have to do it."

"David," Hanna hissed. "Sit down, and be quiet!" Returning her attention to Jozef, she asked, "Is there any more to your plan?"

Shoshana would have to be the one do this. She was the only one who could pass as Polish. With a little rehearsal and preparation she might pull this off and save them all, but the idea could not come from him. He was going to let them come to that conclusion on their own. It would be the only way they would accept putting one of their own in this dangerous position.

"We'll wait for the next full moon, which should be soon, and do most of the travel through the night. I thought it would be best to reach Pińczów at daybreak, when the shopkeepers are just opening their stalls, and the police are changing shifts," Jozef said.

"How do we know what's going on in Pińczów? Who's living in the town? The Jews must be all gone by now," Esther added.

"We'll have to get Stanczyk and his brother involved," Jozef said.

A faint gasp escaped Hanna's lips.

"Look Hanna, don't think for one minute that Stanczyk and his brother have not been enjoying this money every month. Your cash has given them the opportunity to buy food and trade on the black market. Their children are nourished, and both men have liquor in their bellies. This money is a powerful incentive for them, and if they think there is a chance for more, they will bend over backwards to help us."

Hanna took a moment to ponder his words. *He's right. If Stanczyk knows there is an opportunity to get more money, he won't throw us out. He'll want to help any way he can to get his hands on more cash.*

Jozef continued. "Max has connections. He'll use them to find out what's going on in Pińczów before anyone goes there. All right?"

Jozef waited patiently for her response. "Let's give this plan a little time to sink in, Jozef. It's not ideal, and it is very dangerous. None of us wants to make a decision that will end up in a tragedy," Hanna said. The conversation was ended.

CHAPTER 27

Breaking the News
Summer, 1943

Stanczyk finished his breakfast, picked up the usual jug of water and pot of porridge, and prepared to go out to the barn. It was the beginning of July, time to collect his money.

Hanna rehashed the plan over and over playing out different scenarios. It took a long time to come to terms with Jozef's idea. Shoshana had come to terms with going. She would use Nessa's forged kennkarte papers identifying her as Krystina Kominski, a Polish woman born in 1921. The worn, cracked photograph of Nessa on the identification paper would work in their favor. Shoshana looked somewhat like Nessa – same build, same hair color, and same age. She could easily pass for the girl in the damaged picture.

Jozef was elected to break the news to Stanczyk and get him to accept and aid in the plan. Hanna gave two thousand zloty to

Jozef, saying that was all the money they had left. Esther realized immediately that her mother had stashed a thousand zloty. She distinctly remembered her mother having three thousand zloty left for July, but she kept that information to herself.

On the morning the money was due, Jozef stood on the concrete pad outside the enclosure for Stanczyk to bring their usual meal. Opening the barn door, he was startled to see Jozef standing there, waiting.

"Dzień dobry," Jozef said.

"Dzień dobry. Why are you out here, Jozef?"

"Wiktor, we have to talk."

Stanczyk put the water jug and pot down, reached into his shirt pocket, and pulled out a cigarette. "I'm listening," he said.

"Here's the money for July," Jozef said as he held out the wad of rolled bills.

Stanczyk immediately noticed the roll was half the size it should have been. "What's going on?"

"This is all that's left, Wiktor. The money is depleted."

Stanczyk did not speak.

"Trust me, my friend, we had no idea the war would go on this long. I was sure we had enough money to last. I would never have made a dishonorable deal with you, Wiktor. This damned war should have been over by now."

"Shut up, Jozef," Stanczyk said as he grabbed the money out of Jozef's hand and left abruptly.

"Wiktor, stop! We have a plan…" But it was too late. The barn doors closed. Stanczyk was gone.

In the enclosure, the tension level soared as they witnessed the exchange between the two men.

"He's going to throw us out, isn't he?" David asked.

"He needs time to think this through. He's not going to throw us out," Jozef said. "He's a good man. He won't want the blood of six people on his hands. Besides, he'll soon realize if he throws us out we could get caught and then start talking. The SS will want to know where we have been all this time. Give him some time to come to terms with this information."

ᔓ

Wiktor shook with rage. He grabbed a spade from under the barn's overhang and made his way out to the field. He thrashed at the soil, striking it much harder than necessary, hearing the words *the money is depleted* over and over in his head. It took a long time for him to calm down. He was going to have to tell Lujia, who had never really accepted hiding Jews in her barn. *I have no choice; I will have to throw them out,* he thought. There was no way he could feed six extra people without the money. The crops could not be harvested till the fall. What was he going to do with these people? He panicked, pacing back and forth through the rows in the field.

There was no point putting it off. He lit another cigarette as he walked slowly back to the house. Lujia was surprised to see him come through the door. From the sallow look on his face, she knew something was wrong. She sat down at the kitchen table and motioned for her husband to join her.

"Wiktor, talk to me."

He pulled out a chair, sat down, and placed the money on the table in front of his wife. Lujia looked down at the small pile of bills and knew immediately what was going on.

"They have no more money," she said quietly, not taking her eyes off the wad in front of her.

"This is all that's left," he confirmed.

She stood up from the table and puttered nervously around the kitchen, the silence in the room thick and uncomfortable. Finally, she spoke. "We can't let them go."

Wiktor looked up at his wife, surprised to hear those words. "We can't?"

"Of course not, they'll get caught and tell the Germans we were the ones who hid them all these months. What do you think will happen to us then, Wiktor? They will burn down our house and kill us all. Those bastards will slaughter us like they do all the Jew lovers. That's what we are, you know. Jew lovers."

"We have to allow them to stay," Lujia continued. "I don't know how we'll feed them, but it is far better for them to starve right here in our barn than to turn them loose and take a chance they'll get caught."

She was angry and hated her husband for putting their family in this horrible position. The memories of the luxuries they had enjoyed while the money was abundant quickly faded.

Wiktor sat quietly at the table, his head in his hands. Lujia couldn't stand breathing the same air as her husband and left the room.

He sat for a long while, lashing away at himself. *Why did I put my family in this kind of danger?* he thought. *How could I have done this to them? What kind of a man am I?* He tried to think of what he should do. Out of nowhere the words *we have a plan* popped into his head.

He stood so quickly that the chair toppled over. Racing to the barn, he pushed open the door and said, "Jozef, get out here."

Jozef moved the two boards and stepped out. "I'm glad you're back, Wiktor," he said.

"What's your plan?"

Jozef watched Stanczyk's reaction as he outlined his idea. He wasn't sure, but he thought he noticed a slight affirmative nod of Stanczyk's head. When Jozef finished speaking he waited for some kind of a response, but Stanczyk did not say a word. He stared a Jozef until the silence became awkward.

Just as Jozef was about to break the lull, Stanczyk spoke. "It could work. I have to check on a few things," he said as he turned and left, leaving Jozef and the others to wonder what he was going to do.

"Don't worry so much," Jozef said trying to reassure the others. "He'll be back."

Shoshana's nerves were winning the battle, but she wasn't about to trust anyone else to do this. It was her family's money, and she alone had to make sure it went directly into her family's hands. Maybe she could use the opportunity to learn something about her father. David was the only one who managed to lighten her impending journey. He joked about this dangerous mission she was undertaking.

"You'll probably meet a handsome man who will kidnap you and keep you in his mansion, and we will never hear from you again. Typical," he said as his mother whacked him across his head.

Shoshana smiled and winked at her little brother. She knew exactly what he was trying to do, and she loved him for it.

He kept needling her with his bad jokes, and it was exactly what she needed. If this journey was successful, she would not only ensure her family's continued shelter in the barn, but she would find her father as well. *Maybe he is hiding with Marian. I know I'll find him, I can just feel it,* she thought.

ↀ

It took Stanczyk some time to find his brother. He didn't see Max as often as he used to. Max was deeply involved in the underground of the Polish Home Army. Wiktor really needed to update him on this new development and hear his opinion. More and more he was thinking that it might be time to just put these people out and hope that they wouldn't say anything if they were caught.

His entire life was in limbo, not knowing what to do. He left word at Max's house. Since Max was the town councilor, there were always meetings held in his home, whether he was present or not. It was also a place where some of Max's fellow army members gathered. Someone there would know where Max was.

When Max received word his brother was looking for him, he made his way back to Kolkow. It was just after the middle of July when Max entered his brother's home. When Wiktor saw him, he jumped to his feet and held Max in a long, tight embrace.

Max sensed his desperation. *Something is very wrong,* he thought as he tried to lighten the mood and put his brother at ease. "Wiktor, it's been a while. What do you say we have a drink?"

Wiktor took two shot glasses and a half-empty liquor bottle

out of the hutch. He handed one of the glasses to Max, filled it with vodka, and then poured one for himself.

"Let's drink to the fall of Mussolini," Max said, raising his glass. Wiktor raised his glass to meet his brother's, clinked it, and swallowed its contents. The two men sat down as Wiktor asked, "The fall of Mussolini?"

"Two days ago, the United States bombed Italy. Roosevelt and Churchill are stepping up, Wiktor. It's happening, my brother."

Wiktor sat quietly listening to the details. It was news he needed to hear. The war seemed to be standing still. At least this information was a bit of hope for Wiktor to hang on to.

"So Wiktor, what's happening with you?" Max asked.

"A lot, Max. I'm in big trouble," Wiktor said. "The Jews. They've run out of money."

Max refilled his glass as his listened to his brother.

"Without their money I can't feed them. What am I supposed to do with them, Max? If I send them out, they'll be caught and probably be forced to tell where they were hiding. If I don't send them out, I am stuck with six starving Jews in my barn. Before you say anything, Max, we do have a plan," Wiktor added.

Max stood, walked over to the window and looked out at the barn. The news came as a shock. He, too, was upset. It was the Jews' money that allowed Max to travel easily through parts of Poland. His brother had been very generous, sharing a good portion of the cash with him.

"What's the plan?" Max asked.

"They have more money. Back in Pińczów they have hidden gold, American dollars, zloty, and silver. One of the young women, Shoshana, looks and speaks like a Pole. She has Polish papers and is willing to make the journey to Pińczów to get this money. It's very well hidden, but she is almost positive she can find where her father hid it." He watched his brother for a reaction.

Still looking out the window, Max took longer than expected to reply. "You know Wiktor, that's not a bad plan. Pińczów is still a busy town. I was just through there. Almost all the Jews were rounded up and deported to Treblinka in the fall. There are factories running, and the shops are open. Poles from surrounding towns have replaced the Jewish population.

"Wiktor, if the British liberate us, and they see we have saved a family of Jews, it will make us look pretty damn good. Don't you think?" he added as a little perk to the whole scenario.

The men talked and drank, reviewing the plan till late into the night. Finally, Max stood and said, "I have to get back. You'll be fine, Wiktor. Just follow the plan as we've discussed it, and make sure this Shoshana is well rehearsed before she sets out. It's going to work Wiktor, you'll see. It will all be fine."

Wiktor walked Max out to the road and watched his brother stagger off toward his home. Before going back inside, he looked up to the sky and noticed the full moon. They would have to wait until the next full moon for Shoshana to set out on her expedition. This would give him some time to make sure his wife was on board, and it would give Shoshana the time she needed to practice her story and get comfortable with her new identity as Krystina Kominski.

CHAPTER 28

It Must be Perfect

"Crazy Krystina running away, returning to us with money some day," David sang, taunting Shoshana.

Shoshana was a nervous wreck. Although she knew her brother was only trying to make things better, he was now making them worse. Her patience grew thin as his chanting became unbearable.

Standing outside the enclosure, David used his knife to carve something into one of the planks while repeating his little tune, when suddenly he felt a sharp pain in his head as he was pulled from behind.

Esther had grabbed a fistful of David's hair. "One more time, and this hair is going with Shoshana to Pińczów."

"Okay, okay, I'll stop," David said, his head under his sister's control.

"Promise you'll never say that again. Shoshana doesn't need your teasing on top of what she is dealing with," Esther said.

"I promise."

Esther let go and smiled at her sister, and the two of them went back to sit with their mother in the enclosure.

David, having learned his lesson, stood rubbing his head.

"I was only trying to make her laugh," he muttered.

ꟷ

With each day that passed, the time for Shoshana to leave drew closer and became more of a reality. Jozef and Hanna were her main coaches. They all began calling her Krystina. The name had to feel real to her, so she wouldn't falter if she were questioned. Her nerves could not be allowed to separate her two identities.

Jozef and Hanna took turns drilling her.

"Where are you going?"

"To Pińczów."

"Why?"

"To see my uncle."

"Who is your uncle?"

"Marian Wicinski."

"Where do you live?"

"Kolkow."

"Where were you born?"

"Działoszyce."

"How old are you?"

"Twenty-two."

The rehearsals went on day and night. Jozef and Hanna tried to think of every possible scenario Shoshana might encounter.

Her departure date was set for Sunday, August 15. The plan was for her to leave at four a.m. The moon would be full, and the sun would start to peek through the night sky at around five-thirty. Stanczyk and Jozef figured it shouldn't take her longer than three hours to get there, putting her in Pińczów at seven a.m. It would be quiet in town, as most of the people would be going to church, instead of work. Shoshana was to go to Marian's place and hide till she spotted him. She would have to be careful that Wojtek, his brother-in-law, who she assumed was still the chief of the Polish police, didn't see her before she had a chance to come into contact with Marian. He would be outside very early. David remembered from working with Marian that he went to the stables every morning to check on the horses. David said Shoshana should wait for Marian in one of the stalls.

Hanna's troubled thoughts didn't give her a moment's rest. *Marian will take good care of my daughter. He will help her. Yes, Marian will help her,* Hanna thought over and over. For added insurance, she prayed every night, imploring God to take care of her firstborn. She begged and bargained with God for her daughter's safety. The rest of them could hear her whispering, "Please, God, guide my daughter through this journey. Stay with her, give her strength, protect her, and bring her back to us unharmed. Please, God, I'm begging you with all my soul. Bring my Shoshanaleh back to me."

On the night of August 14, Stanczyk came to get Shoshana. It was time to prepare her for the trip. Lujia had agreed and was ready to help. In all these months it would be the first time Lujia would actually lay eyes on this Jew, who had been living in her barn only steps away. The Stanczyks had arranged for their children to sleep at a neighboring farm.

Lujia was surprised when she first saw Shoshana. She wasn't sure what to expect, but from all the propaganda and pictures the Germans circulated about Jews, she certainly did not anticipate the attractive young woman standing before her.

With a slight bow of her head, Shoshana said, "Dobry wieczór."

"Good evening," Lujia replied.

"Thank you for your help Pani Stanczyk," Shoshana added.

Lujia smiled and stared at Shoshana for a moment. *She speaks like one of us,* she thought. "Come with me. We'll get you cleaned up."

Cleaned up. Shoshana couldn't wait. The filth she'd managed to ignore for months suddenly felt like it was weighing her down. Wiktor disappeared, giving the women privacy.

On the kitchen table sat a large bowl with warm water, a small towel, and a bar of soap.

"Take off your clothes and wash yourself," Lujia said.

Shoshana looked around and began to strip. She closed her eyes as her hands touched the warm water. Soaking the cloth, she soaped it and washed one arm, then the other. Systematically, she cleaned her entire body, saving her face for last. She wrung the cloth and with both hands pressed it onto her face. She stood motionless for a moment enjoying this feeling she had missed so much.

"Thank you," she said to Lujia, who immediately handed Shoshana an old housecoat.

"Now your hair," Lujia said as she whittled soap shavings into the bowl.

Shoshana's thick, shoulder-length hair was matted and stiff. It had become a home for bugs and lice, and she hated touching it.

With Shoshana hunched over the table, her head over the basin of water, Lujia poured cold water over her hair. Shoshana worked the soapy water through, scrubbing like she never had before. Lujia emptied the bowl of black water and put it back under Shoshana's dripping hair.

"I'm going to rinse out the soap," she said, and slowly poured cold water over her hair until the soap was gone. She handed Shoshana a fresh cloth and said, "Follow me."

Lujia took her to the bedroom where she had laid out some underclothes, a yellow gingham dress, and a pair of beige open-toed shoes.

"Get dressed."

Shoshana walked over to the dress and touched it. Lujia watched this young woman who had been living on her property for months. *She seems so gentle, so normal,* she thought to herself as she left the room.

As Shoshana removed the housecoat, she spotted a mirror over the dresser and walked over to it, never once taking her eyes off the girl looking back. She didn't look familiar. She had dark circles under her eyes, and she had visible cheekbones where her rounded apple-cheeks used to be. She touched them as if she had never felt her face before. Her eyes moved down to the hollows on each shoulder, where her collarbones protruded. Taking her eyes off the mirror, she looked down at her body and saw hipbones and a flat belly. She knew she had lost weight but hadn't realized how much.

She began to dress. Pulling the yellow checked dress over her head, she noticed the waist didn't fit as tightly as it was supposed to, but she used the belt to cinch it in. The flared, pleated skirt helped to camouflage the loose fit. She slipped on the open-toed, slingback shoes, and her heel jutted out the back just a bit, but they were quite comfortable.

Shoshana turned to look at herself, just as Lujia knocked on the door and came into the bedroom.

"How can I ever thank you?"

"Just do your job, and return safely," Lujia said.

Reaching into the pocket of her apron, Lujia pulled out a hairbrush, a ribbon, some hairpins, and a lipstick. She placed them on the dresser in front of the mirror and left the room.

Shoshana picked up the brush and tried to get it through her wet, matted hair. It took some time to pull apart the knots, but once she could slide the brush through her hair, she felt almost glamorous. Then she pulled her hair together in a ponytail at the back, tied it with the ribbon, and twisted it into a bun, securing it with the hairpins. She saved the best for last. Lifting the top off the lipstick, she twisted the bottom to reveal the small stub of red left in the tube. She dabbed a little on each cheekbone, blending it while admiring the life that returned to her pale face. Her lips were last, and when she was done, she stood back, admiring herself.

Lujia returned and took a look at the results of her efforts standing before her. A sense of pride mixed with emotion overcame her. For the first time she saw Shoshana as a young woman, not a Jew. She handed her a small purse, a sweater, and a kerchief.

"Come, it's time," she said.

Lujia walked out of the house, Shoshana following close behind. She opened the barn door and stood aside to let Shoshana make her entrance. Wiktor and Jozef were speechless at the site of this stranger.

Twirling in a circle, Shoshana broke the silence, "So, what do you think?"

"Perfect," Jozef said.

David quickly removed the boards and came out of the enclosure. The rest of them followed and had the same reaction. Esther pushed her way through them to reach her sister. She was about to take Shoshana's arms, but as she reached out, she saw the dirt caked around her own fingernails and withdrew. In an unfamiliar move, Shoshana reached forward and hugged Esther. It was not something they did often enough.

Hanna stayed back, showing no emotion. Both Nessa and David smiled at the site of Shoshana.

"I'm ready," Shoshana said.

The timing was perfect; it was three-thirty in the morning. Wiktor took Shoshana's purse and placed the identification papers and fifty zloty in the bag. Lujia walked over to Shoshana and handed her the tube of lipstick. Shoshana held Lujia's hand a moment longer than necessary as she accepted the small gift and placed it in the purse. Lujia also gave her a jar of water, which she slipped into the pocket of the sweater.

Shoshana went over to her mother, who was standing stoically off to the side.

Hanna placed her hands on either side of her daughter's face and did not speak. Her eyes filled, and a tear escaped, creating a line as it traveled through the dirt on her face.

"Mameh, I will be fine," she said. "I promise you with everything in me that I will be back. Nothing will happen to me, Mameh. I will be very careful."

Shoshana took her mother's hand and placed it on her chest so her mother could feel her heartbeat. "In a few days I will return with news of Tateh and the money. Marian will help me, Mameh. You know he will."

Still Hanna could not speak.

David gave his sister a loving punch on the arm. "You better hurry back. It's gonna be really boring without you to yell at me all the time."

"If you don't behave while I'm away, I'll kick you all the way to Pińczów when we are free."

"Take this," he said as he handed his sister the knife Marian had given him. "Not that you'll need it. You're scary enough without it."

She took the knife and put it in her purse. She held her little brother's face and kissed his forehead, holding her lips to his skin for a few seconds longer than he expected.

Wincing to fight back tears, David turned and walked away.

Jozef took Shoshana by the arm and led her to the door. She turned one last time and saw them all standing and watching her. Just as she was about to leave, Hanna ran over and threw herself at her daughter. "*Ikh hob dikh lib, mayn tyreh kind,* I love you my precious child."

Jozef separated them roughly. "You have to go now," he said, walking her out of the barn.

Shoshana could hear her mother praying, *"Ye'hi ratson mil'fanecha."* It was the beginning of the Jewish traveler's prayer, said for a safe journey.

CHAPTER 29

Walk of Hope
August, 1943

Four a.m. The plan was on schedule. Holding her elbow to guide her, Jozef ignored Shoshana's trembling and led her toward the back of the barn.

At the edge of the forest he handed her a walking stick and said, "Follow the edge of the trees. It's a straight line; fields on the left, forest on the right."

She looked, but even with the full moon shining brightly, she couldn't see very far ahead.

"Walk straight. The road leading to Pińczów is about eight kilometers north. Follow the line of the trees till you come out to a main road that cuts through the forest. Turn right, and walk on the road for another few kilometers. It will take you over the Nida River and right into Pińczów. Let the sun be your guide.

When it rises, it will be on your right. By the time you see its first light, you will know you're about halfway there."

She liked that. It was a good gauge of direction and time. She was now Krystina Kominski, a Polish woman visiting her uncle, not Shoshana Gold, a Jew in hiding.

Jozef accompanied Shoshana into the forest so she could get her bearings. He walked with her for a few minutes straight up the same path they had used nine months earlier when they fled from Hanosz.

Just before Jozef turned back, he pointed straight ahead. "Stay on this path. Good luck, and stay safe. You should be there in about three hours. Find the money, and get back tonight. Pay attention to where you exit the forest at the road. Memorize it. You will need to find it even in the dark when you return. Mark the place somehow," he said, and without warning, he was gone.

She was alone.

Shoshana started walking. The trees rustled in the wind. The cool breeze sent a chill through her, and she did up the top button on her sweater. It had been a very long time without exercise, and her legs were as heavy as lead. She concentrated on putting one foot in front of the other and watched her feet, not wanting to trip over a tree root or fallen branch. Shoshana was surprised how clear the trail was. From the condition of the path, it was obvious other people had used it. A sudden wave of panic washed over her. *What if I run into someone? What will I do?* But with each minute that passed, she relaxed a little. *I'm actually doing this,* she thought.

When all her senses became accustomed to the surroundings, she was able to quicken her step. Still, her mind raced faster than her footsteps. *What if Marian isn't there? What if the money is gone? What if I hear nothing of Tateh?* Her thoughts were so overpowering, she realized she hadn't been paying attention to the direction. She stopped to get her bearings and figured she'd been walking for about an hour.

Spotting a fallen tree, she went over and sat down. Reaching into her pocket, she pulled out the small jar of water, unscrewed the lid, and took a sip. That's when she saw two small yellow birds flittering from branch to branch. For the first time, her mind was quiet enough to appreciate how loud the forest was. The birds were beginning their day. Their mixture of chirping and birdcalls resonated through the trees. Shoshana took a deep breath and absorbed the beauty around her. Her stiff shoulders relaxed. The dark sky was no longer black, and the moon had faded. Signs of daybreak were all around. Feeling more composed she stood, grabbed the purse and stick, and continued on her trek.

It wasn't long before the sun bathed the forest floor with its first light. Shoshana was halfway there and walked with determination in each step. The path became wider. *I must be close to the road,* she thought. On cue, the sound of a vehicle echoed in the distance. The path inclined slightly uphill, and then she saw the road.

I made it! I'm almost there. She looked down one side of the road and then turned to look in the direction she was about to travel. *Oh yes,* she thought, *I have to make sure I know how to get back into the forest.* She looked at the path she'd just left and saw nothing remarkable. She opened her purse and removed the knife David had given her. She walked forward and counted three trees from where the small path met the road. Using the knife she carved a notch into the tree's bark. Looking around for something she could put at the trail's edge, she saw nothing that would stand out.

Shoshana took the jar out of her sweater. She took a sip of water, leaving some for later, and buried it near the edge of the road making sure the lid was still visible. Standing a few meters away she rehearsed walking back. *Perfect,* she thought, *between the tree and the jar I can't miss it.* She put her walking stick down near the jar, straightened her dress, put the knife back into her purse, and took out the lipstick to freshen the tint on her lips. Before closing the purse, she double-checked her identification paper. She was ready to meet anyone. She was Krystina Kominski, going to meet her uncle Marian Wicinski, and they were going to church together.

The road was deserted. Not one vehicle passed by. It didn't take long before she was out of the forest and into a small village. She thought she recognized it. Yes, this must be Skrzyplow. Sometimes on long walks near the river she had ventured down the road to this tiny hamlet. Walking past a few small farms, she noticed cows and horses and heard a dog barking, but no people were up yet. Then she saw a farmer coming out of a chicken coop. He turned to look at her, and she held her breath as she walked past him.

"Dzień dobry," he shouted.

"Dzień dobry," she answered shyly and continued walking.

Then she saw the familiar Nida River, the same river where she and David almost drowned, the river where Tateh used to take them on Shabbos to play. The wild flowers growing along its banks were beautiful, just as she'd remembered them. She was so close to home, so close to her old life when she was happy, so close to her father.

"Tateh where are you?" she whispered to herself.

Shoshana shook off the memories and the ache in her heart and moved on. She was very close to Marian's. The parks were where she'd left them; the houses and stores looked the same. There were a few people walking about now, but no one paid any attention to her. It wasn't long before she arrived at Marian's farm. The last time she was here, she and Esther had come looking for David. That was the last night any of them saw Tateh.

No one was moving about the farm. She walked around the back of the farmhouse and into the horse stall. The smell of horses was strong. Startled by a voice she hadn't expected to hear, Shoshana froze.

"Can I help you?" Marian said.

She was too frightened to answer.

It only took a second before Marian dropped the bale of hay. "Shoshana?"

"Yes, it's me, Pan Wicinski."

It was like he'd seen a ghost. He was so sure the entire Gold family was dead by now. The last time he'd seen them, he left them with that crook Pilarski in Sobowice.

Running over, he hugged Shoshana tightly, squeezed his eyes shut, and silently thanked Jesus. He put his hands on her shoulders and held her at arm's length examining her face.

"Where have you been? Where is David and the rest of your family?"

"I have much to tell you, Pan Wicinski, and much to ask you."

She was so relieved to feel his protection. *I'm safe. He would never let anything happen to me,* she thought.

"First let me tell you that the rest of my family is in hiding."

"Thank God," Marian said.

"But we may not be safe for long," she added. "Mameh has been paying Wiktor Stanczyk, a farmer in Kolkow, to hide us, but our money has run out, and we're afraid he's going to throw us out now. I've come to find word of Tateh and to take back the money he hid. I know where it is," she said.

"The farmer you're hiding with, did he bring you here?"

"No, I came on my own. I have Polish identification papers, and my new name is Krystina Kominski," she said, opening her purse and handing him the document.

"Krystina Kominski," he mumbled as he looked over the document.

Shoshana swallowed hard before asking the next question.

"Pan Wicinski, where's Tateh? Did he ever show up here? Do you know if he is hiding too?"

Marian looked up at her as he folded the paper and returned it. "I'm sorry Shoshana, the last time I saw your father was when I came to your house to get David. No one has seen or heard from him since." He was not sure if he should add the next part, but he decided to be honest. "You know, my dear, the Germans arrived that day, rounded up the Jews, and marched them to the transports. They were all sent to Treblinka."

Shoshana thought she would faint. She tried to block the words coming from Marian's mouth by fumbling with her purse. Once she felt composed enough, she lifted her gaze. "Did anyone see him going to those transports?"

Marian shook his head.

"With all due respect, Pan Wicinski, there may be many people who believe my entire family was sent to Treblinka, don't you think?"

"Yes, that's true," he said.

"And look at me, standing here in front of you, very much alive."

Knowing there was no point in prolonging this conversation, Marian changed the subject.

"Frania and her husband are in the house, and my niece is visiting from Jędrzejów. She's about your age, Shoshana. Let me go first, you stay here. I want to prepare Frania. My sister has a hard time hiding her reactions, and I don't want her husband to get suspicious."

Shoshana remembered how kind Frania was that night when she and Esther showed up to find David. Almost a year had passed. It seemed like a lifetime ago.

"I'm going to say you're the daughter of an old friend of mine from Gory, and you will use your new name, okay Krystina?"

"Thank you Pan Wicinski. I'll wait right here."

Marian left the stall and walked into the house. He took Frania aside and explained the situation. Once she got over the shock that Shoshana was alive and in the horse stable, she composed herself and said, "Bring her in Marian, she must be hungry."

Marian walked back out to the stable.

"Come, Frania is very happy you're here. Follow whatever I say, Krystina, and no one will suspect a thing."

She nodded and followed Marian into the house.

"Look who I found," Marian announced, as he walked into the farmhouse.

He stepped behind her pushing her forward. "This is Krystina, my good friend Henryk Kominski's daughter. She's walked all the way from Gory to see if her uncle is still here in Pińczów."

"What's all the noise?" Wojtek asked, as he entered the kitchen. Wearing his ripped undershirt and with his unkempt hair, he looked like he'd just rolled out of bed. Zosia, their niece, was sitting at the kitchen table and stood to meet Krystina.

"Dzień dobry, Krystina, very nice to meet you," Zosia said in a soft, welcoming voice.

Making introductions, Marian said, "Krystina, this is Wojtek, my brother-in-law, this is my sister Frania, Wojtek's wife, and this is my niece Zosia. She is visiting too, from Jędrzejów."

"Come eat with us," Frania insisted and practically pushed Shoshana into the chair at the kitchen table. Shoshana didn't realize how hungry she was till she smelled the egg and cereal Zosia was eating.

Frania placed a plate with bread, jam, an egg, warm cereal, and a glass of tea in front of Shoshana.

"Dziękuję," Shoshana said.

"You're very welcome," Frania answered. "Eat up."

Trying not to inhale the meal, Shoshana had to consciously slow down as she ate.

"Where does your uncle live, Krystina?" Zosia asked.

"He lives near the town square. It's been almost a year since I've been to Pińczów. I hope everything is the way I remember it."

Frania looked at Marian.

"It's possible many of the people you may have known are gone now. You'll see many new faces, Poles from the destroyed towns around here have found their way to Pińczów and are living in the empty houses and apartments. Some have made new businesses, and some have taken over abandoned ones," Marian said.

Someone is sleeping and eating in my home? The home that Tateh and Mameh built for us? Shoshana wondered. She put her glass of tea down, and brought her napkin up to cover the lower half of her face as she attempted to hide the feelings rising through her stomach.

"Will you be coming to church with us?" Zosia asked.

Shoshana turned to look at Marian.

"Sure she's coming with us, and then you and Krystina can go for a walk to her uncle's neighborhood. How does that sound, Zosia?"

"I would love to go with you, Krystina," Zosia answered. "I'm just going to finish getting ready, and I'll be right out."

Shoshana was nervous. She had never gone to a church service and wasn't sure what to expect.

Marian saw the panic in her face. "Krystina, it's a beautiful morning. Let's wait outside for the others."

"Thank you for the lovely breakfast," she said, as she followed Marian.

Once outside, Shoshana's nerves got the better of her. "I can't go to church! Someone might recognize me, and I don't know what to do in a church, and what if –"

Marian stopped her in mid-ramble. "Calm down, Krystina. You don't have to worry about anyone recognizing you; almost none of the original people are left. You'll keep your head down, look at the prayer book, and mouth the prayers. No one will be looking at you. It's not like it used to be. The people in this town are mostly strangers. On Sundays they come together to pray for their families, to pray for the end of the war. You will just be another refugee in the sea of transients that gather here on Sundays, searching for a little peace."

Shoshana nodded acceptance as the other three came out of the farmhouse, ready to walk to church.

CHAPTER 30

Buried Treasure

Church was surprisingly easy. Shoshana actually enjoyed the melody of the hymns, and Marian was right. Once the congregation bade each other a cordial good morning, they were all focused on their own thoughts and prayers. She heard weeping throughout the service, and even though she was in a church, Shoshana said her own prayers.

After the service they walked back to the farm and ate a small lunch. Zosia dabbed her lips with her napkin and pushed away from the table. "Wait here, Krystina, I'm going to change. Then we can go for that walk to see if we can find your uncle."

Zosia returned wearing a fashionable hat, tilted over to one side.

What a good idea, Marian thought. "Wait here for a minute," he said, and he went over to Frania.

"Go get me your sun hat, the one with the wide brim."

She nodded and returned in a few minutes with the hat.

Marian hoped it would help disguise Shoshana in case anyone recognized her as the Jew who used to live there.

"Here, Krystina, why don't you wear this for your walk. It will keep the strong sun off your face," he said, handing her the large straw hat. Shoshana placed it on her head and tilted it down over one eye. Marian stood back and looked at her, wondering if anyone could ever recognize her. *No,* he said to himself. *I barely knew her myself. She'll be fine.*

Zosia was still busy primping in the mirror.

"It's a beautiful day," Shoshana said, "I'll wait outside, Zosia. Take your time."

Marian followed her as she walked out toward the road.

When they were far enough from the house, Shoshana turned to Marian. "What should I say to Zosia? I have to get into the cellar of the building. I can't let her come with me."

"First, do you have something you can use to dig with?"

Shoshana hadn't thought about that. "I guess I was going to use my hands," she answered.

Marian walked back into the house and returned with a large soupspoon. "Put this in your purse," he said, "Here's what you're going to do. Walk to the park first. The two of you can sit there and talk. Be careful what you say. Talk about men, clothes, makeup, any subject that two young women would have in common. Stay away from discussing the war if you can. Be very careful not to let your emotions control you, Shoshana, no matter what Zosia says. Remember, she thinks you are a young Polish woman, like her."

Zosia came toward them, swinging her purse. She had a big smile on her face.

"I'm ready," she said.

Shoshana adjusted the straw hat on her head, pulling the brim down a little lower. "Goodbye, Pan Wicinski."

"See you soon," Marian said, as he watched the two girls walk down the road toward the center of town.

ᔓᔕ

"Where did your uncle live, Krystina?" Zosia asked.

"The last time I saw him, he was still living on Plac Wolności, but that was almost a year ago."

As she spoke Shoshana scanned every building and store. Even though it was the hottest part of the day, she could feel the goose bumps dancing on her arms and the back of her neck. On the surface, the buildings, storefronts, street signs – all looked the same. *But it doesn't feel like home,* she thought. Shoshana scanned the faces of the people. Not one looked familiar. Passing the old bakery, she looked inside and saw a strange man and two women talking. A flashback enveloped her. She was five years old, standing at the counter. She looked up, and Mr. Szneider winked as he handed her a cookie.

Shoshana continued to walk, trying to look ahead, but as she passed every store she had to peek in. A wave of panic traveled quickly from her stomach to her throat as she recognized Mr. Gorski in the pharmacy where she used to go to pick up Tateh's medicine. She turned her head away and picked up the pace. *He would surely recognize me,* she thought.

Sensing her tension, Zosia asked, "Krystina, are you okay?"

Shoshana snapped her attention back to Zosia, who had been chatting the entire time, and realized she hadn't heard one word Zosia said.

"I'm sorry, Zosia, it's been so long since I was here. It looks the same, but it's not. I used to visit my uncle quite often, and I have many happy memories from those days. I didn't realize how much coming back here would affect me."

"That's all right, Krystina. Take your time and look around. Do you want to go into any of the stores?"

"No," Shoshana replied. "I don't really have the time to indulge these old memories of mine. I must get back on my way by this evening. As much as I would love to revisit, I think we'd better keep going."

"Sure," Zosia said. "I'm enjoying the walk. It's nice to meet someone like you."

"Like me?"

"You know, I mean someone my own age, to whom I can talk. We have some things in common, you know."

"We do?"

Shoshana spotted two SS officers walking toward them. Her body tensed, and for a moment she thought she should duck into one of the stores. *Relax,* she told herself. *You are not a Jew, you're Krystina Kominski.*

Zosia continued chatting away and didn't seem to care that these two ominous men, dressed in Nazi uniforms were approaching. They were talking to each other, and she could see they were in good spirits. Taking her cue from Zosia, Shoshana straightened her body, put her head up, her shoulders back, and walked with confidence. As the soldiers came closer, almost within reach, the two men looked over at the girls, nodded, and kept going. As they passed, Shoshana felt her legs tremble.

It was then that she spotted the huge willow tree with the bench, exactly as she left it. Leaving Zosia behind, she ran into the park. She sat in the middle of her bench and stretched her arms across the top on either side. With her head back and her eyes closed Shoshana's nervous energy transformed to a sense of peace. Zosia stood back, giving her new friend a minute to herself. Shoshana opened her eyes and snapped back to reality. She waved Zosia over, motioning for her to sit down.

"I used to love sitting on this bench, reading and spending time with my family when I came to visit," Shoshana said. "Sometimes we used to bring our lunch out here and eat under the shade of the tree," she added. Shoshana also remembered sleeping with her family on this very bench when the Germans burned down their house four years earlier.

Shoshana heard Zosia comment, but her voice faded away as she looked up and spotted two strange people across the street leaving her house. *Who are those people?* she wondered. *And how dare they live in our house!*

"I'm sorry to interrupt you," Shoshana said. "Would you mind waiting here while I run across the street? I shouldn't be very long."

"Take as long as you need, I'm fine here."

Walking over to the road, she looked down one side, then the other. The streets were empty. Being Sunday, most people either stayed in, or took their families down to the river. Many of the stores were closed. She walked toward the family grocery store where she'd spent almost every waking minute of her childhood. The handwritten sign in the window said "Closed." She folded the brim of her hat up, so she could press her face closer to the window. Things were out of place, and the shelves were almost empty. *This is not our store,* Shoshana thought and walked behind it to get to the cellar door of the apartment building beside the house where they used to live. It used to be left open to accept deliveries; she was glad at least that hadn't changed.

With her first step, she was consumed by the memory of everyone hiding in this very basement when the Germans first surrounded the town – when her father sent her out to talk to the soldier who threatened to kill them. Descending one step at a time, letting her eyes adjust to the darkness, she stopped for a second on the stair where her father caught her as she fell into his arms after bargaining for their lives.

She shook her head and moved quickly down the remaining stairs. The cellar was practically empty. A few wooden crates were piled against the far wall. She hung her hat on the corner of one of the crates and walked briskly to the back of the cellar. Down on her knees, she removed the spoon from her purse and began scraping the earth. It was loose and easy to move. *This earth has already been disturbed,* she thought, as her anticipation was replaced by a sinking feeling in the pit of her stomach. She discarded the spoon and raked frantically with both hands, as tears fell into the deep hole. A cold, clammy feeling shot through her as she realized the money and other treasures were gone, but she kept digging.

Exhausted, she finally gave up. She sat back against the wall. Everything she had gone through to get here, all her expectations, dissolved into an agonizing cry. Her body convulsed with deep mournful sobs as she realized what this meant. "How can I go back empty-handed? What will happen to us now? Tateh, where are you? We need you. Please come back to us," she cried out loud. No money, no father, no hope. She wrapped her arms around her knees and put her head down, overcome with grief. Shoshana sat in that position rocking, weeping, and thinking only about what this loss would cost her family.

After a long while, she finally lifted her head. Using the sleeve of her sweater to wipe the tears from her eyes and the streaks off her cheeks, she took a deep breath. She stood and looked down at herself. She wiped the dirt off her knees and the back of her dress and did her best to compose herself before she saw Zosia. She grabbed the hat as she walked out of the dark cellar and back into the light.

She squinted as she spotted Zosia in the exact spot where she'd left her. As she got closer, Zosia noticed how disheveled Krystina looked. She got up and ran toward her.

"What happened to you, Krystina? Did you fall? Are you all right?"

It was obvious to Zosia that her friend had been crying, and her dress and legs were filthy.

"You didn't find your uncle, did you, Krystina?" Zosia asked as she pulled a cream-colored handkerchief from her purse.

"No," Shoshana said. "There's nothing left here for me," she added as one last tear escaped down her cheek.

"Why are you so dirty? Look at your knees," Zosia pointed out.

"I went down to the cellar to see if maybe he was there, and

I tripped and fell. I was so upset that I just sat there not even thinking about the mess I was in," she explained.

"Let's sit down and clean you up," Zosia said.

Shoshana sat on the bench as Zosia used the handkerchief to wipe the smudges from her friend's face.

"Here," she said, as she passed the handkerchief over to Shoshana. "Wipe off your knees."

Once cleaned up, Shoshana gathered herself and said, "Come, Zosia, let's go back now."

Zosia gave Krystina her purse and hat, then she stood and held her hand out. She sensed the deep sorrow her friend was experiencing, and the girls walked back to the farm in silence.

Marian was hard at work when they returned. He watched them walking up the road. Shoshana's shoulders were rounded, her head was down, and she was dragging her feet.

He opened the gate and walked down the road to meet them. He put his arm around Shoshana's shoulder and guided her back through the gate and into the house.

"Krystina couldn't find her uncle," Zosia said.

The girls sat down in the kitchen. Frania poured two glasses of milk and set them on the table. Marian picked up Shoshana's glass. "Krystina, come outside with me. Let's talk a little. Maybe I can ask around about your uncle."

He pulled out her chair, and she followed him. He walked her toward the small orchard, looking back to make sure no one followed.

"Shoshana, look at me," he said.

With his index finger, Marian gently guided Shoshana's chin upward and removed her hat. Her eyelids were swollen, her blue eyes were surrounded by red, but worst of all, the light was gone from them. She looked right through him.

"Shoshana, this is not the end, it's just a setback. You and your family have made it through so much, and you have survived. Look at you," he said as he took a step back, "You're a beautiful, strong woman. Your father would be so proud of the way you have taken charge to help your family."

As he spoke, an idea came to him. He had to replace her despondency with hope.

"Shoshana listen to me, only your father and mother knew about that money. Only they knew where it was hidden, right?"

He had her attention.

"If your mother didn't take it, who does that leave?"

"TATEH!" she answered him, the life returning to her voice. "Tateh could have taken that money to pay someone to hide him, just like we are doing," she said.

"That's right," he agreed. "Leib is a very smart man with many connections. Doesn't it make sense that he was the only one who could have taken it?"

"It makes perfect sense," she said, as she wrapped her arms around Marian's neck.

He held her tightly. A wave of emotion released from her trembling body as she sobbed into his shoulder.

He let her cry for a few minutes and pulled away. "Come inside, it's been a long day, and you must eat something and rest," he said.

"I can't rest, I have to get back. They're expecting me. Mameh will be frantic if I don't get back tonight."

"We'll see," Marian said, "First you must eat something,

and then we'll decide. You know, Shoshana, if you're exhausted you will never make it back safely. You can't think straight when you're tired, and you have to be alert. It's a long journey back."

Marian was right. She was exhausted and emotionally spent. "Okay, maybe I'll have just a short rest before I start out."

He didn't argue with her, but he was not letting her go back tonight, not after the traumatic and long day she'd been through. She needed to sleep, and he would walk her partway in the morning, but he wasn't going to say anything now.

It was the four of them for dinner. Wojtek didn't come home. He was probably out drinking as usual. It had become routine for him to stagger in some time after midnight and fall into bed, clothes and all.

Frania placed a bowl of *zupa ogórkowa*, cold cucumber soup with pieces of potato and dollops of sour cream, in front of each of them. Shoshana tasted it. She hadn't eaten this soup in so long she'd forgotten how delicious and refreshing it was.

A plate of *pierogis* filled with potato and cheese and topped with fried onions followed the soup. Frania served bread and preserves with it and tea to wash it down. Shoshana hadn't eaten this well in a long time.

"Did you enjoy your dinner, Krystina?" Frania asked, taking pleasure from watching her devour every last crumb on her plate.

"It was delicious, thank you. I didn't realize how hungry I was," she said.

"Come now, you need to have a rest."

"No, no," she answered as she stood from the table. "I really must be on my way."

"You know, Krystina," Marian said, "it will make no

difference if you leave now or an hour from now. You really do need to give yourself a chance to rest, at least a little bit."

"What's your rush?" Zosia added. "You have a long walk home. Why would you want to walk through the night?" she asked.

"My mother is expecting me and she'll be terribly worried if I don't arrive tonight as planned," Shoshana replied. "But I am a little tired," she finally relented. "Perhaps I will rest, just for a few minutes before I head out."

"That's a very wise decision. Come with me," Marian said as he walked over to the salon. "Lie here on the sofa."

Frania stood back holding a small cushion and light sheet. Shoshana sat on the couch. Frania pushed Marian out of the way.

"Here," she said as she put the cushion on the arm of the couch. "Take off your shoes, and lie down for a short while."

Shoshana did as she was told, and Frania covered her with the sheet.

The cool sheet and soft pillow felt wonderful as she gave up and let herself go. It had been so long since she'd been this comfortable.

"Close your eyes, my dear. You will be surprised how much better you'll feel after a little rest."

It took less than a minute before the deep, steady breathing of a sound sleep took over her body.

CHAPTER 31

The Long Wait

Peering through the slats, Hanna could see the full moon high in the night sky. She could no longer contain her anxiety. Each one of them was nervous and on edge, but they were afraid to discuss it. David thought that if he said anything, he would upset Mameh even more, and that was the last thing he wanted to do. Jozef only worried about the money.

"Where is she? It's been dark for hours," Hanna mumbled.

"Maybe she stopped to rest, Mameh. She must be exhausted. Please don't worry. She'll be fine," Esther said. She was going to add the words *I promise*, but stopped herself.

With each hour that passed, Jozef became more pessimistic. He spoke to Nessa, but loud enough for the Golds to hear.

"It was a dangerous journey for an inexperienced girl, anything could have happened to her. The Nazis could have shot her, or a Pole could have turned her in, or even a nervous partisan might have captured her. Who knows what happened. Poor girl. At least there will be a little more room in here for us, and more food for me. I can talk Stanczyk into letting the two of us stay. I'm sure I can." Jozef had already written off Shoshana. By his calculations, she should have been back a couple of hours ago.

David launched himself over his mother and let his fists fly at Jozef. "Shut up, you pig! This is all your fault." Hanna grabbed David and held him tight in an attempt to smother his rage. Jozef's first reaction was to strike David, but he felt a little badly for the boy. Instead, he turned his back and went to sleep.

It was a long and torturous night. Hanna's body shook with small convulsions as Esther and David lay on either side of their mother, trying to reassure her. All the while, Hanna's mind played tricks. A few times she bolted up, thinking she heard a twig snap or leaves rustling.

"She's back," she would yell, but Esther gently tugged on her mother's shoulders guiding her to lie down.

"It's nothing Mameh, just the wind."

By the time the birds started their morning serenade, Hanna's anguish was so deep she wasn't moving at all. Esther's focus was off Shoshana and onto her mother. She had never seen her so despondent.

"Mameh, look at me," she repeated over and over while shaking her. But Hanna's body was limp, her eyes unseeing. Esther moved closer to her mother and wrapped her arms around her. *Nothing will be the same,* she thought. *First Tateh, then Shoshana, and now Mameh.* She tightened her grip, squeezed her eyes, and wept quietly.

ꕥ

Lujia and Wiktor didn't sleep much, either. Wiktor kept getting up to stand at the door and watch for Shoshana's return. Leaning against the door frame, staring out at the trees, he smoked cigarette after cigarette.

ꕥ

It was just after four a.m. when Shoshana leapt off the sofa. It took a second or two for her to realize where she was. "Oh, my God, what have I done?" she said out loud. Marian was afraid this would happen, so he'd spent the night in the chair beside her.

"Quiet, Shoshana, you'll wake the others," he said.

"Mameh must be frantic! I can't believe I did this."

"You did nothing, Shoshana. You had to sleep. There was no way you could have made it back safely without some rest."

She knew he was right. Her legs had barely carried her weight last night, when she was ready to leave. Deep down she was glad Marian made her rest, but the guilt of what this change of plan must be doing to her family was overwhelming. She broke into a cold sweat and nervously tried to straighten her clothes and hair.

Just then Frania appeared in the salon holding a candle. She put it down on the table and spoke softly to Shoshana. "Come, my child. You have to take a deep breath and pull yourself together. We will fix you up and you will be on your way in just a few minutes."

Strands of Shoshana's hair had fallen out of her neat bun. "Sit here, let me fix your hair. We don't want you to look like a wild woman on your journey home. You still have to be composed and comfortable. No running, no panicking, okay Krystina?" Frania said as she brushed Shoshana's hair, pulling it back into a perfect bun.

Looking around, Shoshana realized Marian had left the room.

"Thank you, Frania, you've been wonderful to me. I don't know how I can ever repay you."

"You can repay me by visiting again after the war is over," Frania said. "While you use the outhouse, I'll make you a quick sandwich that you can eat on your way."

Shoshana nodded. She had to come to terms with being late. There was nothing she could do about it now. *I have to be careful and make sure I get home safely,* she thought.

She used the outhouse and returned to the kitchen to say good-bye to Frania. Shoshana hugged her tightly and thanked her again as she took the paper bag with the sandwich. Looking around, she realized she didn't have her purse or sweater. She found them both at the end of the sofa. She put on the sweater and was ready to leave.

"Where's Marian?" Shoshana asked. "I can't leave without saying good-bye."

Frania had no idea where Marian was. Leaving Shoshana standing in the salon, she walked quickly to his room, but he was not there.

"I don't know where he is, I will tell him good-bye for you. It'll be light soon, you should head out," she said.

Shoshana nodded, but was unhappy about not thanking Marian for everything he had done. Still, she couldn't waste any more time.

She stepped outside, and there he was, waiting for her.

"I'm coming with you," he said.

Shoshana looked at him as a surge of relief rippled through her. She was very nervous having to walk through town when it wasn't even light out yet. Where would she say she was going if a soldier stopped her? She had thought of a weak excuse about going to visit her sick aunt in Gory, but she didn't have all the details worked out, and she knew it was poorly planned.

Without thinking, she threw her arms around Marian. "Thank you, thank you," she repeated.

"I'll walk with you till you are safely out of town and back in the forest," he said, guiding her toward the gate.

She was so relieved. For some reason, the forest didn't scare her. In fact, she felt a sense of calm and peace inside its protective cover. She was at one with her thoughts in the forest – with the trees, the birds, and the sky. Even though it was for a short while, she felt free in there. If Marian accompanied her that far, she was confident she could get back on her own.

Marian knew no one would bother him. He was still well known in town. He was one of the original residents of Pińczów, a respected council member, and the brother-in-law of Wojtek Grabowski, the head of the Polish police. He had walked and driven down this main road leading to the forest hundreds of times. It was only about three kilometers, and he would have Shoshana safely in the forest by the time the sun peeked over the horizon. This was the least he could do for Leib.

He opened the gate, and they began walking down the dark road toward the main street, which would take them back over the Nida River. The sky displayed the pinkish hue of daybreak. The full moon, straight ahead, lit their path.

"Tell me more about your situation and how you got to…" his voice trailed off to let her fill in the name.

"Wiktor Stanczyk," she said. "So much happened to us after you paid that farmer, Pilarski, to keep us in Sobowice. Did you know him?" she asked.

"I knew *of* him, Shoshana. I knew your father had made arrangements and paid for him to keep David safe. Other than that, I had very few dealings with the man. Was he not good to you?"

"He was an awful man. It wasn't long after you left that he threw us out and stole the money you gave him and most of our belongings. Then he told other farmers that he had released Jews. They terrorized us and almost killed us. One of them stabbed David in the hand with a knife. Then from nowhere two men, one with a gun, stopped them."

"I heard that Pilarski was taken away by the Germans," Marian said. "Maybe they heard he was making money hiding Jews."

Divine justice, Shoshana thought and continued with the story. She told Marian about Działoszyce, living with cousin Aaron, the labor camp David worked in, how they met Nessa and Jozef, the trek through the sewers, the deal they worked out, and the murderous Hanosz. She explained that Stanczyk was Jozef's connection. Marian listened, amazed. He couldn't fathom the horrors they had been through.

"It was Jozef who found Wiktor Stanczyk. He made the arrangements for Stanczyk to hide all of us for seven thousand zloty a month."

Marian stopped walking. "Seven thousand zloty? That's a fortune! No wonder you ran out of money. What was he thinking?"

Nudging Marian to move on, Shoshana said, "I guess he thought the war would be over by now. We all hoped it would. Now I am going back empty-handed, and I don't know what will happen to us."

Marian thought for a moment about trying to hide them with him, but he knew that would be impossible. With Wojtek living under his roof, they would have a better chance living in the forest than in his stable. He felt sick that he couldn't do anything, but the reality of his situation made it impossible.

His thoughts were interrupted by the faint sound of a vehicle coming from behind.

"Keep walking," Marian said.

As the vehicle came closer, Marian turned to see a jeep with two German police officers.

"I'll do the talking. You stay calm," he said in a low, authoritative voice.

The jeep swerved slightly around the two pedestrians and came to a stop on the side of the road a short distance ahead.

Both officers got out of the jeep and stood in the middle of the road, waiting for Marian and Shoshana to reach them.

"Guten Morgen," one of the men said, "Where are the two of you off to so early this morning?"

Marian took one step forward. "My name is Marian Wicinski, and this is my niece Krystina Kominski. I'm taking her to Gory. That's where her mother, my sister, is. She's not well, and we want to get there as early as possible," he added.

The officers stared at them. From her outward appearance

Shoshana was holding up quite well. On the inside, however, her heart pounded so hard, she could barely hear what they were saying.

"Papers please," the officer said.

Marian reached into the inside pocket of his jacket as Shoshana opened her purse, willing her hands to stop shaking. She handed her identification paper over to Marian, who, in turn, passed both papers to the police officer.

The officer looked up at Marian and Shoshana. Once again her blue eyes served her well as she returned his gaze.

"Everything is in order," he said, handing the papers back to Marian.

Marian took them. "*Danke*."

"It should be a glorious day," the officer said, "I hope your mother feels better," he said directly to Shoshana.

With a nod of her head she answered, "Danke."

They returned to their jeep and drove away. Neither Marian nor Shoshana moved until the vehicle was completely out of sight. Shoshana's body went limp, and she leaned hard into Marian.

He supported her weight easily. "You did great. You're an amazing woman, Shoshana. Your father would be very proud of you. Come, we must get you back to your family," Marian said as he handed the identification document back to her.

She took a deep breath. *I did it,* she thought. *They didn't have a clue I was Jewish, I really did it.* Something changed in her at that moment. She felt a new sense of power and confidence that radiated through her posture. *Tateh would be proud of me.*

It wasn't long before they reached the edge of the forest. "I left myself some markings to get back onto the forest path," she told Marian.

"That was clever. What should we be looking for?" he asked.

"It's still about a kilometer in, but on the left I used the knife you gave David to make a mark on a tree."

He stopped walking. "David still has the knife I gave him?"

Shoshana reached into her purse and handed it to him.

"It came in very handy. David loves it, and it was hard for him to part with. He keeps it close all the time. It helps to occupy his time in the barn. He's made carvings with our names and dates. He's quite a handful," she added.

Staring at the knife, Marian smiled thinking back at some of the antics David pulled. He really missed the boy. Marian returned the knife to her. "Please make sure to tell David how proud I am of him for taking such good care of his family."

"I'll make sure he knows," Shoshana said, putting the knife back in her purse. "He misses you too, Marian."

He put his arm around Shoshana's shoulder and pulled her into a short, tight squeeze. "Let's keep moving," he said.

It was only about ten minutes later when she found her tree. "Here it is!" she said and ran over to embrace it. She then ran a couple of meters ahead, and there was her jar and stick. Marian caught up to her. The two of them stood for a moment, silent, staring at each other, not wanting to say good-bye.

"I have something for you, Shoshana," Marian said, as he reached into his pants pocket and pulled out a wad of bills. He stretched out his hand to give it to her.

"There's one thousand zloty here. I'm sorry it couldn't be more," he said.

She didn't make a move to take the money.

Marian took her hand and placed the money in her palm. "Give this to your mother. She will know how to use it."

Holding the wad in her hand, she whispered, "Thank you."

He kissed her on one cheek and then the other. "We will see each other again. Go now. Be safe."

A heavy lump rose in her throat, and she found it difficult to speak. Instead, she nodded, then turned away and began to walk. She took a few steps before she turned to see Marian still watching her. She waved one last time, tucked the jar back into her sweater, and, using the stick, she started down the path back to the barn.

CHAPTER 32

Decisions

Thoughts of seeing her family pushed Shoshana through the forest quickly. As she moved through the trees and bushes, her thoughts replaced the sounds of nature. *How am I going to tell them I found nothing? They will be so disappointed, and Jozef will be angry.*

The closer she got to Stanczyk's barn, the more nervous she became. The responsibility of her family's safety was more than she could deal with. She forced her legs to keep moving. The sun illuminated the forest floor, and the temperature rose. As she stopped to remove her sweater she noticed a clearing on her right. She recognized that field; it was Hanosz's farm. She was almost home. She snickered. *Home. That jail we're living in is our home. But if that's where Mameh, Esther, and David are then it is my home, at least for now.*

I'm not really returning with nothing. I have the thousand zloty Marian gave me. Shoshana didn't want Jozef and Nessa to know about that money. She stopped, opened her purse, took out the cash and shoved the wad into the waistband of her undergarment. *I'll give it to Mameh when Jozef is asleep.* She twisted her hips back and forth to make sure the money was secure, then straightened her skirt and continued to walk. There it was, the side path that led to the back of the barn. She'd made it. Shoshana closed her eyes, and with a heavy sigh said a short prayer. "Please God, *please* keep us safe."

The cow and horse were grazing, there were two pigs snorting and nudging the ground with their snouts, the chickens scattered in different directions, pecking at the earth, but there was no sign of any human. *Where's Stanczyk?* she wondered. Trying not to disturb any of the animals or foliage, she tiptoed around the back of the barn. The door was not locked, so she pushed one side open just enough to squeeze through.

David was the first to leap up from his prone position in the enclosure. He leapt over his mother to remove the slats and stepped out to see his sister standing in front of him. "Shosh!" he said louder than he should have and wrapped his arms around her waist. She held on to him. Tears welled in her eyes as she blinked them shut.

"Mameh, Shoshana's back!" Esther said shaking her despondent mother. "She's come back to us, Mameh. She's safe."

It only took seconds before they were all out of the enclosure. David moved away from his sister, and Hanna took his place. She read her daughter's distraught features and knew what was behind them. She didn't care. She had her Shoshanaleh back.

Hanna held her daughter whose silent tears flowed at the sight of her mother. "Everything will be fine Shoshanaleh. We're all together again, and we'll stay that way. You came back to us, and that's all that matters."

At the first sight of Shoshana, Jozef knew she had nothing. She was not carrying a sack or case. He knew the gold and silver would not fit in that small purse. He swore under his breath as he returned to the enclosure. He needed to think before Stanczyk came out.

Nessa squeezed Shoshana's hand. "I'm glad you're back," she said and then followed her husband back into the hole.

Esther embraced her sister. "It's so good to see your face," she said. "We expected you back last night, and Mameh thought you would never return. I told her you'd be fine. I told her." She had been petrified, too, that Shoshana was gone for good, but she never let on how she felt.

Esther took a step back from her sister. "Did you hear anything about Tateh?" she asked.

"Not really," Shoshana answered. Hanna and David moved in closer to hear what news she had brought back about Leib. "When I got to Pińczów, I went straight to Marian's." She looked at David. "He really misses you, David. He wanted to make sure you knew that."

David looked down and thumped at the ground with his shoe. Shoshana reached into her purse and pulled out the knife. "Here," she said to her little brother. "He was very happy to know that you've kept it all this time."

Shoshana continued. "Marian's the reason I'm so late, he wouldn't let me leave last night. He made me rest. He insisted it would be too dangerous for me to go when I was so tired."

Esther interrupted impatiently. "What about Tateh?"

"I'm getting there," Shoshana said. "Marian's niece Zosia was visiting from Jędrzejów. He arranged it so that she would come with me to the house. He didn't want me walking alone through Pińczów. He thought it would look better if two girls were strolling together. Nothing is the same; the people are all strangers. The only person I recognized was Mr. Gorski from the pharmacy, but I was careful not to let him see me. Zosia waited in the park, while I went to look for the money."

Shoshana glanced at her mother. "It was all gone. The dirt was loose, and I knew someone had dug it up before me. I kept digging anyway, just to make sure," she said.

Hanna could see the toll this was talking on her daughter. "You did very well, Shoshanaleh."

"I went back to Marian's with nothing, and I was terribly upset. Marian thought that Tateh might have taken the money. He said Tateh was the only one, besides us, who knew that there was hidden gold and money buried there. Marian thinks Tateh may have used the money to pay someone to hide him, just like us."

Esther gave Marian's theory some thought.

Shoshana purposely left out the part about the Germans rounding up all the Jews and transporting them to Treblinka. What good would it do to tell them that all their relatives, neighbors, and friends were taken to Treblinka? *Besides,* she thought, *deep down they already know.*

She wasn't quite finished telling her story when the door opened, and Stanczyk entered the barn. Hanna started to walk toward him. Her daughter had been through so much, and she was going to be the one to let him know there was no money. But Shoshana pulled her mother back and approached him, instead.

"Pan Stanczyk, I regret to inform you that I've returned empty-handed. The money I went to retrieve was stolen by someone else, sir. We are at your mercy, Pan Stanczyk."

Inside the enclosure, Jozef listened like a coward, letting Shoshana do the pleading for him.

The blood drained from Stanczyk's face as he put both hands around his head as if he was preventing it from exploding. Before Stanczyk could say a word, Hanna spoke up.

"We may have nothing now, Pan Stanczyk, but as you know, we were wealthy people before this war. We still own a house in Pińczów, it can be yours if you continue to keep us here. As soon as the war is over, the house will be yours."

He dropped his hands and glared at Hanna. He hated her in that moment, and he hated himself for putting his family at risk for six Jews. Hanna shuddered as she saw the look on his face. His jaw was clenched so tight she could see the muscles protruding all the way down his flushed neck. She took a couple of steps back and motioned for her family to get into the enclosure.

"Pan Stanczyk, think about my proposal. This war can't go on much longer. The German army is being defeated. If you keep us, you will have something at the end of all this to give your family a new start after this war."

Without answering, Stanczyk left the barn, but he was thinking about Hanna's words. He would have to discuss this with Lujia. He wasn't about to make another major decision about these Jews without his wife's input. He lit a cigarette and bolted the door shut with the iron bar.

ꟷ

There was no point in putting off the news. Lujia was cleaning up after breakfast. "Where are the children?" Wiktor asked.

"Fredek is outside, and Kassia and Gita went to Gory to visit with their friends."

"We have to talk, Lujia."

"The girl is back?" Lujia asked excitedly.

He took his wife's arm and led her to the kitchen table. "There's no more money," he blurted out.

Lujia leaned back in her chair, narrowing her eyes as she glared at her husband.

"She made it to town, but someone else got to the money before she did. She came back with nothing," he said, as he put his arms on the table and buried his face in them. His body began to quiver, and Lujia knew he was crying.

She made no move to comfort him, but his anguish managed to defuse her anger a little. There was no point in punishing him further.

"Pull yourself together, Wiktor. We have to work on this problem together, and we must put our children's safety above the lives of those people. Do you understand?"

He nodded as he composed himself. "I'm so sorry, Lujia."

"Save your apologies, Wiktor. We have to deal with this right now. We need to think." She stood and began pacing back and forth.

Thinking out loud, she said, "Nothing has really changed. So the girl didn't bring back money, what does that really mean to us? It's doesn't change anything for us. It changes *everything* for them. We were going to use that money to buy food on the black market. We can't do that now. We have enough to eat. It's the Jews in the barn that we have no food for. We can't let them go because if they get caught, they'll expose us." She turned to Wiktor and spoke directly to him. "So, we will keep them here and not feed them," she said, as if she had found the perfect answer.

"Not feed them? You want to starve them to death?"

"Do you have a better idea?" she barked.

Wiktor could see that his wife was desperate. She wasn't thinking straight. This was his fault, and he would have to be the one to come up with a solution. He didn't bother to tell Lujia about Hanna's proposal. It would do them no good at the moment, anyway. He lit a cigarette and left the house. Even walking through his open fields, he felt trapped. He thought about what Max had said about the British liberating them and exonerating them for rescuing six Jews. Six dead Jews would not produce the same reception. But Lujia was right about not letting them go: it would be a certain death sentence for his family.

Hours and several cigarettes later, he was no closer to a solution. Then he started to reason. *We can only take one day at a time. We have enough water, people can live a long time on water,* he tried to convince himself. *We can give them a little food, maybe a potato or two once in a while. Lujia can still give them bread, just not as often. We can offer them the broth that we boil our potatoes and kluski in. There will be nutrients in that. We'll have to do the best with what we have. We have no choice and neither do they.*

CHAPTER 33

What Goes Around, Comes Around

Stanczyk did not return to the barn for the rest of the day. With no food or water, they would have to make do with the little bit of bread they still had. Jozef took Nessa's portion, and this time there was not enough left for the Golds to share with her. By the end of the night, it was all gone.

They exchanged hunger and thirst for sleep. Before succumbing to the escape of her dreams, Hanna thanked God that Shoshana was back. *Whatever Stanczyk decides to do with us, at least we're together.*

ᔕ

The morning light woke David. Carefully stepping over his mother and sisters, he exited the enclosure and walked over to peer through the slats to the outside. He saw two pigs devouring the contents of their trough. Pangs of jealousy rose in him. *Look at them, free to roam, their bellies full, a home to sleep in, and they have each other.* He watched them for a long while before Shoshana came out to join him.

"What are you looking at?" she asked.

"Nothing," David answered as he turned and slid down the wall, landing hard with a thump.

Shoshana positioned herself beside her little brother. "David, whatever happens, at least we have each other," she mumbled, trying to convince herself.

ᔕ

A month later, the fear of being thrown out had been replaced by apathy. It was obvious Stanczyk had decided to let them stay, but it was also clear he was not going to feed them – at least not like he used to.

Lujia continued to supply one loaf of bread every couple of weeks, and their daily jug of water arrived every morning. As for other food, their three meals a day had now dwindled to one. Usually it was a large pot of starchy water with either a few noodles or a couple of potatoes.

ᔕ

It was October when the bustle of the harvest took over the town. Suddenly, Stanczyk's empty barn filled with storage for winter. Wooden crates containing cabbages were stacked high against the far wall, and bundles of oats sat on top of the enclosure. The six people below them stayed quiet and motionless until the daily action in the barn subsided.

As the bone-chilling rains of November set in, it was time to retrieve the winter clothes they used under the straw as padding. They never thought they would have to put those layers on again. The easterly winds howled at night as they huddled for warmth. Esther noticed how much more room they had even with their coats on – a sign of how much weight they had all lost since this hole had become their home a year earlier.

David couldn't sleep and left the enclosure to sit by the wall that faced the road. It became his usual spot. It was the closest he could get to the outside world without stepping foot in it. Through the slats he watched people walking, horses and wagons traveling, even the odd German vehicle zooming by. It was his window to a life he could watch but never participate in.

It was getting light when David was roused by an unusual sound. *What is that,* he wondered. *Could it be the wind?* He couldn't make it out, but thought it sounded like the cries of a woman. The open fields carried the chilling sound through his bones, and an eerie wave ran through him. He sat listening, his imagination running away with him. *Maybe it's an injured cat,* he thought, and the memory of his own cat, Yoel, came rushing back. *Wind doesn't sound like that. Something or someone is hurt.* The voice didn't get any louder or closer, just a steady anguished howl. Finally, with no answer and nothing to do, David crawled back to the enclosure and fell asleep to the mournful sound.

When he woke with the rest of his family some time later, the noise that had puzzled him earlier was drowned out by the usual morning activity on the road outside.

"Did any of you hear that crying noise a while ago?" David asked.

"I didn't hear anything," Esther replied.

The rest of them ignored him, hoping that maybe this morning Stanczyk would show up with food.

The day continued like any other, but David had trouble shaking an odd feeling in the pit of his stomach. He positioned himself in front of his favorite slat. Not much light streamed in as the day was cloudy and gray. Then he heard it again, the sound of a woman crying, but this time he heard more than one voice, and the voices were coming closer. He thought he heard a melodic hymn too.

"What is that?" Shoshana asked.

"I told you I heard crying," David said. "Something's going on."

They all came out of the enclosure and found a slat to look through. Even Jozef, who did little more than grumble and complain these days, came out.

The noise became clearer as it approached. Shoshana thought she heard a man say "*wieczne odpoczywanie*."

"It's a funeral," she said. "I heard someone say something about eternal rest. Didn't you hear it, Esther?"

"Yes, but I couldn't make out what it was," she answered.

It makes sense, David thought, *that's what I heard earlier; it was the sound of a woman crying.*

"Shhh," Hanna said. "They're coming closer. We need to stay silent."

A gasp escaped David's lips as he shook his sister's shoulder and pointed up the road. Coming around the bend were four men carrying a coffin on their shoulders. A woman and young girl followed behind, weeping. Jozef tried to make out who the widow was, but her head was covered with a black kerchief, and she had her hands up to her face.

Then came a second group with another coffin in tow, a widow with two small children following; then another group, and still another.

"What the hell happened here last night?" Jozef muttered. He recognized one of the women. It was Pani Solecki. He'd had business dealings with her husband, a gruff and miserable man. *No great loss,* he thought.

The procession continued in the direction of Gory, one coffin after the other in single file. It seemed to go on forever. Then David spotted her. It was Marta. Pulling on his mother's coat, David whispered into Hanna's ear and pointed at the woman who was following the second-last coffin. Stone-faced, looking straight ahead, she was not weeping like the others.

"Hanosz is in that coffin," Hanna whispered to her daughter, who quietly whispered the news down the line.

Marta's last words to David had shaken him to the core, and he remembered them clearly. *I feel sorry for you Jews. We have no choice. You must die. All of you Jews must die.* The words were as loud in his head as if she was saying them now. *How ironic that it's her husband who is dead, and we're still very much alive,* David thought.

There were twelve coffins in all. Stanczyk was a pallbearer helping to carry one of the wooden boxes. It was a dark day for the small community of Kolkow. As the last person disappeared from sight, they were finally able to speak.

"What could have happened?" Hanna said, looking to Jozef for answers.

Jozef, dazed by what he just witnessed, was speechless. He recognized at least half of those widows.

"Jozef," she said louder, trying to snap him out of his daze. "Why them? It couldn't have been an illness, it must have been a mass murder. Who would have wanted to murder those men?"

Esther stepped in. "Jozef, were all the dead men like Hanosz?"

"What do you mean?" he asked.

"I mean did they all hate Jews like Hanosz did? Did they *kill* Jews?"

Jozef didn't answer. Instead, he went back to the enclosure and remained silent for the rest of the day and night. He didn't even fight his wife for her portion of bread. Seeing the funeral of these men he used to know had touched a personal place in Jozef.

It was just before dark when Stanczyk arrived, carrying a big pot of broth. Shoshana waited for him. They hadn't spoken since the day she returned from Pińczów almost three months earlier. But he was their only connection to the outside world, and after what they witnessed, they needed answers.

He opened the door and was startled as he saw movement near the back of the barn.

"I apologize, Pan Stanczyk; I didn't mean to startle you."

There was a new uneasiness about him. He was usually so placid, but tonight he seemed alert and agitated.

"We saw the procession today. We know you've lost many of your friends, Pan Stanczyk. I'm very sorry, this must be a difficult day for you," Shoshana said in a kind and gentle tone, hoping he would open up to her.

"What happened to those men? How did they die?" she finally asked.

Wiktor removed a cigarette from his pocket and joined her near the back of the barn. Leaning on one of the cabbage crates, he lit the cigarette. "They were all murdered in the night."

"Murdered?"

"Yes, murdered in cold blood. Beaten, stabbed, and killed in front of their wives and children."

"But why would the Nazis kill those men? What was their crime?"

Stanczyk took a long, hard drag of his cigarette, the ember glowing brightly as it burned. "They were not killed by Nazis, they were murdered by Jews," he said, looking at Shoshana for a reaction, and she did not disappoint him.

She gasped, bringing both hands to her face. He saw her body stiffen and the horror in her eyes.

Jews, she thought, *how could that be?* She wanted to speak, but the words were stuck in her throat. Wiktor let her squirm; he wanted her to be uncomfortable with the news. It was her people who had done this. It took a few minutes before Shoshana composed herself enough to ask more questions.

"I don't understand," she finally managed to choke out. "What Jews? From where? How?"

"Jewish partisans. Seems like they were planning this for a long time. They knew exactly who to target," he said.

She looked puzzled. "What do you mean?"

"All the murdered men were known for hunting Jews, or

turning them in to the Nazis. Each one of them had a reputation for hating Jews. They made no secret of their hatred. In fact, they boasted about it. They were proud Nazi collaborators and thought their actions would bring them great recognition.

"You know, Hanosz was one of the men killed. Did you hear that Jozef?" Stanczyk said, expecting this coward Jew to come out and face him.

"We saw Marta walking behind his coffin," Shoshana confirmed.

Jozef was listening carefully. He knew about these partisan groups. He'd seen evidence of their existence a long time ago, when he walked through the backwoods. He knew they were escaped Jews from surrounding towns. They had become secret armies, fighting to stay alive and keep as many Jews safe as possible in the process. They were freedom fighters, out for revenge, and surviving as best they could.

Shoshana reasoned that Stanczyk was not one of the dead farmers because of them. He was hiding Jews – saving them – not turning them in. *What goes around, comes around. You saved us, now we've saved you,* she thought, but didn't dare share that thought with him.

CHAPTER 34

Cold and Starving
January, 1944

Shoshana stayed out of the enclosure long after Stanczyk left. Disturbed after watching the long funeral procession, sleep was the last thing on her mind. She propped herself up against the barn wall, barricading herself between two crates for protection from the wind that whistled through the open slats. She sat alone, her mind leafing through old memories and adding these new ones of the dead farmers.

Hours had passed when Hanna started out of a deep sleep. Feeling beside her, she realized Shoshana was not there. Worried, Hanna got up, removed the boards, and felt her way in the dark, whispering her daughter's name.

Shoshana leapt to her feet. "I'm here, Mameh."

"Why aren't you sleeping?"

"I can't sleep, Mameh. My body is tired, but my mind won't

switch off." Then Shoshana remembered something. This was the perfect time.

"Mameh, sit here with me. I have something to tell you."

She reached into her undergarments where she had stashed Marian's money. Sitting down beside her mother, Shoshana reached over and took Hanna's hand. Opening her clenched fist, she laid the money in it.

"What's this?"

Shoshana gently put her hand over her mother's mouth. "Shhh," she said. Leaning in closer, Shoshana pressed her lips against her mother's ear and used her hand as a sound barrier to muffle the whisper. "It's from Marian, one thousand zloty. He wanted you to have it, Mameh. It was the best he could do."

"God bless him and keep him safe," Hanna said as she removed her shoe. She lined the sole neatly with the wad and put it back on. Hanna ran her hand lovingly over her daughter's hair, "Come, mayn tyreh meydaleh, my precious girl, let's try to get some rest before the others wake."

Returning to the enclosure, Shoshana accidentally tripped on David's leg. He woke instantly and suddenly felt very crowded. As the women lay down, he felt an urgent need to get out of there and stretch. Sometimes he felt so claustrophobic he couldn't breathe. He stood in the middle of the barn and inhaled deeply. He couldn't stomach the thought of returning to the tiny crawl space, so he went to sit near his favorite slat facing the road. An hour later he heard voices.

It was the first Sunday in December, and Stanczyk appeared directly in front of the barn with one of his neighbors. They began to discuss politics while they waited for their wives and children to be ready for church. The neighbor said something about a meeting in Tehran.

"Stalin, Roosevelt, and Churchill," the farmer said.

David pressed closer to the opening. *This is really big,* he thought. *Russia, the United States, and Britain all meeting together.* He needed to hear more.

The two farmers continued talking. "They're working together to bring down the Nazis. They've reached an agreement on a second front," the neighbor told Wiktor. "They said, 'We came here with hope and determination. We leave here friends in fact, in spirit, and in purpose.' How much longer can this go on?" The farmer took a last deep drag of his cigarette and then flicked it down the road.

David struggled to hear more, but the women and children had joined their men, and together they walked out of earshot. *It doesn't matter. I heard enough,* David thought. *I have to tell the others.* He waited until there were no more people heading in the direction of Gory. It was safe to talk now, so he went to the enclosure and peered in.

"Mameh, come out here. I overheard some good news." These were words they all longed to hear. It had been so long since they'd heard any news at all. With all of them standing on the concrete pad, David shared the information.

☙

January arrived with blowing snow, dipping temperatures, and cold wind whistling through the cracks. They used the heavy feather blanket to try to keep warm, but unlike the previous winter, they had no insulation left on their own bodies to aid in retaining heat. With less than eight hours of daylight, the cold nights were long and agonizing. There was nothing left to talk about, nothing to eat, no more news to give them hope. The vermin and lice were relentless and caused unbearable pain and itching.

The oppressive hunger consumed them, but they tried not to speak of it. Jozef seemed to suffer the worst, and the lack of food drove him insane. One night he ripped through the barricade Stanczyk had built at the far end of the barn where he stored the cabbages. Jozef took one and tried to gnaw through the tough outer leaves. Concerned about how sick he would feel, devouring this fibrous vegetable on an empty stomach, Esther attempted to talk him out of it, but he would have no part of it. A madman, he gorged on the cabbage until finally he dropped the remaining chunk on the ground in front of him. He leaned back against the wall, satiated, the wildness gone from his face. Nessa nudged him to come into the enclosure. With a hard jerk of his arm he flung off his wife's gentle gesture, as if he was repelling a bee from stinging. She retreated and left him alone.

It didn't take long for the effects of the cabbage to take hold. It started with a muffled moan and grew to an agonized bellow. Nessa and David tried desperately to stifle his sounds. David put his hands over Jozef's mouth, while Nessa pleaded with him to be quiet. Jozef pushed them away with ease. His stomach pain was so severe he couldn't stand. Once he released some of the built-up gas, he felt a little better. But that was short-lived.

Even with the fresh wind blowing through the barn, the stench was unbearable. It hung in the air. Shoshana gagged and wretched, but her empty stomach produced nothing.

David reacted with anger. “You weak coward, how dare you put us all in danger and make us endure your stink!”

Hanna held her son back, but this time she was not upset at his disrespect. Jozef deserved it.

Nessa apologized over and over for her husband’s actions, and Esther just prayed quietly that it would all be over soon. Jozef was far too loud, and he was putting them all in danger.

Stanczyk burst into the barn and was instantly taken aback by the foul odor. Bending down, he picked up the half-eaten cabbage and regarded Jozef, doubled over in pain. “*Dupek!*” he swore angrily. “What’s the matter with you? You’re like an animal!”

We’re nothing like animals, David thought. *I wish we were. They’re free to go outside, and you make sure to feed them.* He knew better than to speak it out loud.

The next morning, Stanczyk promptly removed all the cabbage from the barn. He wasn’t taking any more chances. They could not survive much longer with the bits they were given to eat. It was just a matter of time before their bodies gave in to this merciless torture.

ᔓᔕ

Besides the obvious weight loss, the vitamin deficiency took a heavy toll. The women noticed clumps of hair coming out along with the filthy rodents they extracted from their heads every morning. Their splotchy gray skin thickened, and their lips bled from the deep, dry cracks. The cruel conditions chipped away at their will to live. Seeing the despair defeat her mother and siblings, Esther did her best to give them a reason to endure the torment.

"Mameh?" she would say, as she shook her mother to open her eyes every few hours. "Mameh, what do you think Tateh is doing right now?" Just the mention of Leib's name brought back a little strength. They had to stay alive so they could reunite with Leib. Esther used her father's memory to instill hope in them, and it worked, at least for a few seconds every day.

By spring their misery turned to real desperation. Not even memories of Leib could penetrate their suffering. Hanna spent endless hours trapped in her thoughts, wondering and planning how she could help her children. It was up to her to end their suffering. She knew what had to be done.

CHAPTER 35

When Hope is Gone
May, 1944

It was time to share her plan. David was too young and didn't need to know about this horror until it was upon him. Hannah waited for the right time, when David was safely sitting in front of his slat watching the road. Jozef and Nessa were asleep. She motioned for her daughters to come closer. They sat up and shifted themselves into a tight circle facing their mother.

Staring at her daughters, Hanna examined one, then the other. She barely recognized them. Esther's skin was gray and leathery, and Shoshana had dark circles around her sunken, cloudy eyes. The two girls could barely maintain focus, staring at their mother through half-open, swollen eyes. She'd gone over this speech a hundred times in her head. She was doing the right thing.

"Shoshana. Esther. I look at my children and see only suffering. There's no more life, no hope left for us. We're dying a slow, agonizing death. We're starved for food, for news, for dignity, and for freedom. We sit here fighting with the mice, scrounging for every crumb, while parasites feast on our bodies. We are terrified that the Nazis could arrive at any time and kill us all. We need to prepare, my sweet children. We need to be able to escape to God on our own terms."

Esther's brows furrowed, and her expression changed. Hanna saw the disapproval on her face. Shoshana barely listened, her stare vacant. Hanna wasn't sure Shoshana even heard her words, but she was determined to get through. Her family was not going to die like dirty animals at the hands of the Nazis. She was taking control.

Using her index finger Hanna guided Shoshana's chin and forced her daughter to focus on her.

"Shoshana," she said louder. "Shoshana, are you listening to me?" Hanna detected a slight affirmative nod.

"Shoshana, you're going to go back to Pińczów." When Shoshana pulled away, Hanna put her hands on either side of her daughter's face and demanded her attention.

"You are going back to Gorski's pharmacy. You will remind him who you are and how much money your father gave him. You will give him this thousand zloty for four cyanide capsules, and you will bring them back here to us," she said as she shoved the folded wad into Shoshana's coat pocket.

Esther started to speak, but Hanna let go of Shoshana's face for a second and stretched out her hand, palm facing toward Esther in a gesture for her to keep quiet.

Shoshana didn't acknowledge her mother's words or actions at all.

Trying a different approach, Hanna began stroking her daughter's hair. "Shoshanaleh this is the last mitzvah you can do for your family. You have the ability to end our suffering, Shoshanaleh. Only you can help us escape this hell, *mayn zis kind*, my sweet child."

Hanna watched as the expression on her daughter's face changed. She looked directly at her mother, instead of through her.

Esther blurted out, "Mameh, how could you do this? Shoshana won't come back if you send her out like this. She can barely sit up, let alone walk all the way to Pińczów. Look at her, Mameh! She's weak and tired. She's not alert enough to make it there and back. Why are you doing this, Mameh? Tell her she doesn't have to go. TELL HER!"

Shoshana neither acknowledged nor refused her mother's proposal. She jerked her head away from Hanna's hand and lay down on her side, curled into a fetal position. She closed her eyes and did not move for many hours.

The tension between the women was obvious to David when he returned to the enclosure. Esther sat with her back to her mother. Shoshana lay facing the wall, her knees drawn up to her chin. Hanna's jaw was clenched, and her arms were crossed in front of her.

"What's going on?" David asked.

"Quiet, David," Hanna said. "This doesn't concern you."

She didn't want him to ask questions. She had to get him out of there.

"David, we're in the middle of something important. You're too young to listen to this. Go back out, and I'll tell you when you can return."

Hanna watched her dejected son leave to sit by himself near the outside wall. She felt badly for him, but this was too important.

As the day went on, Hanna had second thoughts about the pressure she'd put on Shoshana. She was so frail. Hanna weighed the options over and over. She couldn't stand to see her children deteriorate and suffer more each day. It was the only way out of this hell. But in Jewish law it is forbidden to take one's life. Would God understand and forgive her?

The day dragged on. Esther and Hanna did not speak. Shoshana barely moved from the prone position she had taken earlier in the day. Hanna continued to rehash her plan. The more she thought it through, the more she realized she had waited too long. She couldn't send Shoshana out there in her condition. Why hadn't she thought of this eventuality months ago, when they still had some strength – some conviction? *It is too late. Esther is right. Shoshana is long past being able to perform a task of this magnitude.* Both girls were sleeping. Hanna decided she would release her daughter from this burden in the morning.

"David, you may come back now," Hanna whispered to her son.

David crawled into the space and was enfolded in his mother's arms. They slept that way, huddled together, giving each other what warmth and comfort they still possessed.

ᘓ

Sounds of morning filtered into the dark barn. Birds began their singing, and the faint drilling of a woodpecker echoed in the distance. The call of the rooster woke Hanna. She lay still, contemplating the new day. As soon as Shoshana was awake, she would relieve her daughter of the insurmountable task she'd forced on her yesterday. She was resigned that their fate would lie in the hands of God.

As the morning light crept in, Hanna watched the boards on the top of the enclosure become more defined. The sun hit the side of the barn, and the air around her began to warm. Hanna sat up when she heard the iron bar being removed from the door. She saw Stanczyk's worn boots through the slats. As usual, he said nothing as he put a jug of water down on the concrete. He didn't leave any bread with it.

The light was still dim in their tiny compartment, but she could see the outline of everyone still sleeping. She looked at David, close beside her, and then over to Esther and Shoshana. She stopped breathing. Shoshana. She wasn't in her spot. Hanna crouched onto her feet and leaned over Esther to touch the place where her daughter should have been. Esther woke to her horrified cries. "Shoshana! Shoshana," she repeated. They were all awake now. Jozef mumbled and rolled over.

"What's happening?" Nessa asked.

Esther glared at her mother. Hanna could see the hatred in her daughter's eyes.

"She's gone, Mameh. Why are you so upset? You got what you wanted."

"Where is she?" David demanded.

"Ask your mother," Esther said before she lay back down. She couldn't look at her mother for fear of what she might say.

ᔓ

Shoshana was well into the forest by the time the light danced through the tall trees. There was a strong sweet smell of fresh growth, and the forest floor was softer than she remembered it. Still, she had a hard time walking and had to rest every few steps. Her legs buckled as she moved from tree to tree, hanging on for support. Her mother's words played in her head like a worn record stuck in one spot. *This is the last mitzvah you can do for your family, this is the last mitzvah you can do for your family.*

This time Shoshana looked like a Jew. There was no facade. No lipstick or fancy dress, no Polish identification papers. She looked like a starved, disheveled Jew who had been in hiding for the past year and a half. If a German soldier saw her, he would shoot her on the spot. She welcomed that thought for a moment, but then she thought of her family and how they would suffer, not knowing what happened to her. That guilt was a powerful force. Her legs moved forward.

For some reason, Shoshana wasn't afraid this time. She walked a little and then rested, repeating this pattern throughout the day. She drank from tiny puddles of dew that had formed on leaves. She found herself fighting off sleep every time she stopped to rest. Sometimes she lost the battle and dozed before moving on. It had taken Shoshana three hours to walk to Pińczów the last time. Now she was eight hours into her trek, and she was just nearing the end of the forest.

She stopped to think of her timing. *There's no point in going to Pińczów now, Gorski's store will be closed by the time I get there. I can't go to Marian's like this. If his brother-in-law is there, I will put his whole family in danger. No, I will sleep here and go to see Pan Gorski in the morning.* Shoshana walked back into the forest to a grassy area off the path where a broken tree trunk lay on the ground. She would rest up close to it and use it as shelter. Shoshana lay down close to the mossy trunk and covered herself with foliage. She didn't fall asleep though; once her body was at rest, her mind became very active. Here she was, trying to sleep in the middle of a forest, in the middle of a war, completely alone for the first time in her life.

As darkness fell over the forest, a whole new set of noises filled the air. She heard every blade of grass rustle, every wing flap, and every cricket. She started humming a soft melody and lulled herself to sleep.

ᔕ

The sound of a breaking branch startled her awake. She could hear the slow footsteps of someone approaching. She was paralyzed with fear. Perhaps they would pass and not see her. The steps seemed to come closer and then stop. Shoshana lifted her head ever so slightly to peer over the trunk. Her fear melted as she saw a deer picking at the trees. The elegant animal filled her with peace and hope as she watched it eat. She didn't move until it wandered out of sight.

Shoshana stood and brushed herself off. The kerchief she had in her pocket was still there. She pulled it out, folded it into a triangle, and placed it on her head, tying it tightly under her chin. She pulled the top forward as far as she could to conceal her face.

Shoshana exited where she had buried her water jar the last time she was here. She found the old cut in the tree she'd made with David's knife. Now it was more like a healed-over sore, and it almost blended with the trunk. She thought back to her last encounter with Marian and how he'd given her the thousand zloty. The words, *Give this to your mother. She will know how to use it* came back to her. In her wildest dreams she never thought the money would be used to buy her family's death.

"Cyanide capsules," she whispered to herself. "We're going to kill ourselves. I am here, so I can bring back poison so we can kill ourselves." The sudden realization of what she was doing hit her hard.

What about Tateh? What will he think when he finds out his family was found dead in a barn? He will be all alone. Shoshana panicked and wanted to turn back. Her mother wasn't thinking straight. *This is the last mitzvah you can do for your family.* Her mother's words argued with her own thoughts.

Shoshana continued walking, her mind ablaze with conflict. *Mameh can no longer see past our suffering, or past the end of this war. She thinks it's the best thing for us. She never talks about Tateh anymore. She may have lost all hope, but what about the rest of us? I'm not ready to die, and I know Esther's not. Mameh didn't even let David know what she was planning – because it's just too horrible.*

She looked up and saw the river. She was in Pińczów. The shops wouldn't be open yet, so she needed to find a hiding place until Pan Gorski arrived at his pharmacy. She would get the capsules and then decide what to do. Shoshana was familiar with the homes in the area and knew many people had wooden sheds and outhouses in their yards. Walking behind the homes, she found a shed where she could hide and watch the stores.

It was ten o'clock when Gorski finally unlocked his store. Shoshana looked down both sides of the street, walked as quickly as she could to the pharmacy, and stepped inside. There he was, Marek Gorski, her father's old friend. She remembered when she was a little girl, overhearing a conversation between her parents about how Moshe Gorski had converted to Christianity because he had fallen in love with a Christian girl. He had changed his name to Marek years before the Germans took over.

Gorski's back was to the door; he was placing something on a shelf in front of him. "I'll be right with you," he said, without turning around.

Shoshana glanced out the window and saw no one in the street. She removed the kerchief from her head and began twisting it nervously around her fingers.

Shoshana saw the horrified look on Gorski's face when he finally turned and saw her. "Who are you? What do you want? Get out of my store!" he said, pointing toward the door.

Her voice meek and cracking, Shoshana said, "Pan Gorski, perhaps you remember me. My name is Shoshana Gold. My father is Leib Gold."

Gorski took a few steps closer to Shoshana. He removed his spectacles and squinted, staring at her face. Shoshana noted the second he recognized her.

"Shoshana? Is it really you?" he said. "We thought your whole family was transported to Treblinka." Looking outside his window, he pushed her farther into the store and said, "Come to the back." He pulled open a curtain to reveal a room filled with shelves containing small jars and bottles. There was a table and two chairs against one wall and a counter, sink, and small stove against the other. "Sit here. I'll be right back."

She leaned forward to watch as he locked the door and put a closed sign in his window.

"Sit here, my dear," he said, pulling out the chair.

Shoshana's mouth was so dry she could barely speak. "I'm so sorry, Pan Gorski. Could I trouble you for some water?"

"Of course," he said, embarrassed that he hadn't offered it himself. He poured her a glass and handed it to her. Then he lit the stove and prepared two cups of tea. He opened a paper bag and pulled out some sponge cake. Placing both in front of her, he sat, ready to listen.

Shoshana held the cup between her trembling hands and enjoyed the heat as it warmed her icy fingers. Then she grabbed the cake and was about to shove the whole thing into her mouth when Gorski clasped her arm.

"Slowly, Shoshana. You haven't eaten in a long time. If you swallow this all at once, you'll make yourself sick."

Shoshana put the cake down on the table and broke off a small bite, savoring the burst of sweetness in her mouth.

Shoshana felt Gorski's stare. "Dziękuję," she said.

"You're welcome, Shoshana. Now tell me, why are you here? You took a terrible chance coming back."

Shoshana reached into her pocket and pulled out the thousand zloty. She calmly put it on the table in front of Gorski and said, "I want to buy four cyanide capsules."

She was surprised to see no reaction. Gorski wasn't shocked or horrified at her request.

"Four cyanide capsules?" he asked. "Are there not five of you?"

"Tateh is not with us. He must be in hiding somewhere, like we are."

Gorski observed her for a long time. He walked over to one of his shelves. Reading label after label he finally picked up a small canister. He came back and plunked it down on the table in front of Shoshana. She jumped a little in her chair.

"This canister contains the poison you're looking for, but before I give it to you, I want you to know exactly what it means to die of cyanide poisoning."

He sat back down. "First you will feel sick, and your heart will pound so hard you will think it is exploding in your chest. Then you will get dizzy and experience a headache worse than any pain you have ever had. Then come the seizures. You may bite through your tongue and –"

"Stop!" Shoshana blurted. "I can't hear any more."

"But you must hear this," Gorski said. "You walk in here to buy cyanide capsules, and you really have no idea what you're asking for. It's my job to make sure you know."

Shoshana tried unsuccessfully to fight back the tears. "I don't want to know," she said standing abruptly. Her palms supported her weight as she pressed them into the table. She leaned closer to Marek Gorski and shouted into his face, "This is the last mitzvah I can do for my family!"

They stared at each other for a long moment before Shoshana broke down completely. Gorski got up, and gently guided her back into her chair. He gave her a handkerchief as she sobbed uncontrollably. He pushed the bit of tea left in the cup closer to her and sat quietly while she cried.

Shoshana finally composed herself, but she was ashamed to look up at him.

Gorski finally spoke. "Look, Shoshana, the Red Army is coming. They're close. It won't be long before they defeat the Nazis and liberate the camps and towns. You and your family will rebuild your lives. Have faith, Shoshana. Your life is not yet over, my dear. You're young and have a strong spirit. Think of what you've accomplished today alone. So many others are gone, but you and your family are still alive. If you can just hang on to a little bit of hope, Shoshana, you *will* survive."

He made sense. *The Russians are moving slowly, but they are coming. It can't be much longer. We can do this, we will all be together with Tateh one day. Free. We will live like we used to,* she thought.

Gorski waited before he spoke again. "So, Shoshana, do you still want to buy these four capsules?"

She stared at him and stood, her body stiff, her stance straight and confident. "No." She said it with conviction.

Marek Gorski took the canister off the table and placed it back on the shelf. He walked over to the table, picked up the money and the paper bag, which contained the remainder of his lunch and handed it to her. "Go. Be with your family, Shoshana. If it's God's will, our paths will cross again."

She accepted the money from his outstretched hand. "You're a very smart man, Pan Gorski," she said, placing the zloty in her pocket. Gorski watched Shoshana tie her kerchief under her chin, walk to the front door, and leave. She didn't look back.

CHAPTER 36

In God's Hands
Fall, 1944

Esther didn't know if she was more angry or worried. Against Hanna's wishes, she filled David in on what their mother's plan was. All alone, Hanna propped herself against the back wall. She had trouble breathing and continually rubbed her fists together in nervous agitation. What had she done? How could she sacrifice her child like that? Guilt was ripping her apart.

It was almost dawn two days later, and David sat up hoping and praying for his sister's safe return. He was crouched behind a stack of bales when he heard movement at the back entrance. He could just make out the shape of his sister. Without a thought David ran out and threw himself at Shoshana, almost knocking her over. No words were exchanged. She held him and rested her cheek on top of his head. They stayed that way for a long time.

Esther and Hanna heard the movement and rushed to get

out of the crawl space. Esther's pent-up anger turned to tears at the sight of her sister. She stood in silence, watching her siblings embrace.

Still holding her brother, Shoshana reached out her hand to Esther. She joined the two in a long embrace and thanked God for her sister's return.

Hanna stood back watching her children. She, too, clasped her hands to her chest and thanked the Almighty for returning her daughter, but her shame held her back from the reunion.

Shoshana finally noticed her mother, unclasped David's arms, and walked over to her. Shoshana's face exuded a powerful energy. There was an air about her that hadn't been there before. She spoke first.

"Don't regret the decision you made for us, Mameh. You made it because you love us."

Esther and David listened intently as Shoshana continued.

"I've had a lot of time to think these last two days, Mameh. I've learned a great deal about my strength – about *our* strength, about our will to live, and our determination to survive this atrocity together. We are going to walk out of this barn one day, Mameh. We will find Tateh, and we will be a complete family again. I know that in my heart, and I want you to know it in yours."

"I'm so very proud of you, Shoshanaleh." Hanna pressed her lips to her daughter's cold cheek. She had learned an important lesson today. Hanna returned to the enclosure, leaving her three children together to resolve their own thoughts about the events of the last couple of days, while she retreated to wrestle her demons alone.

There was never any mention of the cyanide again.

ᔓ

Spring turned to summer. News of the Russian army's advancement became more regular. There were more German vehicles coming through Kolkow as the Germans tried desperately to hang on to their conquered land; to accomplish the Final Solution.

It was late afternoon, on a Tuesday, when two German jeeps came down the road. Stanczyk noticed them stopping in front of every farm. He pretended to work as the men surveyed each property. They would talk to each other, pointing and discussing each farm, before moving on to the next parcel of land. Finally they were in front of Stanczyk's iron gate. One soldier pointed at the small hill on the edge of the forest near the back of the barn. Stanczyk continued hoeing, all the while watching the men.

He was somewhat relieved when they moved down the road to the next farm, but Stanczyk felt uneasy for the rest of the day. The Germans were scouting out the area. What did it mean?

ᔓ

In October 1944, Stanczyk went to a meeting at his brother Max's home. Max was still very involved in the Polish Home Army. The mood was somber. Some of the men were drunk, some were angry, and others sat quietly. It was the man sitting alone in the corner that caught Stanczyk's eye. He looked defeated. He had white streaks down his face where tears had washed away the dirt. The man looked up to the ceiling. His lips moved as though he was talking to someone. *He's praying,* Stanczyk thought, captivated by this man's sorrow. Stanczyk flinched when he felt Max's hand on his shoulder.

"What's going on, Max? What happened? Talk to me."

Max motioned with his head for Wiktor to follow him. He took his brother to a quiet area at the back of the house.

"We tried to take back Warsaw from the Nazis before the Red Army got there. We thought once we had some control the Russians would come in and help. They didn't. They let us do their dirty work for two months – and we lost – thousands of our men and women.

"We thought it was working, Wiktor. We were gaining control, but then those Russian bastards stopped coming. They wanted us slaughtered so they could occupy Poland and not have to deal with the Germans *or* us. The Germans sent in bomber planes and more troops. It was a slaughter, Wiktor," Max said, his voice cracking.

"How many did we lose?" Wiktor asked.

"I don't know, but some are saying between the dead and wounded the resistance lost more than twenty thousand. The civilian loss was much higher – in the hundreds of thousands."

Wiktor went cold. There was nothing more to say. He put his arm around his brother's shoulder and they sat quietly, mourning their comrades and their people.

ꕥ

The fall harvest brought a little more food. Stores of cabbage, grains, and potatoes were replenished. The starchy soup Stanczyk provided had a little more substance. There were a few more potatoes, and sometimes a few kluski were left in. The emaciated cow no longer produced milk. Lujia relied on some of her neighbors to share a little milk, but even that was not happening much anymore.

The approaching winter would be the third that the six hidden Jews would endure in this tomb. They all knew they would never survive it.

There seemed to be a bustle of activity in the tiny village. Every day more military vehicles passed through the town. Sounds of gunfire in the distance broke the silence. More and more planes flew overhead. Signs of battle were all around them.

It was a cold, sunny day in December when David bolted up from his prone position.

"Listen," he said. "There are soldiers outside. Do you hear them talking?"

Esther sat up too. "Yes, but I can't make out what they're saying."

Hanna pulled David back down. "Quiet," she demanded.

They didn't move a muscle as they heard the men's voices move to the back of the barn. They were very close now, and David could make out Stanczyk's voice clearly. He wasn't doing much talking, but he heard him say "*Tak*" every few seconds, agreeing to everything the soldiers said.

Shoshana listened intently to the conversation.

"You can see the road from this spot," one of them said.

"This barn is good, it will hide the cannon," the other said. "Schmid, go down and see when we come into view from the road."

"Jawohl," the soldier answered. She heard his heavy steps bound past the barn.

Shoshana was able to make out enough of the conversation that she knew what they were doing. She nodded to the others in the barn to let them know she understood.

Schmid was back. "The barn covers the area, but only for about twenty meters. As soon as you pass that clump of trees, the cannon will be in view."

There was a moment of silence before the next voice. "We'll put a Howitzer on this spot, pointing toward the road. From here we can see the Russians before they see us."

Shoshana heard a faint *tak* escape Stanczyk's lips.

"Weiter, let's move on," the soldier said. "We need to find the next spot for more artillery."

Shoshana listened till they drove off. She turned to her family. "They're putting a Howitzer on the hill behind the barn. They're moving on to find more places to place weapons so they can be ready to ambush the Russians."

"They must be getting very close, if the Germans are looking for strategic areas in this little village," Jozef said.

"What's a Howitzer?" David asked.

"It's a big cannon on wheels. They're going to roll it up the hill and fire it at the Russians," Jozef answered.

David thought for a moment. His eyes wide, he got up on his knees, "The Russians will shoot back to destroy the cannon and kill the Germans. The barn is in the middle. They'll shoot right at us, and what if the barn catches fire? We'll be trapped in here!"

Esther felt her brother's panic. She knelt beside him, put her arms on his shoulders, and brought him back to a sitting position.

"David, you can't think the worst. We'll make sure Stanczyk leaves the bar off the doors so we can escape. We've survived in this barn for over two years, and now that the Russians are so close, we are *not* going to die in here," Esther said.

David didn't answer. He lay on his side, his knees tight to his chin. Esther saw him mouthing the *Shema*, a Jewish prayer he'd said every night since they'd been in this hole. It brought him comfort and helped him fall asleep.

∽

The ground rumbled. The Golds and Lanskis awoke, startled. Jozef perked up. "It's a tank," he said.

David stepped over his sister to get out of the enclosure. Over to his slat near the road, he blew on his frozen fingers. The air was frosty that eighth day of January in 1945, so he pulled his coat sleeves over his hands and leaned close to the crack between the boards. He saw the first German vehicle, then the next, followed by three motorbikes with sidecars – each vehicle filled to capacity with armed soldiers. The rumbling became stronger, and the tank rolled into view. It shook the ground beneath David and reverberated through his body. Dust that had been lodged in the boards for years filled the air, forming a thick cloud of particles. A soldier stood upright sticking out of the hatch behind the huge gun that protruded from the front of the tank. A mixture of dirt and snow surrounded the enormous belts that propelled the vehicle forward. David had never been this close to a tank, and he watched as it thundered past.

Then he saw six soldiers moving the Howitzer toward him. He knew they were headed for the hill behind the barn. His worst fears were about to be realized. He saw past the first group to a second group with another cannon. They were both coming this way. Hanna called her son to come back inside, but David ignored her. He was focused on the huge, spoked wheels grinding beneath the weight of the enormous gun. David recoiled. All he could visualize was a battle with that powerful weapon on one side, a battalion of shooting Russians on the other, and him and his family caught in the middle. David began to hyperventilate. His concentration broke when Esther pulled him gently away from the slat. It was at that second he saw it. He wriggled his shoulders free of his sister's grip and darted right back to his spot. The German soldiers didn't stop at the gate! They continued to push the weapon past the barn, down the road. The second group followed close behind.

He turned to Esther. "They're not stopping here! Look, they kept going. They could never turn that thing around, they're going somewhere else." His elation was contagious. The fear of burning to death had consumed David ever since he'd heard that a cannon was to be placed behind the barn.

It was almost six years ago, when David was only nine, that he'd witnessed Mr. Zimmerman running past him, blood pouring from the gunshot wound in his stomach. The vision of that man's suffering had never left David. His fear of dying a slow painful death was the only thing he was truly afraid of.

CHAPTER 37

The Russian Army Arrives
January, 1945

Sounds of gunshots and explosions were close. Planes roared through the skies above. The tiny town of Kolkow was about to become a battlefield. The twenty-five-kilometer stretch of road between Pińczów and Działoszyce passed by many small towns, that the Red Army would invade in their effort to push the Nazis out of Poland.

It was two days later, when the first Russian battalion arrived in Kolkow. David hadn't moved from his crack. It became his permanent window on the world, and he reported to everyone what was happening. First he heard them – then he saw them. They didn't look like the German soldiers; they were easy to identify. These new uniforms were not as pristine, the hats were not metal, and the coats were a different color; a lighter, moss green. The decals and shoulder boards were different too, and there was no mistaking the shouts he heard in Russian.

David, sitting out in the open, made Hanna very nervous. It would only take one bullet to sear through the weathered wood and kill her only son. David was not obeying her orders to come inside, so she decided not to give him a choice. She stepped through the opening and stood over him, her hands on her waist.

"David," she raged, "get in there right now." She pointed to the enclosure where the rest of them were taking cover.

"I have to see this, Mameh. Look! The Germans are losing. They're finally getting what they deserve. How can you expect me not watch this? It's the best thing I've seen in years, Mameh. See for yourself."

Hanna could barely hear David above the artillery fire, but she didn't care what he had to say. She grabbed his ear and forcefully brought him to his feet. Then she shoved him toward the enclosure. David had never seen his mother this angry. He went in without any further argument and stayed put. Hanna replaced the boards to seal them in: to try to keep her family safe for the last time in this barn.

The shooting continued through the night and into the next day. There was no sign of Stanczyk. No one came in or out of the barn or the farmhouse.

They heard soldiers running past on either side of the barn. There was a thump as someone sat on the ground and leaned against the barn to rest. From the sound of his metal helmet hitting the wood, David figured it was a German. The weary, frightened soldier had stopped to rest where he thought no one would know.

They stayed very quiet. Hanna fought back the urge to

cough as the smell of gunfire filled her lungs. They were in the thick of a Russian-German confrontation, and each man out there was fighting for his life.

By the second nightfall the gunfire had died down. Were they resting? Had they moved on? No one knew, and no one dared to wonder aloud. The six Jews remained silent in their tiny pen, afraid to move, afraid to make a sound. By morning, shouts were heard among the men outside. They were not in German. The only language spoken was Russian. David whispered to his mother, "I have to go out, Mameh, I have to see what's going on."

"No!" Hanna replied emphatically.

"Mameh, let David peek through the crack. We have to know what's going on," Esther implored.

"No! He's not going anywhere," Hanna said, clutching David's coat.

The day continued with the same noises and language they'd heard earlier that morning. There were still no German voices, and the only gunfire was far off in the distance.

∽

Late that evening, the sound of the barn door opening startled the group. Hanna looked through boards to see Stanczyk's familiar boots. He tapped on the board signaling for someone to come out. David was eager to go, but Hanna kept a tight grip on him. Jozef removed the boards and stepped out.

His first sight was Stanczyk holding a jug of water, a cigarette dangling out of the side of his mouth. He took the jug and gulped the water.

Wiping his mouth with his filthy sleeve he said, "What's happening, Wiktor?"

Stanczyk put his hand on Jozef's shoulder. "They're gone," he said, laughing like a madman.

"Gone? The Germans are gone?"

"Nothing but Russian soldiers as far as the eye can see!"

With that, Hanna finally let go of David, allowing him to bolt out of the enclosure. He went straight to his slat to survey the scene for himself. The women remained inside listening to the sound of their liberation.

"Come see for yourself," Stanczyk said, inviting all of them to step outside.

What they thought would never happen *had* happened. Now, Hanna realized, they could move out of this cramped, rat-infested enclosure and find a new place. They could go back to Pińczów and search for Leib. In the morning they would all make their way back home. Hanna shared her plan with her daughters and would tell David, as soon as he came back in to sleep in this cramped cave on his bed of compressed hay for the last time.

ꕤ

Hours passed, but David couldn't sleep. He felt his sister's restless body next to his. "Shosh, are you sleeping?" he whispered.

"No, I can't sleep. I can't stop thinking about what we're going to find."

"Do you think we'll find Tateh?" Esther asked, joining in the conversation.

Shoshana remembered what Marian had told her, about how

the Nazis came in and marched all the Jews of Pińczów to a transport headed for Treblinka. She'd never shared this information with the others. Maybe now she should.

"I have to tell you something," Shoshana said. "Remember when I went back home to get the money, and I stayed with Marian? He told me something that day that I've kept to myself."

They listened carefully.

"The morning Tateh was supposed to meet us at Marian's house, the Nazis rounded up all the Jews from the town and sent them on transports to Treblinka. Remember how Tateh never arrived, and we had to leave without him?"

"That doesn't mean anything," Esther blurted out angrily. "Tateh was a brilliant man with many connections. Didn't you say that Marian thought he might have been the one to take the money that was buried under the house? What about that?"

Shoshana lay in the dark quietly for a moment. "I just thought you should know," she muttered under her breath.

Hanna, pretended to sleep but heard every word. With her eyes still closed she listened to her daughter confirm the feeling she already knew deep in her heart. She wiped the tears that pooled in the corner of her eye.

ଓ

The cold air still had a faint smell of gunfire the next morning. The six Jews in the enclosure looked at each other and spoke only with their eyes. It was time. With Jozef leading the pack, they exited the tiny enclosure that had served as their home for over two years. Jozef had been outside the barn regularly to empty the bucket, and Shoshana had been out twice in the last two years, but Hanna, Esther, and David had never left it. For twenty-six months they lived like breathing corpses, side by side in an oversized coffin. Now, they all stood together on the concrete pad and waited until Wiktor Stanczyk slid the bar from the doors and opened them. Standing to the side, he motioned for them to come out. One at a time, they emerged into the bright sunlight.

Using her hand to shield her eyes, Hanna looked around. There was still some action in the town, but only a few Red Army vehicles with Russian soldiers were left. She turned and saw her son – eyes closed, arms outstretched, face pointed up to the sun – absorbing the rays he had not felt on his skin for a very long time.

Jozef was talking to Stanczyk. Nessa stood behind her husband, listening in. Hanna gave them a few minutes to finish their conversation before she approached.

"Pan Stanczyk, may I speak to you for a moment?"

He looked at this tiny woman in daylight. She couldn't weigh much more than thirty kilos. He removed the cigarette from his mouth and waited.

"You and your family were very brave to hide us this whole time. We're so grateful to you and will never forget the chances you took daily. I'm almost embarrassed to ask you for one last favor, but it's very important, Pan Stanczyk."

He looked at her and waited to hear what this favor was.

"When we arrived, we gave you a bag with all that we had in it. You can keep everything. I just ask that you let me have my husband's Kiddish cup. It may be the only thing I have left of him," she said, her voice cracking.

Stanczyk looked down at this frail but unbroken woman.

He looked over her shoulder at her three children who were now two years older than when he first met them. They had nothing and nowhere to go, yet they had survived unspeakable hatred and tyranny. *To say they have nothing is wrong,* he thought. *They have each other.*

"Wait here," he told Hanna.

He turned to go inside his house, but standing at the doorway was Lujia, holding the etched silver Kiddish cup. She handed it to her husband, and he carried it back to Hanna. Lujia stood at the door, her arms over Fredek's shoulders. Pinning him tight against her apron, she watched the exchange between the two. It was the first time her son realized these six Jews had been living in his barn. Fredek's two sisters stood at the doorway watching in amazement. Kassia's suspicion that her father was harboring Jews had just been confirmed.

Hanna couldn't take her eyes off the silver glinting in the sunlight. She saw Leib's lips touch the cold metal as he sipped from it. She could feel his warm hand as he passed it to her to sip the wine of the Shabbos Kiddish prayer. She quickly shook the ghosts from her head and looked over at Lujia. Hanna smiled and nodded her head. It was the first time she'd actually seen Lujia's face. Even when Lujia had brought the kettle of soup to the barn, she always set it on the concrete pad and left quickly, without speaking a word.

"*Dziękuję bardzo*, thank you very much," Hanna said, bowing her head. She put the cup into her deep coat pocket. Shoshana, Esther, and David joined their mother. Shoshana, having established a bond with Stanczyk, spoke for the rest of her family.

"How can we ever thank you for hiding us? We owe you our lives." She picked up his hand, brought it up to her lips, and kissed the back of it. "We will never forget the kindness you and your family extended to us."

Hanna had not forgotten the promise she made to Stanczyk. She'd promised him their house. Neither of them mentioned it in that moment, but Hanna was a woman of her word. As soon as she could find a place to settle her family, she would be in contact with him.

Stanczyk swallowed hard, fighting his mixed emotions. He was so relieved to finally be rid of them, but at the same time he felt good that he was responsible for saving these six lives.

Without much more than a quick good-bye to each other, the Golds and Lanskis parted ways. There was no love lost between the two families. Jozef and Nessa's original goal was to trade the lives of the Golds for money. That kind of savagery from anyone, let alone a fellow Jew, could never be forgotten.

The two families opened the iron gate and stepped onto the road. The Lanskis turned to walk toward the farm they once owned. The Golds interlaced their arms, partially for support and partially in solidarity and set out in the opposite direction – to go home, to search for Leib and the life they'd left behind.

PART FOUR
Many Years Later

CHAPTER 38

After the War

David never imagined he would be back on this road in Kolkow of his own free will. With his grandson sitting beside him, he stared out the car window, the breeze blowing in his face. He closed his eyes and allowed his mind to wander back to when he walked down this very road with his mother and two sisters. That last time was when they had been freed after twenty-six months of hiding in a cramped barn. David remembered how excited he was to finally go home and be reunited with his tateh. But there was no home to go back to. No tateh. No family. No friends. Nothing was the same. The Poles had taken over Jewish homes and businesses, and anti-Semitism was everywhere. Pińczów was no longer his hometown. His house no longer belonged to his family. The four of them, like so many other Jews with nowhere to go, ended up in Foehrenwald, a displaced persons camp. From there, each one would move on to a new life and try to leave the horrors of the Holocaust behind.

ശ

David reminisced about each one of his family members and thought first about his oldest sister, Shoshana. She met her husband Fishl Burakowski in Foehrenwald. She and Fishl made their way to Palestine on Aliyah Bet, the illegal immigration, ships. Shoshana was finally able to fulfill her father's dream of living in the Holy Land.

But after eleven years of living in a constant state of war with the Arabs, Shoshana, Fishl, and their two daughters decided to join Mameh and David in Canada where they felt more secure, until one cold Shabbos in January 1972.

David remembered that day vividly. He was walking home from shul with Mameh when he saw red flashing lights and emergency vehicles on the street. The footprints in the snow pointed to the front door of Shoshana's house. He remembered the mournful cry his mother let out at the site of her daughter's lifeless body splayed on the floor.

At the age of fifty-two, after finally living in a place where she felt safe, Shoshana died of a massive heart attack. At her funeral Hanna, David, and Esther huddled together in the cold again, to watch yet another horror unfold in their lives. A piece of their soul was buried and lost forever.

ശ

Then David's mind wandered to Esther. He was proud of his sister for all she'd accomplished after the war. Esther and her husband, Feivel Biel, were married in Bergen-Belsen. In the very place where so many Jews were murdered, they began a new life together. They moved to America and had three sons whom they raised with a strong Jewish faith. There was nothing more important to Esther and Feivel than education. They knew that, unlike material items, knowledge was a powerful weapon no one could ever take away. They raised their boys to be proud Jews and respected doctors.

Through hard work and determination, Esther and Feivel built their American dream. But everything changed when Esther was diagnosed with non-Hodgkin's lymphoma. In 1984, at the age of sixty-two, Esther succumbed to cancer, but not before building a proud legacy. Esther left behind her husband, three children, and nine grandchildren.

ൿ

David knew his strength and courage came from his mother. Hanna never forgot her husband, Leib. His memory lived in her heart and in the hearts of her children. Leib never returned, nor did the family find any evidence of his death. But no matter what life threw at Hanna, she was a survivor. After Shoshana's and then Esther's passing, Hanna became very frail and eventually moved to a Jewish home for the aged. David visited after work every day to feed her dinner. He spoke to her in Yiddish and stroked her hair, trying to calm her, as her mind regressed back to the days of Hitler and hiding in the barn – the very barn he was about to lay his eyes on after all these years.

He thought about the hard life his mother had and how she had outlived her husband and both of her daughters before she died at the age of ninety.

ೞ

Then David looked back on his own life. From the day he arrived in Canada, he struggled to build a future for himself and his family. He never forgot the sacrifice the Stanczyk family made, and he never gave up trying to reclaim the house in Pińczów that Mameh had promised them. But the Polish government was uncooperative, and he wasn't able to reclaim his former home. To this day, David continues to send the Stanczyks regular care packages consisting of clothing, medicine, and money.

David married Esther Eisenstat and had three sons.

He remembered vividly the day he was told that their middle son, Jordan, had leukemia. It was August 25, 1967, when Jordon was only four years old, that God took his baby boy. Unlike surviving the Holocaust, David would never recover from that loss.

Life changed after Jordan's death, and David threw himself into his work, spending long hours and days building up his business, Golden Bay Sportswear, where he employed more than twenty people. He never closed the shop early, except for that one memorable day when he received a phone call to come quickly to the hospital. He picked up the family photo, which had survived the war, kissed it, locked up quickly, and raced away.

Just as he stepped off the hospital elevator, the doors before him swung open, and there stood his wife, Esther, his youngest son, Doron, Shoshana's two daughters, Sarah and Ella, and Ari, his oldest son, holding a tiny bundle swaddled in a blue blanket. Ari walked straight to David and placed the newborn baby in his arms. David carefully accepted the tiny, red-faced child. Bustling hospital noises ceased to exist. All David heard were Ari's words, "Daddy, meet your new grandson, Jordan." David couldn't take his eyes off this miracle cradled against his body. He raised the infant closer to his face and placed his lips on the baby's forehead. He was cradling his first grandchild, the namesake of the little boy he had lost to leukemia a lifetime ago. "The Gold legacy will live on," he whispered, knowing that somewhere, somehow, his tateh was watching.

ಌ

Reality set in when the driver turned to David and said, "We're here."

David's eyes settled on the barn beyond the iron gate. It was intact and unaffected by the decades that had passed since he'd last laid eyes on it. It was as though time had stood still. He wanted to step out of the car, but his legs felt like anchors. Jordan gently shook his grandfather's shoulder and asked, "Are you okay, *Saba*?"

David looked straight into the child's bright, blue eyes and lied. "Yes Jordan, I'm okay."

They got out of the car and hesitated in silence for a minute. David took a deep breath to calm himself, but couldn't help thinking this was the same air he'd breathed in 1942, when he was hidden in this ominous, dilapidated barn that stood before him. He could almost see his mameh and sisters standing there too.

David had an overwhelming impulse to protect his grandson

from the terrors this place held for him. He was the same age as Jordan was now when he entered this barn for the first time. David put his arm around Jordan's shoulders, pulled him close and guided him slowly toward the barn that had both entombed and protected him for over two years.

He finally said, "Come, *mayn zis kind*, my sweet child, and I will show you how your saba survived the war."

GLOSSARY

agronom – (Polish) deputy in charge of agriculture

auf den knein – (German) [get down]on your knees

bris – (Yiddish) circumcision ceremony

Cheder – (Yiddish) religious school

Danke – (German) Thank you

Dobry wieczór – (Polish) Good evening

dupek – (Polish) swear word – ass

dziękuję – (Polish) thank you

Dzień dobry – (Polish) Good morning

Gut Shabbos – (Yiddish) Good Sabbath

Guten morgen – (German) Good morning

forshpeits – (Yiddish) appetizer

Jawohl – (German) Yes, sir

Judenrat – (German) Council representing Jewish community, often forced to represent, mediate or liaise with the Nazis

Judenrein – (German) free of Jews

Junakies – (Polish) Polish auxiliary guards

kasza – (Polish) grain cereal

kotletin – (Yiddish) meat patties

Kiddish – (Yiddish) prayer over the wine

Kaddish – (Yiddish) Jewish prayer for the dead

kennkarte (papers) – (German) labeling identification issued by the Third Reich and color coded, Jewish papers were yellow kluski – (Polish) noodles and fried onions

Kristallnacht – (German) Night of Broken Glass, November 9, 1938

Mameh – (Yiddish) Mommy, Mother

matzo(s) – (Yiddish) unleavened bread

mazel tov – (Yiddish) congratulations

mayn tyreh kind – (Yiddish) my precious child

mayn tyreh kindeh – (Yiddish) my precious children

mayn tyreh meydele – (Yiddish) my precious girl (endearing)

mayn tyreh meydl – (Yiddish) my precious girl

mayn zis kind – (Yiddish) my sweet child

mitzvah – (Yiddish or Hebrew) good deed done out of religious duty

Raus! – (German) [Get] out!

Rosh Chodesh – (Hebrew) the beginning of the month

Rozumiesz – (Polish) understand

Saba – (Hebrew) Grandfather

Schnell – (German) quickly

Shabbat – (Hebrew) the Sabbath

Shabbos – (Yiddish) the Sabbath

Shema – a Jewish prayer said when one is ready to die

Shemini Atzeret – (Hebrew) a Jewish holiday

shidduch – (Yiddish) an arrangement leading to marriage

shtiebel – (Yiddish) a makeshift place to pray

shul – (Yiddish) synagogue or worship

soltys – (Polish) village councilor

Tateh – (Yiddish) Daddy, Father

Tak – (Polish) yes or uh-huh

wieczne odpoczywanie – (Polish) rest eternally

zloty – (Polish) currency

zupa ogórkowa – (Polish) cucumber soup

As a boy, David Gold wore the armband all Jews were forced to wear, so that they could be easily identified and persecuted by the Nazis.

The paper below, bearing a Judenrat stamp, identifies David Gold as a habitant of the Działoszyce ghetto. The identification paper under David's belonged to his mother, Hanna.

JUDENRAT in DZIALOSZYCE

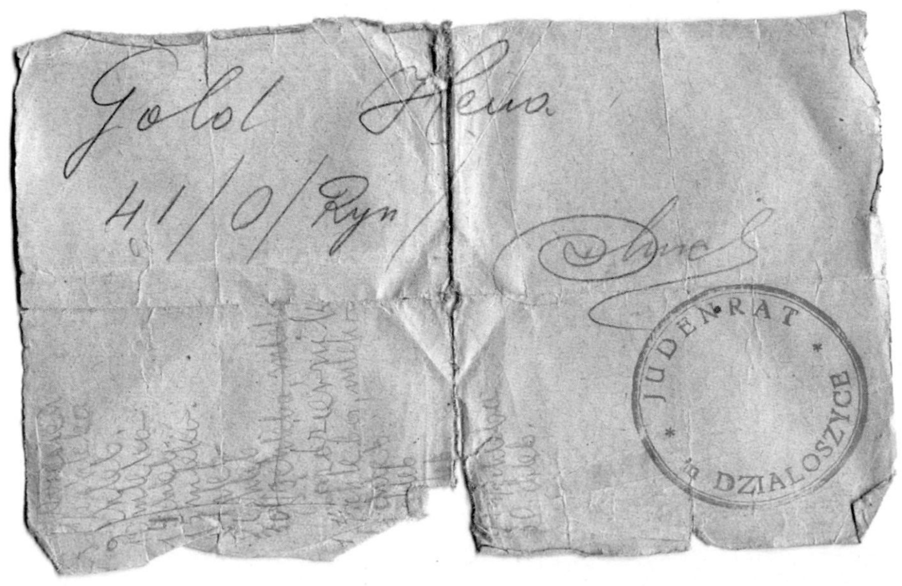

41/0/Ryn

JUDENRAT in DZIALOSZYCE

Jews being marched out of the town of Pińczów to Treblinka.

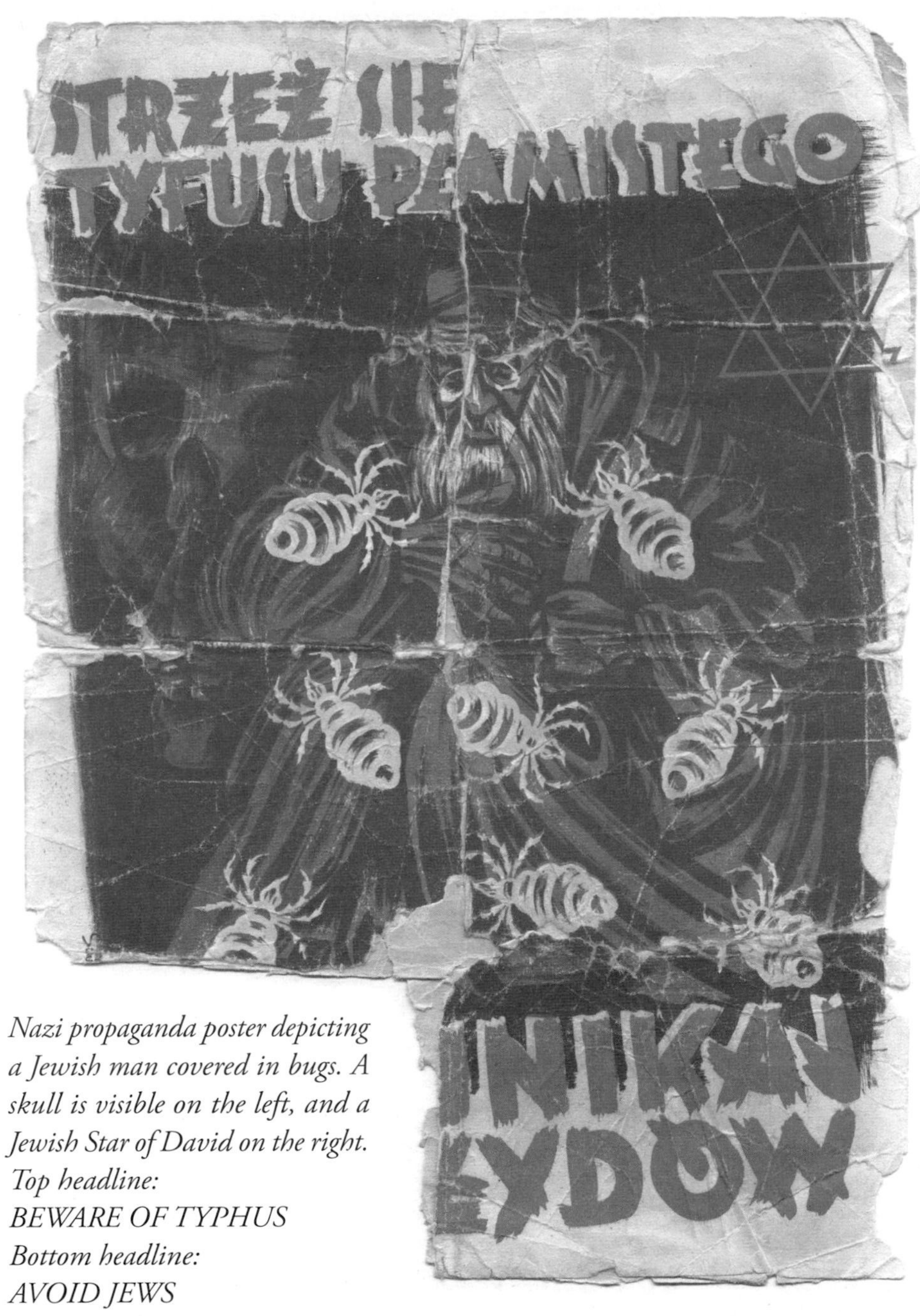

Nazi propaganda poster depicting a Jewish man covered in bugs. A skull is visible on the left, and a Jewish Star of David on the right.
Top headline:
BEWARE OF TYPHUS
Bottom headline:
AVOID JEWS

Wiktor Stanczyk's old barn where six people hid for 26 months, still stands in silent testimony to the events that played out within it and to the horrors of the Holocaust. The end of the barn was so close to the road that a careless word, spoken at the wrong time from within, could have betrayed the presence of the people hiding inside.

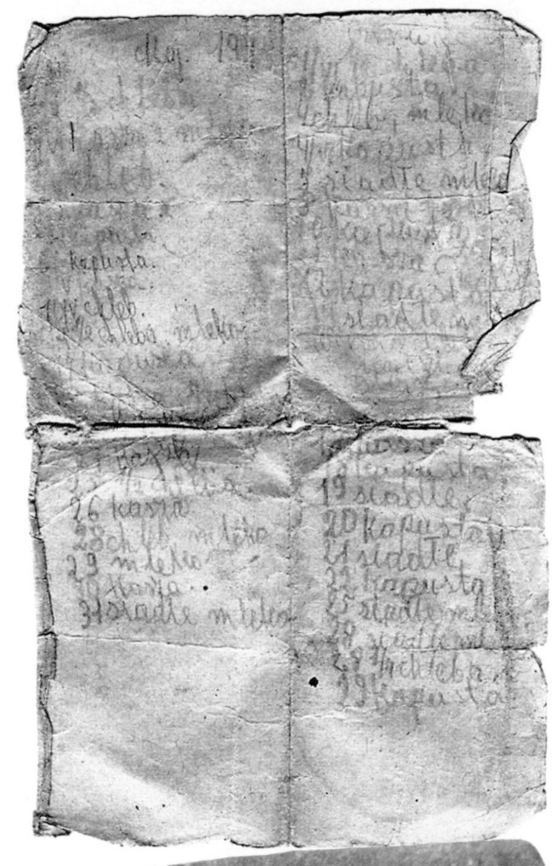

One of David's food lists written by him to try to pass time in the barn.
The same foods are repeated;
Cabbage
Bread
Milk
Groats.

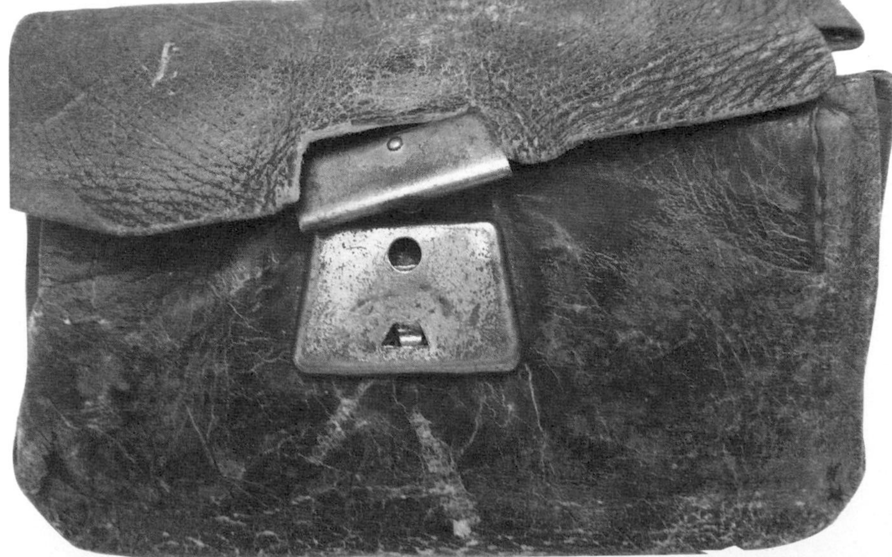

David's tiny wallet that he kept in his pocket throughout the war.

L. Gold
1927
1930
RADA MIEJSKA I ZARZĄD MAGISTRATU M. PIŃCZOWA w 10-TĄ ROCZNICĘ NIEPODLEGŁOŚCI POLSKI

The Town Council of the Polish town of Pińczów from 1927-1930. Leib Gold is circled at the top.

Leib's silver Kiddish Cup not only survived the war, but was returned to Hanna when she asked if she could have it as the single physical reminder of her husband.

The only existing photo of the whole Gold family: Hanna, David, Leib, Shoshana, and Esther.

The remaining four members of the Gold family after the war: David, Shoshana, Hanna, and Esther.

Acknowledgments

I would like to thank my Uncle David Gold. It is through his memories I was able to piece together the story of my mother's family during the Holocaust. At the age of eighty-five, he relived his terrifying experiences so that future generations would never forget one of the most horrific events in human history.

A special thank you to my sister, Sarah Burakowski, who contributed her input and insight as a teacher who has taught the Holocaust to many students. She was the only one who could truly share and understand my emotional journey, as we relived our mother's harrowing experiences. My mother, Shoshana, died when I was a young teen. Writing this book, has allowed both Sarah and me to reconnect with her and walk in her shoes through the darkest time of her life.

Thank you to Drs. Larry, Stanley, and Merrill Biel, sons of Esther and Feivel Biel, who contributed what they knew about their mother's history through the war.

My warmest thanks to Richard Archbold, author, editor, teacher, and friend, who took me under his wing, helping me prepare a proper proposal to present to a publisher. Rick took the time to read my book and encouraged me to try a mainstream publisher. He helped me through the process of writing a compelling query letter and synopsis that would get my book noticed.

The support of my *Canadian Jewish News* family, both old and new, was invaluable.

I want to thank Margie Wolfe for recognizing *Hidden Gold* as a story worth telling. I am honored to be among the authors published by Second Story Press. My sincerest gratitude goes to Kathryn Cole, my editor, who did an incredible job editing my manuscript. Kathryn was never too busy to answer my questions, guiding me through the many steps involved in having my book published. Other Second Story staff members, Michelle Melski and Melissa Kaita, were equally supportive and a pleasure to work with.

Most of all, I would like to thank my husband, Marshall Cohen, my rock for thirty-one years, who listened as I read him every paragraph out loud. He used his keen gift of visualization and guided me through each scene to make it as authentic as possible. It was Marshall who came up with the title *Hidden Gold*, he was as emotionally vested in every word as I was. Marshall cheered me on when I was ready to quit and picked me up through the difficult realizations I made as my family's story came to life on paper. His strength and encouragement kept me grounded and determined to make sure the story of the Gold family will live on.

About the Author

ELLA BURAKOWSKI has been writing a column in *The Canadian Jewish News* for the past twenty years. Now the Operations Manager at *The CJN*, Ella has learned the newspaper business from the ground up.

Born in Israel to Holocaust survivors, Shoshana (Gold) and Fishl (Burakowski), Ella was compelled to write *Hidden Gold* while her Uncle David was still able to describe the family's experiences during the Holocaust.

Ella lives in Toronto, Canada with her husband, Marshall Cohen.